Teacher's Guide

WORLD RHYTHMS! ARTS PROGRAM

WEST AFRICAN DRUM & DANCE

A Yankadi-Macrou Celebration

KALANI
RYAN M. CAMARA

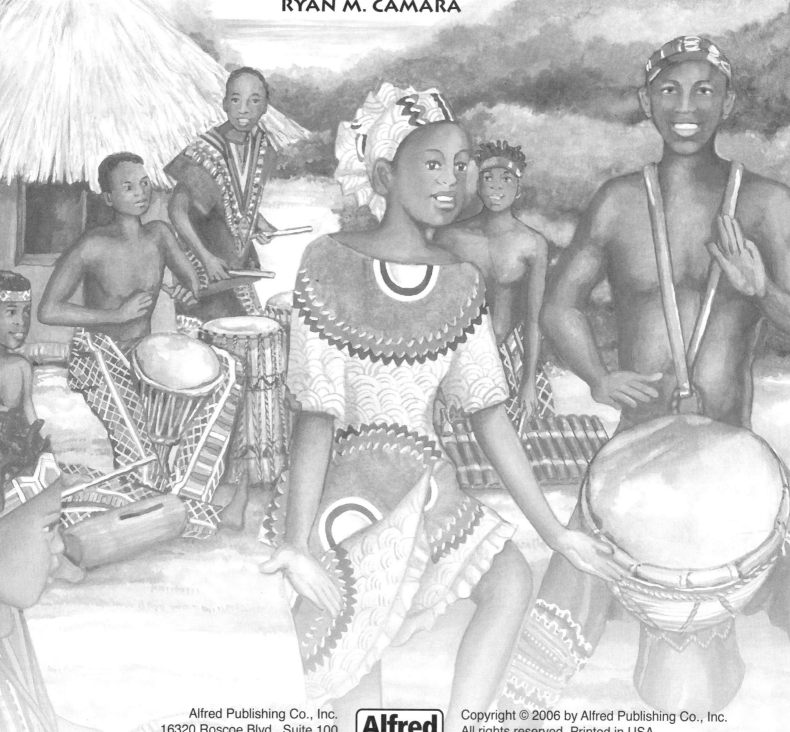

Alfred Publishing Co., Inc.
16320 Roscoe Blvd., Suite 100
P.O. Box 10003
Van Nuys, CA 91410-0003
alfred.com

ISBN-10: 0-7390-3869-9
ISBN-13: 978-0-7390-3869-7

CONTENTS

ABOUT THE AUTHORS

KALANI

Kalani is a master percussionist, world music composer, award-winning author, and Orff-Schulwerk specialist. He is featured on recordings for Disney, Warner Bros., Tri-Star Pictures, Paramount Studios, the Nature Company, and Jim Hensen Records. He has worked with such music legends as Kenny Loggins, Max Roach, Barry Manilow, Vic Damone, and John Mayall, and is the featured percussionist on the Yanni: Live at the Acropolis *video and CD. He released two CDs of original music:* Pangea and Insights.

Kalani has authored several books for Alfred Publishing Company including All About Congas, All About Jembe, All About Bongos, The Amazing Jamnasium, *and the award-winning drum circle facilitation book and DVD* Together in Rhythm. *Other DVDs include* Kalani's Ultimate Bongo Jam, Ultimate Conga Jam *and* Ultimate Jembe Jam. *He is a featured percussion instructor at WorkshopLive.com and the founder and director of programs and training for Rhythm Gym, a 501c3 non-profit organization dedicated to promoting fitness through active music making (rhythmgym.org).*

Kalani offers Drum Circle Music™ certification training and other professional development programs in the U.S. and abroad (drumcirclemusic.com). More information can be found on his website, kalanimusic.com

RYAN M. CAMARA

Ryan M. Camara is the adopted son of Master Drummer M. Lamine Dibo Camara from Guinea, West Africa, and a recognized and respected performer and educator of the traditional music and culture of Guinea, West Africa. He received formal training in ethnomusicology as a student at UCLA and has studied in Guinea annually since 1996, training extensively and performing with master artists including Mamady Keita, Boka Camara, Ousmane Sylla, Sekouba Camara, and Ballet Matam, and with members of Guineas National Ballet companies Les Ballets Africains and Ballet Djoliba.

Ryan has performed with such African legends as Prince Diabaté, Mouminatou Camara, Yamoussa Soumah and Oscar Camara. He has numerous recordings to his credit, including a variety of instructional CDs and Forè-Foté's acclaimed Wonbéré with members of Les Ballets Africains.

Ryan has presented workshops at the University of California, Santa Barbara; the University of Colorado; the University of Montana; and Southern Oregon University; and elementary and secondary schools throughout California, Oregon and Montana. He currently serves as the Artistic Director for the non-profit cultural organization Denbaya, Inc., is the founder of djembelesson.org (an on-line lesson resource for djembe and dundun drumming), and continues to perform with Forè-Foté and his own percussion and dance ensemble, Wakili. He balances a busy touring schedule with teaching traditional West African music through Southern Oregon University, the Denbaya School of Drum and Dance, and the Ashland Schools Foundation.

THE WORLD RHYTHMS STORY

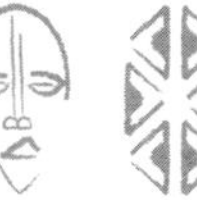

It is both astonishing and inevitable that Kalani and Ryan would collaborate around the jembe. Astonishing, because both men began their musical careers on quite different paths; inevitable, because the world of serious jembe players is a small one, and people in it eventually find each other.

Kalani's and Ryan's journeys with the jembe began in the '90s. They were both living and working in Southern California. Kalani was a percussionist; his drums were congas, bongos and timbales, but when he saw the jembe, he knew he had to bring it into his setup. "I was taken with it immediately: the shape of it—and the sound. It was such an exotic-looking instrument and had such a wide range of sound; unlike any other drum I had ever seen or played."

In those days, Ryan was playing drumset. "I felt very limited by the rock, reggae and top-40 styles of music I was playing—but it was how I made my living while I went to school. Then, one day I saw someone play a jembe at a NAMM show in Los Angeles. That music evoked such power and feeling. It changed my life! I liked how a jembe player wasn't stuck behind a drumset! I began seeking out master teachers like Mamady Keita and M. Lamine Dibo Camara, and, a year later, I sold my drumset and bought a ticket to Guinea, West Africa, where I have traveled and studied every year since."

Kalani and Ryan would not meet until the new millennium, but, in the meantime, they traveled parallel paths with the jembe and West African rhythms. They studied with some of the same jembe masters—at different times. They were both using the jembe, but from different approaches.

Ryan M. Camara (middle) studying on the island of Roume with Master Drummers Ousmane Sylla (Left) and M. Lamine "Dibo" Camara (Right) during his first trip to Guinea in 1996.

Kalani incorporated the jembe into his CDs *Pangea and Insights*. "I started using it with more mainstream music, including in my percussion setup with congas and bongos. It seemed natural to me to take the jembe on the road and play it alongside other percussion instruments."

When Kalani played his jembe with Yanni at the Acropolis in Greece, that one show, which was both a TV broadcast and a video, introduced millions of pop music fans to this extraordinary drum.

Ryan followed the jembe into its own ethnic world. He spent months at a time in Guinea studying with the country's top music teachers, then toured California and other states with the West African troupe Forè-Foté. Ryan's second visit to Guinea deepened his ties to that culture: "My teacher, Dibo Camara, invited me into his family, and gave me the name 'Baba.' I learned from him a deep appreciation and respect for the culture he came from, not just his music."

By the late 1990s, Kalani and Ryan were both prominent in their chosen specialties. Kalani was taking the jembe to a growing and diverse audience. As a master teacher, he toured the United States and Taiwan giving drumming workshops and clinics and made his first presentation at the Percussive Arts Society International Convention. He also formed his own band and toured California. Between gigs, Kalani developed drumming programs with Kaman Music and Toca percussion and played on movie and TV soundtracks—all with the jembe now solidly installed in his lineup.

Company Forè-Foté 2001 Tour photo. From left to right: Aboubacar "Miguel" Camara, Aboubacar "Lopez" Soumah, M. Lamine "Dibo" Camara, Ryan M. Camara, Nene Soumah.

In these same years, Ryan was fully committed to Forè-Foté. He performed with them on the CD *Wonbere* and in the World Festival of Sacred Music and the Watts Tower Day of Drum Festival. He also became the principal U.S. organizer for the Forè-Foté School of Drum and Dance in Guinea and was widely recognized as a major force in traditional music and dance of his adopted country.

The new millenium found Kalani and Ryan both working in the northwest United States. Ryan moved to Ashland, Oregon, to open the Forè-Foté School of Drum and Dance Northwest. Kalani accepted an invitation to be a presenter at the Seattle World Rhythm Festival. They were still on parallel paths, and they would not meet until the following year.

In 2001, Kalani created Drum Camp (drumcamp.com) and recruited Ryan to help staff it. "I wanted someone to teach West African drumming and dance.

A mutual friend suggested I get in touch with Ryan, so I called him up. We were comfortable with each other from the very first conversation." That first Drum Camp would be followed by many others. "I was so impressed with Ryan—his mastery of the music and the technique and also his work ethic. He gives 110 percent."

Drum Camp 2005

Drum Camp also changed Ryan's life. "Until Kalani invited me to teach at Drum Camp, I rarely did anything related to jembe that was not through Forè-Foté. In fact, I was on tour with Forè-Foté and had to schedule a week break to go to the first drum camp. I felt like a teenager out on his own for the first time again. It was really a turning point in establishing my own professional career."

Wakili with special guest Kalani at Oregon's Britt Festival 2005. From left to right: Kalani, Angela Parkinson, Sean Grace, Ryan M. Camara, Paul Riley.

For the next few years, both Kalani and Ryan would continue to develop their particular interests in the jembe and the culture it represents.

Ryan would continue spreading the traditional music, dance and culture of Guinea through workshops, residencies, and performances. He continued to work with Forè-Foté, but also founded his own performance troupe, Wakili. He then became Artistic Director of the non-profit Denbaya, Inc., and led educational tours to Guinea.

Kalani was drawn more and more into music education as a way of broadening the base of interest in world music. Encouraged by Sylvia and Andrew Perry of Peripole-Bergerault Educational Instruments, he completed his Orff-Schulwerk levels training and began building a reputation as a top presenter at conferences for such organizations as the National Association for Music Education, the American Orff-Schulwerk Association, and the American Music Therapy Association. He also authored the book and CD *All About Jembe* for Alfred Publishing.

In 2004, the WRAP project began to emerge as Kalani and Ryan saw how their individual areas of expertise complemented one another's, and they began talking about collaborating to create something very special for students and communities. Kalani says they are both excited about WRAP's potential. "Ryan brings an understanding and love of the West African culture to the project that is very special and totally authentic. He makes it possible for students in this country to take on the roles of young drummers, dancers, and singers in Guinea and feel the same things they feel when performing these songs and rhythms. In 2005, through a grant from the International House of Blues Foundation, we shared the WRAP curriculum with students at Markham Middle School in Watts, California. They were so excited to have the opportunity and caught on quickly. Even those with no prior drumming experience showed great improvement in skills and confidence. The staff was amazed with the transformation.

Kalani with students from Cold Springs Elementary School, Santa Barbara, CA.

Kalani with students from Markham Middle school, Watts, CA.

"My whole orientation with music has been to share the joy of it with other people, so I have concentrated on teaching, presenting, and writing. Ryan and I designed the WRAP project in teachable units to present the music in its appropriate ethnic context, culture, dance, song, even food. This will give students a much deeper experience in other cultures than has been done in the past.

"Not only is the WRAP curriculum tied directly to an authentic source, but Ryan and I have been formulating the material for teachers and students at workshops, festivals, clinics, camps, in all kinds of venues and for all kinds of audiences. We then used the feedback we received to make the lessons available to a wide range of students, regardless of their prior musical experience. We're pleased to offer a program that brings the culture of West Africa to so many people and helps them apply the spirit of the music to their lives."

WHAT THE EXPERTS SAY

"I was very happy to be a part of this book. My son, Ryan, put so much of his heart into capturing the true and authentic account of my culture's music and dance traditions. To gather correct information and translate into English in such depth was a very challenging task. But it was done very well and with respect for our traditions. I give my thanks to Ryan, Kalani and the sponsors of this wonderful project. Inuwalli khi fanye."

—**M. Lamine "Dibo" Camara**, Master Drummer and founder of Company Forè-Foté in Guinea, West Africa

"I was very excited when Ryan and Kalani asked me to be a part of this project. I have been sharing my country's culture through dance for many years and am so happy to know that more people will be able to enjoy it as much as I do. This curriculum brings together the drumming, dance, songs, background and culture of Guinea. I am looking forward to seeing many people drumming and dancing together in the future.

—**Djibril Camara,** Master Dancer from Guinea, West Africa, formally of Ballets D'Afrique Noir

Ryan Camara, Djibril Camara, and Kalani

WHAT THE KIDS SAY

"I'm very happy to see American foreigners come here to study my culture's music and dance. However, I only see adults! I'd love to meet and share with American kids my age. I'd love to learn about them and their culture and have them learn about me and my culture."

—**Aminata Bangoura**, student at Ecole Primaire de Roume, Guinea, West Africa

"The music and dance is very special here [in Guinea] and something that we do as part of our normal day. We dance after school, after work, at marriages—all the time. That's what our parents taught us. I've never seen an American kid. I hope that some come here one day so we can dance together."

—**Mohamed Lamine Conté**, student at Ecole Primaire de Roume, Guinea, West Africa

"Learning to drum for the first time was harder than I expected and it was more fun than I expected! I liked the rhythms. I liked drumming and dancing and the different arrangements and the patterns that we played."

—**Kitty Mularz**, Ashland Middle School

"I liked learning about the Susu people who created the rhythms, and I especially liked knowing what that rhythm was used for in their culture. It made it more fun to play the rhythm here, knowing why they played the rhythms there."

—**Delaney Swink**, Ashland Middle School

"When I'm playing and dancing, I feel great. I like to learn the Susu words and enjoy singing in other languages."

—**Heather Hansen**, 4th-grade student at Solvang Elementary School, Solvang, CA

"I think it's great that we got to learn this music. It's unique and the dance steps are really fun. I'd like to meet some children from West Africa someday. I could learn a lot from them."

—**Karina Uribe**, 4th-grade student at Solvang Elementary School, Solvang, CA

ABOUT THE CURRICULUM

The World Rhythms Arts Program (WRAP) is a multiple-discipline curriculum that incorporates drumming, singing, dance, and culture. Rooted in traditional West African music and dance, WRAP develops arts and life skills through a holistic approach to music and movement education. Students play their way through 20 developmentally progressive lessons, learning authentic drumming and dance skills, traditional rhythms, an artist's vocabulary, Susu language, culture, geography, and essential life skills.

WHO CAN USE THE WRAP CURRICULUM?

- Music teachers
- Dance teachers
- Community music teachers
- Music and dance facilitators
- Music and dance therapists
- Ethnomusicologists
- World art and cultures teachers
- Music history teachers
- Cultural performance organizations

WHO CAN PARTICIPATE IN WRAP?

People of all ages and abilities can participate in the WRAP curriculum. The curriculum is suitable for students from upper-elementary through college levels, and allows teachers to customize lessons to meet the needs of their students. Prior experience will be a factor in determining to what depth and rate a teacher will move through his/her program. In addition to being a multiple-discipline curriculum, WRAP may also be used as a stand-alone drumming program, dance program, and as a social studies, history, or language unit.

WHAT CAN THE WRAP CURRICULUM BE USED TO TEACH?

- Drumming skills
- Xylophone skills
- Vocal percussion
- Body percussion
- Rhythm patterns
- Dance steps
- Ensemble playing
- Music and dance arrangements
- Performance skills
- Music vocabulary
- Language skills
- Social skills
- Life skills
- Aspects of West African history and culture
- Aspects of music history and appreciation

P.R.I.D.E. AND THE WRAP CORE VALUES AND BEST PRACTICES

The following are the WRAP core values with the best practices listed for each.

Progress

We can make and acknowledge our progress by

- keeping our curiosity alive—pushing to learn more;
- motivating everyone to improve—even by the smallest measure;
- showing initiative and courage by trying new things and taking risks;
- showing resiliency and a sense of humor when we are challenged;
- discussing our accomplishments at the end of every session.

Responsibility

We can show that we are taking responsibility by

- being on time, well prepared, and actively listening to each other;
- treating the instruments and each other with care;
- being respectful of ourselves and each other;
- learning about other cultures from reliable sources;
- showing up early to set up and staying late to straighten up.

Inclusion

We can agree to help everyone feel included by

- greeting each other and finding out how everyone is doing;
- helping those who need or ask for it;
- being patient with those who may need more time;
- cooperating with our fellow musicians and dancers;
- communicating our thoughts, feelings, and opinions.

Diversity

We can agree to celebrate diversity by

- acknowledging that everyone has different skills and needs;
- using our different talents to create the best possible outcomes;
- trying out different approaches before making conclusions;
- welcoming all ideas and perspectives, even when we may disagree with them.

Excellence

We can agree to work together towards excellence by

- paying attention to every detail of the performance;
- showing perseverance—even when it's difficult;
- trying to improve in every way—even in ways no one else may notice;
- being accountable for our actions;
- never settling for less than our best effort.

The WRAP core values help students create enduring understandings of the many benefits of participation that extend well beyond the music and movement skills. You may find it helpful to create posters or signs for your music room that show each value. It's a great way to create and show your P.R.I.D.E. (You can share your photos, PDFs, and good news through the WRAP website: drum2dance.com.)

WRAP OBJECTIVES

The following are some of the objectives in creating this program:

- Expand students' capacity for effective communication in a variety of modalities (aural, visual, verbal, kinesthetic, interpersonal, etc.)
- Build confidence and self-esteem by validating creative input and by offering and encouraging students to participate in public performances
- Demonstrate the value of skill building and the artful application of techniques through the process of study, practice, and performance
- Demonstrate the value of creative thinking and improvisation though group interaction and guided play
- Instill respect and appreciation for the music, instruments, and traditions of other cultures by offering the highest quality information and resources
- Understand how music and movement reflect other aspects of community life including art, literature, politics, economics, social patterns, and popular culture
- Identify musical elements, styles, and forms, and be able to analyze and synthesize those elements
- Improve listening skills through active call and response, echoing, pitch and timbre recognition, and pattern identification
- Develop leadership skills, initiative, and determination through dynamic music-based interactions
- Improve citizenship through mutual sharing and support, open dialogue, and reflective thinking
- Foster a desire to continue exploring the music, dance, and traditions of other cultures
- Create a deep and satisfying connection to the social arts, and maintain an active connection to drumming and dancing throughout one's life

BECOMING A WRAP TEACHER

Just as the WRAP curriculum helps students to appreciate the music and dance of another culture while improving their overall musical and movement abilities, it also provides an authentic and rich learning experience for the teacher. Music educators the world over are embracing the jembe for teaching rhythm, ensemble playing, and the development of essential life skills through group drumming. Through the WRAP curriculum, you now have the opportunity to complete your African connection by learning the authentic jembe drumming language straight from the source. As a WRAP teacher, you gain authentic drumming and dance skills that will serve you throughout your entire career—no matter what kind of music you play.

Once you have mastered the program content, you will find that learning new rhythms will be easier and learning new dance steps will feel more natural. (Surprise your friends with some of your new moves the next time you hit the dance floor!) One of our primary goals in designing this program is to raise the level of "musicianship through drumming" and help our peers gain the skills they need to embrace world drumming with both hands (and feet). Reaching that goal means learning new skills and taking time to develop them until they are integrated with your existing skill set. Before you begin teaching the World Rhythms Arts Program, it is essential that you take time to review the curriculum and develop your personal skills and knowledge. We understand that teachers cover a broad range of subjects, so we've designed this material to be easy to learn and fit into your busy schedule.

COURSE PREPARATION

The following course preparation outline will help you make the most of the program:

- **Jembe:** Start right away! Use the DVD to learn how to produce the sounds and play the rhythms. Use the audio CD as a practice companion. Playing jembe is at the core of the curriculum and perhaps the most challenging skill you will develop. Practice at least 10 to 15 minutes per day (more if possible).

Tip: For a more comfortable, low-volume practice session, cover the drumhead with a piece of cloth.

- **Dundun:** Learn from the DVD and practice with the CD. Allow adequate time to become comfortable with each rhythm before you begin your program.

- **Xylophone:** Learn and review before each lesson.
- **Dance:** Start right away! Learn and practice the steps using the DVD. Once you have the routines memorized, you can try using the audio CD.
- **Songs:** Learn and review before each lesson. Practice with the CD, with xylophone, and a capella.

DVD

The WRAP DVD features a wealth of resources to make learning the curriculum both easy and effective for you and your students.

Features

→ Cultural overview of Guinea
→ Playing techniques and rhythms for all instruments
→ Jembe rhythm patterns through body percussion
→ Dance instruction (front and back view, plus a commentary track)
→ Village performances (the youth troupe from Guinea)

CD

You may use the CD for learning and practicing the rhythms and arrangements, and, in some cases, for performance. For a complete list of CD tracks, see appendix O.

Features

→ Performance arrangements
→ Rhythm patterns for each instrument at slow and performance tempo
→ Layered parts with échauffment and break
→ Dance practice tracks
→ Language examples

Using the Student Enrichment Book

Every WRAP participant should receive his/her own copy of the Student Enrichment Book at the beginning of the program. At the end of each lesson, the student completes an assignment, providing an opportunity to deepen the learning experience. The lesson assignments include a variety of topics which can include; providing notation and lyrics, filling in missing words, identifying geographic items, reciting Susu language, and completing a word search. The SEB contains important study material and serves as both a notebook and personal reference guide for future performances and/or projects. Upon completion of the WRAP program, each student receives a signed Certificate of Achievement, which he/she can display with pride. It is very important that each student receive his/her personal SEB on or before the first WRAP session. We recommend that each instructor complete his/her personal SEB before beginning the program.

TEACHING THE WRAP CURRICULUM

The WRAP curriculum provides you and your students with a comprehensive learning experience—complete with movement, drumming, singing, and performance skills. We know your time is valuable and have organized the lessons into manageable sessions that flow naturally from one topic to another. Lesson content is based on sessions of 45 to 60 minutes, but is flexible enough to be delivered at any pace that is suitable for you and your group.

Each lesson is organized into the following categories:

Objectives

Skills and competencies your students will learn:

- **Musical skills:** Skills and techniques that pertain to music competency, many of which transfer to other instruments and areas outside of the WRAP performance.
- **Life skills:** Important social skills, values, and strategies that are woven into the curriculum. These are often brought up as specific discussion topics at the end of a session.
- **Movement skills:** Balance, timing, motor and loco-motor movements that will help students in many areas outside of dance, such as sports and many jobs that require physical coordination.
- **Materials:** What your group needs to complete the lesson. This may include drums, xylophones, a movement space, CD player, etc.
- **Vocabulary:** Words that reflect the core material and concepts of each lesson.

Process

Steps to presenting the lesson material:

- **Let's Speak:** Students learn and review Susu language and dialog. All words and dialogues are written and referenced to their appropriate track on the CD. Additional information about the language lessons can be found in appendix H, along with the "Susu Language Pronunciation Guide."
- **Let's Move:** This section involves all students in an inclusive movement activity in which they learn traditional dance steps to the arrangements. Dance notation is included as a supplement to the DVD.
- **Let's Drum:** Rhythms and techniques are outlined with photos and notation that support the materials on the CD and DVD. Patterns are presented using a methodic approach of vocalization, body percussion, rhythm construction process, and traditional Western notation.
- **Let's Sing:** Songs are presented in sections and built over several lessons. Traditional notation supports the audio CD and DVD examples.
- **Let's Play:** To complete and celebrate the learning process, a mini-performance arrangement is offered at the end of each lesson. These not only provide a rich context for expression, but build towards the final performance arrangement for your WRAP celebration.
- **Wrap-Up:** Preparing for discussion and review of lesson topics.
- **Evaluation:** Assessing what learning took place and addressing challenges.
- **Discussion:** Deepening the experience through thoughtful reflection and sharing.

We know there are many styles of teaching and that your educational/performance goals may not be the same as someone else's. Your unique approach to music and movement education will determine how you present the WRAP curriculum. No matter how you pace your lessons, which entry points you use to dive into the material, or what performance goals you set your sights on, we are confident you will find the WRAP curriculum both rich and rewarding for you and your students.

BEYOND THE STANDARDS

The WRAP curriculum supports the National Standards for both music and dance education. Numbered Icons for both dance [dance icon] and music [music icon] standards can be found throughout the lessons. Additionally, most states have their own standards for arts education. Note that standards are simply placeholders for curriculum development and assessment. They identify areas of focus that together, support a complete and comprehensive education.

National Dance Standards for Dance Education

1. Identifying and demonstrating movement elements and skills in performing dance.
2. Understanding the choreographic principles, processes, and structures.
3. Understanding dance as a way to create and communicate meaning.
4. Applying and demonstrating critical and creative thinking skills in dance.
5. Demonstrating and understanding dance in various cultures and historical periods.
6. Making connections between dance and healthful living.
7. Making connections between dance and other disciplines.

The National Standards for Music Education

1. Singing, alone and with others, a varied repertoire of music.
2. Performing on instruments, alone and with others, a varied repertoire of music.
3. Improvising melodies, variations, and accompaniments.
4. Composing and arranging music within specified guidelines.
5. Reading and notating music.
6. Listening to, analyzing, and describing music.
7. Evaluating music and music performances.
8. Understanding relationships between music, the other arts, and disciplines outside the arts.
9. Understanding music in relation to history and culture.

MAKING THE MOST OF YOUR PROGRAM

The following suggestions are designed to help you and your students get the most out of this material. You can share your tips and see more through the WRAP website: www.drum2dance.com.

Movement

- Warm up with rhythmic stretching.
- Encourage students to fully extend arms, legs, and smiles.
- For young students, it may help to practice the dance by saying the moves, saying them and moving together, then moving without talking.
- Encourage dancers to learn the drum parts. This will help their timing, inflection, and precision.

Drumming

- Warm up with hand and arm stretches. Use body percussion rhythms to get the blood flowing.
- Emphasize three keys to successful ensemble drumming: knowing your part, knowing your neighbors' parts, and knowing how all the parts fit together.
- Encourage drummers to learn all the dance steps and how they are sequenced. (By doing them!)
- Rotate students through the different instruments as much as possible.
- Have students who are waiting to play drums support and learn the patterns through body percussion or vocalizing the rhythms.
- Rather than using words to start and stop the group, play the breaks on the whistle or drum. This non-verbal approach supports active listening and musical intelligence.
- Remind students that speed comes with accuracy. (Don't beat the drum—drum the beat!)
- Take time to practice the drumming parts and ensembles using only voices ("vocables"). Discuss how the dynamics, listening, and awareness of self and others is different from that of using drums.

Singing

- Warm up with breathing exercises.
- Encourage students to project their voices.
- Emphasize the importance of correct pronunciation and pitch.

Performance

- Remind students that audience members will remember one thing from your performance: how they felt when it was over. Ask, "How do you want them to feel?"
- Show your enthusiasm by smiling and projecting to every member of the audience.
- Practice good body language habits.
- Maintain your professional attitude before, during, and after being on stage.

<u>If possible:</u>

- Practice in front of mirrors to help dancers synchronize and work as a team.
- Videotape rehearsals and performances to provide objective feedback for students.
- Bring out the xylophones and vocals by using an amplifier or small PA system.

Discussion

Use P.R.I.D.E. as talking points:

- How did we (you) make PROGRESS?
- Where did we (you) take RESPONSIBILITY?
- In what way(s) did you or others demonstrate INCLUSION?
- How was DIVERSITY represented?
- How did you reach your standards of EXCELLENCE?

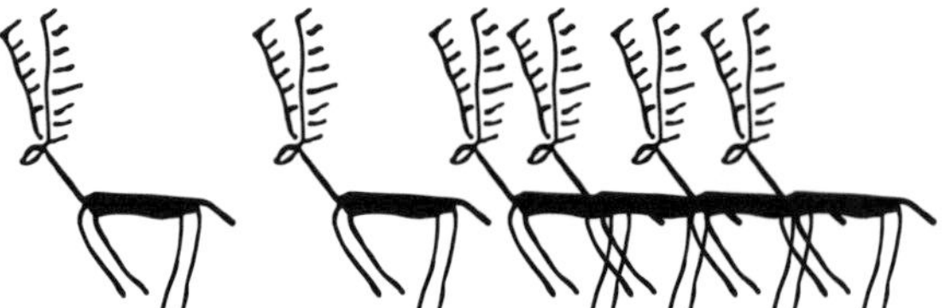

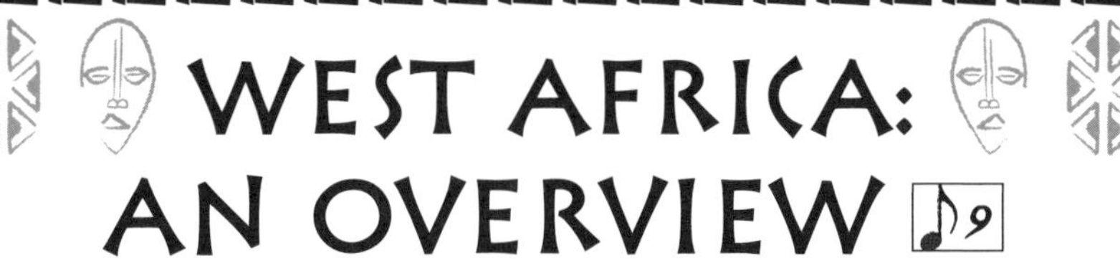

WEST AFRICA: AN OVERVIEW

The West African Region

West Africa covers a vast area of the sub-Saharan region of the African Continent often referred to as the "Bulge of Africa." The colonial boundaries of the 14 contemporary countries cut across ethnic and cultural lines, often dividing single ethnic groups and even past empires into many different sections. West Africa features a widely diverse geographical landscape and a multitude of ethnic groups, each with its own language. Each ethnic group has unique musical instruments, rhythms, songs, dances, and stories that help define and preserve their cultural identity.

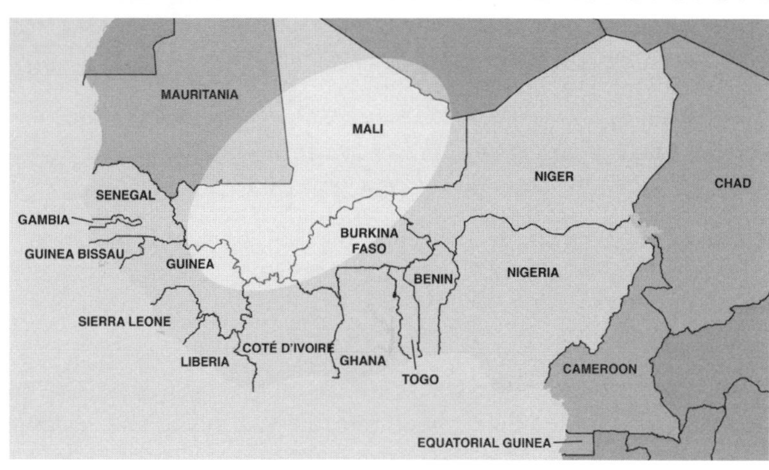

Mali Empire (12th-14th Century)

The Mandé Ethnic Groups of the Mali Empire

The instruments, rhythms, songs and dances of the WRAP program all originate among the Mandé speaking ethnic groups who trace their heritage directly to the former Mali Empire of the 12–14th centuries. The Mali Empire was famous for its scholarship, tremendous wealth and amazing music and dance. Today, Mandé speakers inhabit portions of the present-day countries of Guinea, Mali, Cote d'Ivoire, Burkina Faso and Senegal. The major Mande ethnic groups responsible for the traditions learned in the WRAP program are the Malinke and Susu, largely located within the country of Guinea.

Guinea and the Isles de Los

The Republic of Guinea is a beautiful, vibrant and culturally rich country, with four distinctive geographic regions and home to over 36 different language/ethnic groups. While major cities like Kankan, Labe and the capital city of Conakry boast many modern amenities, most Guineans live in small villages, in much the same way they have for centuries. The WRAP program, in conjunction with the Foré-Foté School of Drum and Dance, has developed a special relationship with the small Susu fishing village of Roume–the smallest of the three inhabited islands known as the Isles de Los, located just off the coast of Conakry.

Did You Know?

Roume was called Crawford Island until the end of the 19th century, named after the notorious slaver, Crawford, who was executed in an 1850 uprising that liberated the former slaving base. Tales of treasure buried by Crawford and his men are said to be the inspiration for Robert Louis Stevenson's famous novel Treasure Island.

Roume: Our Village

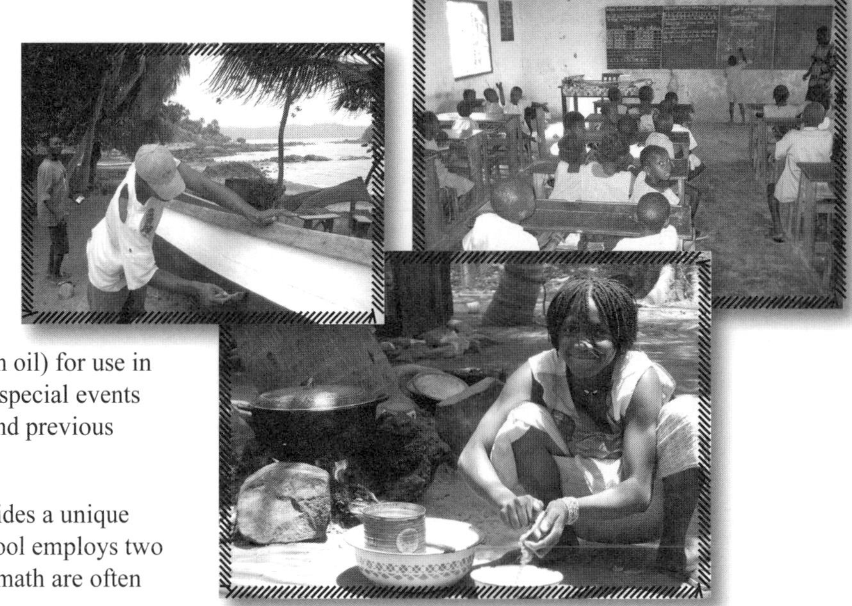

On the island of Roume, virtually everything revolves around the work of fishing. Most men work daily, repairing their boats and fishing nets. They will often take their boats out overnight to catch enough fish to bring back to their families. In the morning, women will take the fish that will not be eaten to the markets in Conakry. They sell the fish and buy mainly rice, vegetables, and breads. Everything else that grows on the island is consumed. Roume has plentiful mango, banana, coconut, and orange trees. The fruit of the *tugi gbili* (palm tree) is used to produce *ture gbeli* (palm oil) for use in cooking and *tugiye* (palm wine), which is consumed at special events and ceremonies. Some families grow *yucca* (manioc) and previous inhabitants grew their own rice and peanuts as well.

The new Ecole Primaire de Roume, built in 2001, provides a unique educational opportunity for Roume's children. The school employs two teachers, and academic subjects including reading and math are often taught in both the Susu and French languages.

All school-aged children are expected to work with their families after school. Boys work with their fathers, repairing boats and fishing lines and cleaning up around the village. Girls will cook, wash clothes and take care of the youngest children. All young people pull water from the wells and gather wood for making fires to cook.

Favorite sports include swimming and soccer, and the island team competes against other teams from nearby villages or Conakry. The island is home to a group of local musicians who also work as fishermen. When music is needed for a particular traditional event—marriage, naming ceremony, boat launch, or even a Yankadi-Macrou party—the families involved will bring cola nuts to the musicians, and, as it has been done for centuries, ask them to play for the ceremony.

For more information on the history and culture of Guinea, visit the WRAP website: drum2dance.com.

Students with school teacher Alexandre Bazil Morgan (left), drum instructor M. Lamine Dibo Camara (center), and school director, Facinet Camara (right).

A Gift Between Communities

On March 24, 2004, Ryan Camara presented a gift from the authors, Alfred Publishing, and Peripole-Bergerault Educational Instruments of nearly 2 million GNF (Guinea francs), accepted by the school director, teacher, and village chief. The majority of funds went directly to the Ecole Primare de Roume (primary school), and were used for classroom materials and tuition by those who could not afford it. Other funds were used to buy costumes for the Roume ballet. This heartfelt gesture was to acknowledge the many gifts we, in distant countries, receive from people whose names we may never know, whose faces we may never see, but whose spirit touches us in places words alone cannot reach. It is through mutual respect and sharing that we all benefit and thrive.

WEST AFRICAN MUSIC

We cannot study West African music without studying West African culture, and we cannot play West African music without feeling as though we've become a small part of West African culture. Unlike Western music, where the sole purpose is often entertainment, West African music is an integral part of people's daily lives. Traditionally, there is not a separation between artist and audience; rather, music is a participatory communal experience shared by all members of a village. The music of Guinea is truly the music of the people and offers great insight into their traditions, life, and culture. By participating in this culture's music, we are offered insights into our own sense of self, community, and the process of creating the feeling of a "village," whether we live in a rural or urban setting.

The National Ballets of Guinea

Much of what we know of Guineas traditional pre-colonial music and dance is a result of the "Cultural Socialist Revolution" that former President Sekou Touré instituted after Guinea's Independence. The movement was designed to reconnect Guinea with its pre-colonial cultural history and celebrate its ethnic diversity, while unifying the country with a sense of nationalistic pride. Touré reached out to villages all over the country, often forcing them to give up their sacred rhythms, dances and rituals for the benefit of Guinea's cultural heritage. Hundreds of local artistic groups were organized throughout the country and national orchestras, choirs, theater groups, and ballets were formed. School children were trained in their traditional music and dance, and competitions were held throughout the country to find the best artists. These artists, who represented different ethnic groups, were brought to Conakry and eventually formed into the three National Ballets of Guinea: Les Ballets Africains, Djoliba National Ballet, and the National Ballet of the People's Army. These ballets bring choreographed routines interwoven with stories of village life and African history to the stage, to spread the culture of Guinea and of West Africa to modern audiences. They have toured for the last 50 years to nearly every continent on earth, becoming true cultural ambassadors of Guinea, and of Africa as a whole.

INSTRUMENT GUIDE

Many traditional West African instruments are used throughout the WRAP curriculum. In addition to particular rhythm patterns, students will learn the history, techniques and typical uses of these instruments during the WRAP course. This broad and thorough approach empowers students with a greater knowledge and appreciation of West African music, and, because music and dance is such an integral aspect of daily life, imparts a more accurate representation of West African culture.

PRIMARY INSTRUMENTS

Jembe

The *jembe* (JEM-bay), called the *sanbanyi* (SAHN-ba-nyee) by the Susu people, originated by at least the 13th century among the Mandé-speaking ethnic groups located in and around present-day Guinea. Its goblet shape comes from the large mortars used to pound millet. (See photo in "The History and Purpose of Jembe Rhythms" on page 20.) Carved from a single piece of wood with goat or antelope skin stretched across the larger of the two openings, the jembe is traditionally played with the hands while standing. The three primary notes played on the jembe cover a large sonic spectrum, making it both a solo and accompaniment instrument.

Traditionally, jembe ensembles usually consist of two to three jembe accompanists and one or more soloists. More modern "ballet" music may have up to five or six jembes. The soloist's drum is pulled the tightest and has the highest-pitched sound. Although the accompanying jembes are not tuned to a specific pitch, their tuning and tonality reflect the parts they play in the ensemble. For example, the designated primary accompaniment or first jembe pattern will be played on a drum tuned lower than the soloist's, but higher than the one playing the second jembe accompaniment pattern. Many traditional jembe rhythms include a "bass" jembe accompaniment, which is played on the lowest-pitched drum. (The three "ears" on the jembe are called *sèssè,* or, in some regions, *ksing ksing.* They are sometimes attached to a soloist's drum to produce a rattle effect, giving the perception of increased volume and differentiation or coloration of sound.)

Dundun

The *dundun* (DOON-doon) family of double-headed drums are cylindrically shaped with cow skin covering both ends. The three drums, from largest to smallest, are called *dundunba* (DOON-doon-bah), *sangban* (SAHGN-bahn), and *kenkeni* (KEN-ken-nee). Together, the dunduns provide the rhythmic and melodic basis for the ensemble. They are said to have developed simultaneously with the jembe. Dunduns are traditionally played horizontally, fitted with a strap and slung over the shoulder. The heads of the dundun are played with a large stick (16" to 17" long). They are sometimes placed vertically (see center drum in photo) and played by one person using two sticks. This arrangement is often referred to as "ballet style." In some areas a bell, called a *kenken*, is attached to the drum and played with a metal rod or bolt.

The sangban is the middle-sized/pitched drum, and specifies the rhythm that is being played through its unique patterns and phrases. The kenkeni is the smallest drum in the ensemble and produces the highest-pitched note. It most often plays a repetitive rhythmic *ostinato* (repeated pattern) that serves to keep the pulse for the ensemble. The largest of the three drums is the dundunba, and it produces the lowest note. While it has specific patterns for every rhythm, it is also free to improvise within the rhythm and accentuate the movements of the dancers as well as the phrases of the jembe soloist.

The three dunduns and kenken are not found in every region in Guinea. The jembe, however, is always accompanied by at least one dundun, usually the sangban, whenever it is played.

Krinyi

The ***krinyi*** (KREEN-yee), also called the ***krin*** (KREEN*)*, is a type of log drum that originates from the forest region of southeastern Guinea, and it consists of a hollowed-out section of tree trunk. The main opening and two side slits create two bands of varying pitch. It is played with two wooden sticks and produces a variety of tones depending upon where it is struck.

Seke-Seke

The ***seke-seke*** (SEH-KEH SEH-KEH), also called the ***kese-kese***, is a basket-shaped shaker from eastern Guinea comprised of small rocks or seeds housed in a woven covering of burlap and leather. They are always played in pairs using alternating hand motions.

Bala

The ***bala*** (BAH-lah), called ***balafon*** in French, originates among the Susu ethnic group but is found throughout West Africa. It is an instrument associated with the ***griot*** or ***jeli*** caste of professional musician/historian/praise singers. Considered by many to be the precursor to the modern xylophone, the bala consists of a frame from which 21 wooden bars are strung in decreasing length, each with guard resonators attached to the bottom. The bars are tuned to a ***heptatonic*** (7-note) scale, with each bar an equal interval from the others of about 120 cents, and they are struck with hard rubber-covered mallets. The bala can be played either while standing (attached with a strap), or while seated on the ground.

MUSIC AND THE MANDÉ CASTES 9

At the time of the Mali Empire, Mandé society was separated into three distinct classes of people: farmers called ***heron*** (who would eventually make up the noble*[1] class as well), groups or castes of specialized professionals known as ***nyamakala***, and slaves. There are four distinct castes of nyamakala: the ***Garangé***, leather workers; ***Funé***, mimes; ***Jeli***, bards or griots (oral historians who tell the history of people through song and playing of special instruments); and the ***Numu***, blacksmiths and woodcarvers. Nyamakala castes are strictly hereditary, meaning you would have to be born and initiated into a nyamakala family to perform the specialized roles inherent to the caste. The two important nyamakala in Mandé musical history are the Jeli and the Numu.

The Role of the Jeli

The ***Jelis*** are the keepers of the oral traditions and have three main roles: chronicler or historian, entertainer, and preserver of social customs and values. While the Jelis are considered to be the "professional musician's caste" in West Africa, they do not typically play jembe. The primary Jeli instrument is the voice, with which they impart the oral histories of the Mandé. Jelis will often accompany themselves on the bala, kora, or bolon.

While in the role of entertainer or historian, the Jelis will often perform solo, though they do have a role in the music of the jembe ensemble. They are called upon to sing appropriate songs for the specific rhythm and dance being played. During the song they are expected to sing ***matogoli*** (improvised flatteries) for important members of the village. They may accompany their singing by striking a long iron tube called a ***karignan*** with a metal rod to keep time.

*Noble classes are those belonging to a hereditary line of high social or political status.

The History and Purpose of Jembe Rhythms 

Unlike the music and instruments within the Jeli caste, the jembe has no hereditary restrictions placed upon it. It can be played by anyone, though it is thought to have originated in the Mandé nyamakala of blacksmiths and woodworkers known as the Numu. Historical accounts of jembe origins often state that women were the originators of many early traditional rhythms. Often working in groups of two or three, they would alternate pounding their pestle into large mortars, accompanied by hand clapping, thereby creating complex rhythms through their labor (see photo). Typically, other members of the village would dance and sing to these rhythms that were being created while working. Only members of the Numu caste possessed the necessary ***gundow***, or trade secrets, to carve the first jembes and other percussion instruments to accompany these dances. While there are many great Numu jembe players—notably members of the Camara, Kante, and Doumbia families—the Numu did not create the jembe just for themselves. The jembe is really the instrument of and for the people.

Women pounding millet in a mortar on the island of Roume.

The jembe and its family of percussion instruments were created to accompany dance. In Mandé society, there is a traditional rhythm and dance for virtually every event in a person's life. Imagine you are a child born in Guinea. The drums roar as you are given your name. They help you meet new friends as you dance to the beat under a full moon. They whisk you off to undergo initiation and welcome you home after you've been away. The music is the "soundtrack of your life," and by listening and participating, you learn not only about yourself, but also about the people around you. The drums wail to gather the village together for weddings. They cry out to help settle disputes. They can be heard encouraging workers in the fields, and they are the focal point for all the biggest feasts and celebrations.

Notice that we're referring to how the drums *are* played, not how they *were* played. In many regions of Guinea and the surrounding areas, specific rhythms are still played only for the sacred and secular events, as they have been for centuries. The musical culture is not static, though. Every year, variations are made on older rhythms and new rhythms are created. The jembe has become one of the world's most recognizable hand drums and can be heard in popular music throughout the world; however, it is while accompanying the "dances of our lives" in villages throughout West Africa that the jembe fulfills its true purpose. Perhaps, by experiencing the essence and feeling of the traditional music and dance of this culture, we can discover more about our own.

INSTRUMENT TECHNIQUE

Learning to play any instrument is like learning a new language. In the past, "world music" drums were often lumped together into the same category, inadvertently promoting the idea that they are all played in the same way. This is not the case. Every drum has a unique voice and proper playing technique that is particular to its culture. Learning these techniques is crucial for being able to communicate with others, to accurately play the rhythm patterns, and to enjoy using the instruments while avoiding injuries. All the basic techniques are shown on the accompanying DVD and outlined in the following section. Although the hand-drumming techniques in the WRAP curriculum are specific to the jembe, they can serve as a solid foundation for learning to play hand drums from other traditions such as congas, bongos, ashiko, doumbek, and timbau.

Tip: If you or your students have no experience with jembe or world percussion instruments, see appendix E, which outlines some simple, engaging activities, and games designed to introduce students to the instruments in an informal and fun way. These activities will help students gain confidence and familiarity with the instruments, and they can be added to any lesson during the course.

JEMBE TECHNIQUE

The jembe drum is a versatile instrument capable of producing a wide variety of sounds. Traditionally, there are three basic tones that comprise its language. By learning to properly produce just these three sounds, you can play virtually any traditional rhythm pattern.

Note: It is important to make sure your drum is properly tuned to get the best possible sound. If you have not yet tuned your drum, please refer to the tuning section in appendix C.

Body Position

The first aspect to good technique is proper body position. Traditionally, the jembe is played while standing. It is hung from the shoulders with a cloth strap that positions the drum at approximately a 45-degree angle between the legs (see photo). When playing in the standing position, adjust the strap so your hands can just reach the center. It is now common in drumming classes and ballet performances, when dance is the focal point, for jembe players to sit. In the seated position, approximate the same 45-degree playing position you have when standing. This will allow the bottom of the drum to remain open for air to escape. In both positions, keep proper body posture by having a straight back and the head and eyes facing forward, not tipped down at the instrument.

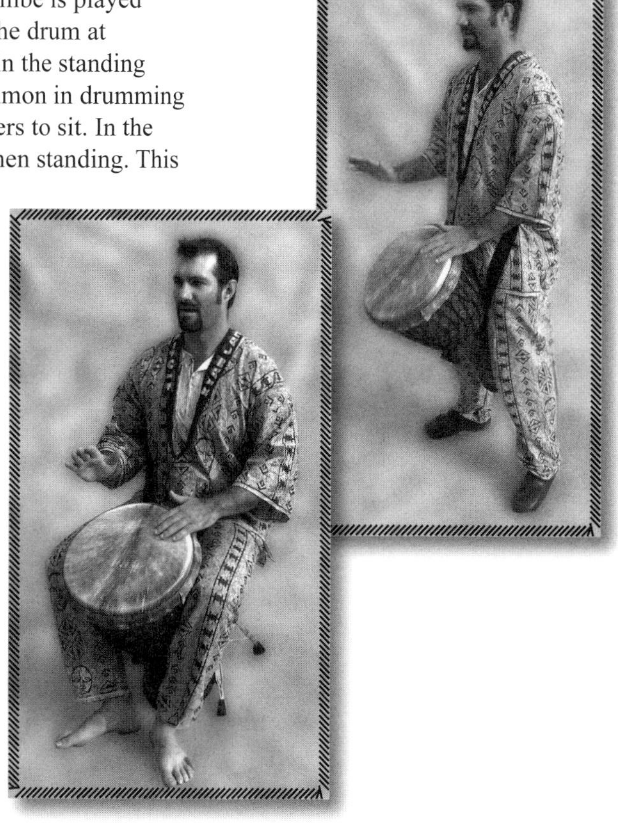

Bass Tone

The ***bass tone*** is the lowest-pitched note of the jembe, and when played correctly, produces a deep, full, resonant note. To produce the proper sound, position your hand so your palm and fingers are all just within the circumference of the drum, between the center and the edge. Keep your hand and fingers flat (but relaxed), and your thumb up and out of the way. Avoid placing your hand directly in the center, because this is a node or "dead spot" that will not produce the best possible sound.

To play the bass tone:

1. Start with your arm in a relaxed position at a comfortable height above the drumhead (10"–14").
2. With palm down, raise your hand and arm from the elbow.
3. Allow gravity to pull your hand towards the head.
4. Strike the drum with your hand flat, just off-center. Make sure the entire portion of your hand is within the circumference of the head.
5. Allow your hand to rebound back to the starting position as the drum resonates.

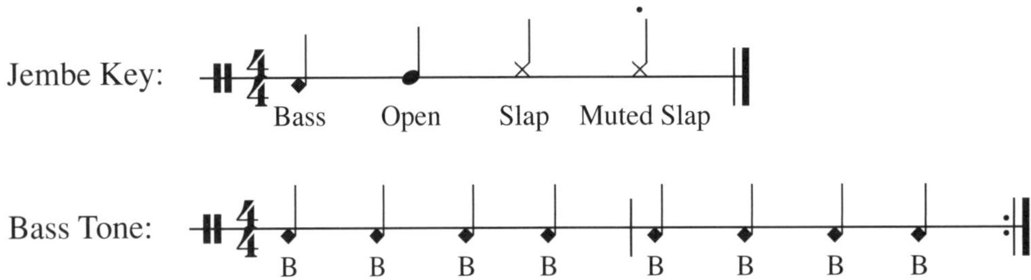

The most important concept to grasp when playing the bass tone, or any tone, is to think about ***pulling*** the sound out of the drum, not ***holding*** it or ***pushing*** it through. To get the best possible sound, pull your hand away from the skin as quickly as possible when striking the drum.

Open Tone

The ***open tone*** provides a rich, full, natural sound that is higher in pitch than the bass tone. Depending on the diameter of your jembe's head, you may have to turn your hands slightly so all portions of your fingers are in contact with the skin. The thumb is held up and back so it doesn't interfere with the sound or get bruised on the rings of the drum. Keep your fingers together and your wrist and hand flat in line with the head. (Be sure to concentrate on pulling the sound out and not letting your hand rest on the drum.)

To play the open tone:

1. Start with your arm in a relaxed position at a comfortable height above the drumhead (10"–14").
2. With palm down, raise your hand and arm from the elbow.
3. Allow gravity to pull your hand towards the head.
4. Strike the drum with your fingers together (except for the thumb), crossing the edge of the drum right where your fingers meet your palm. Focus the weight of your hand to the lower part of your fingers.
5. Allow your hand to rebound back to the starting position as the drum resonates.

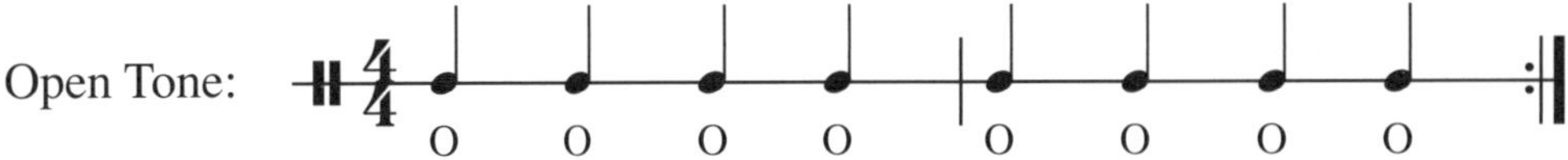

Remember to keep your hand position consistent, and try to strike the drum in the same place every time. Try to match the tone and volume between both hands as you practice.

Slap Tone

The ***slap tone*** is the highest-pitched note of the jembe and is produced in much the same way as the open tone. To play the slap tone, cross the drum in exactly the same place as you did for the open tone, right where your fingers meet your palm. Unlike the open tone where your fingers are together, the slap involves relaxing your hand and allowing your fingers to naturally spread. You should notice a slight curvature in your hand and fingers. Your fingertips are the main point of contact with the skin. It is this relaxed position of the fingers that creates a more complex vibration in the head, producing a tonal/pitch change without affecting dynamics.

Note: The slap tone is not a louder note, but rather a higher-pitched or harmonic sound. Don't try to "beat it" out of the drum, but practice proper technique and let it come naturally.

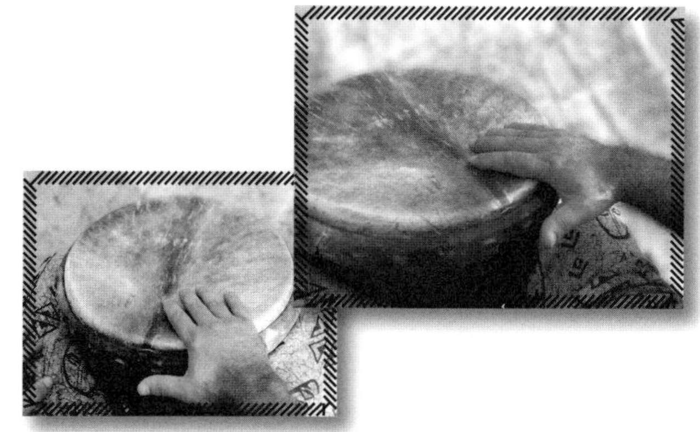

To play the slap tone:

1. Start with your arm in a relaxed position at a comfortable height above the drumhead (10"–14").
2. With palm down, raise your hand and arm from the elbow.
3. Allow gravity to pull your hand towards the head. Strike the drum with your fingers relaxed, crossing the edge of the drum in exactly the same place as you did for the open tone, where your fingers meet your palm. Focus the weight of your hand to the fingertips, producing a higher pitch (harmonic).
4. Allow your hand to rebound back to the starting position as the drum resonates.

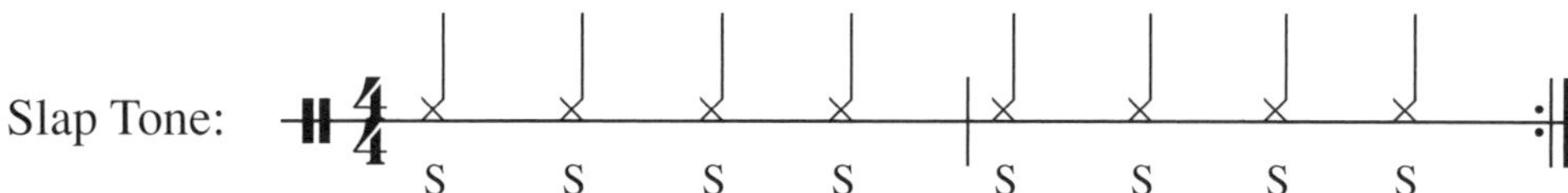

Drums take time to learn, just like any other instrument.

Here are a few tips to help you get the most from your practice time:

- Start where you are. Give yourself permission to be a beginner, and enjoy the journey to better technique.
- Give yourself time to improve. A little bit each day is better than a lot once a week.
- Practice all tones with both hands and at slow tempos. Never sacrifice technique for speed or volume.
- Resist the temptation to create variations of the techniques as we've outlined them. While you may gain some immediate gratification, you will have greater success in the long run if you master proper jembe technique.

DUNDUN TECHNIQUE

The dundun drums provide the rhythmic and melodic foundation for the ensemble. They are played in different ways (horizontally or vertically) and in different configurations (one, two, or all three drums) within the various regions of Guinea and the surrounding countries. The ***dundunba*** is played with large sticks (15"–16" long), and the ***sangban*** and ***kenkeni*** are played using sticks that are gradually smaller in diameter. It is important to strike the head near the center of the skin, allowing the sticks to bounce from the head, and not to hold or press them into the head (unless playing the muted stroke).

While it is common in Mandé music to play the dundun drums horizontally with the kenken (bell), some traditional music, and nearly all ballet music, is played with one or all of the dunduns in the vertical position. Susu music, such as Yankadi and Macrou, would often have only one dundun placed vertically with no bell. These traditional dundunba patterns are shown in the WRAP curriculum for both rhythms. In Guinean ballet music, Yankadi and Macrou are often performed with all three dundun drums and bells in various vertical and horizontal playing configurations. One of the most common configurations is to play the dundunba vertically and the sangban and kenkeni

horizontally with kenken. We have adopted this approach for the WRAP ballet, offering students the chance to see and practice both vertical and horizontal styles of dundun drumming while still remaining consistent and true to the cultural origins of the rhythms.

Vertical Dundun Technique

When playing the dundun vertically, adjust the height of the top head to be at waist-level. You can do this by placing the dundun on a stand, pieces of wood, a box, or something similar. If the drum is large enough, placing it on the floor will do. When playing all three dunduns in "ballet style," the sangban and kenkeni are strapped to the sides of the dundunba with rope or straps so the top head of each is at the same height as the dundunba.

Horizontal Dundun Technique with Kenken

The sangban and kenkeni drums are played horizontally, with a stick in one hand to strike the head and a metal beater in the other to play the bell. Traditionally, dunduns are hung over the shoulder with a cloth strap, but they can be strapped easily to a chair or stand. Usually, your dominant hand will play the skin, while your other hand will play the bell.

There are two types of sounds that are played on the dundun: open and muted. The ***open tone*** is produced by striking the drum in the center, allowing the stick to rebound. The ***muted tone*** is played by striking and then firmly holding the stick against the center of the skin. The kenken is played by tapping the middle of the bell with the tip of the beater.

Tip: Use two folding chairs to quickly create a horizontal dundun stand (see photo).

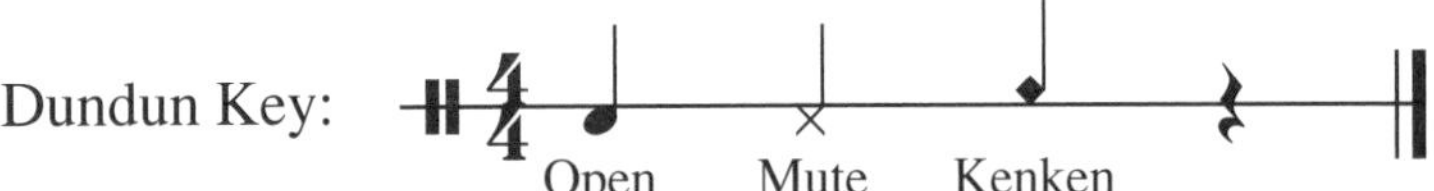

KRINYI TECHNIQUE

The krinyi is capable of producing a wide variety of sounds depending on where it is struck. Traditionally, krinyis are placed on the ground and played while seated with the instrument between the legs. In modern ballet productions, krinyis are sometimes worn around the waist by attaching a strap to the sides of the instrument with nails or bolts.

Krinyis are played using two medium-sized sticks. The proper krinyi sound is produced by striking the entire ***tone bar*** with the shaft of the stick (not the tip), then allowing the stick to bounce freely off the wood. If using tone blocks to imitate the krinyi sound, the same technique is used, striking the edge of the block with the shaft of the stick in a consistent manner.

SEKE-SEKE TECHNIQUE

Seke-sekes are always played in pairs and utilize an alternating, or bouncing, hand motion. To produce the correct sound, hold as shown and play in an up-and-down motion.

About Vocables 

It's been said that "If you can say it, you can play it." We strongly recommend adopting the practice of introducing and practicing tones and rhythms using the voice. This not only helps students gain a feeling for rhythm patterns and different instrument sounds, but helps create confidence when using their voices in a creative way. Vocalizing rhythms can also help produce stronger singers and speakers. While there are no codified vocal systems used in jembe cultures, it is common for teachers and students in African cultures to create their own syllables to represent the sounds played on the drums, and to string those sounds together to create patterns. Throughout the lessons, we refer to this method as using vocables. *A vocable is a vocal representation of an instrument or rhythm. Vocables are meant to convey the pitch, duration and timbre of a drum or percussion instrument.*

Below are two examples of verbal representations of a drum pattern. The first is based on Babatunde Olatunji's "gun/go/pa" method (see "Myths and Misconceptions" in appendix D). The second is a set of basic vocable sounds. We encourage you and your students to create your own system that makes sense for you.

Other examples of vocables:

- Dundun open: "doon"
- Dundun muted: "det"
- Krinyi high/low: "tah-kah / tu-ku"
- Seke-seke: "chah"

Note: Another way to verbally represent instrumental patterns is through chant, words, and phrases arranged in a particular rhythm. Chants can include rhymes, poems, songs, and "nonsense" words.

BALA (XYLOPHONE) TECHNIQUE

Playing Technique

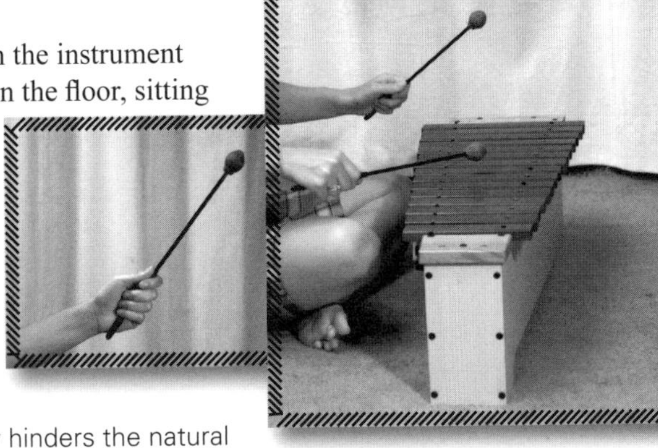

The African bala is either played while sitting on the floor or while standing with the instrument strapped to the player. Orff xylophones are played in one of three ways: sitting on the floor, sitting in a chair, or standing with the instrument in a stand. Adjust your body or the instrument height so the elbows are slightly higher than the instrument. The wrists should be flat and the mallets at a slight angle in from the arms.

Hold one mallet in each hand, placing the shaft between the index finger and thumb. Lightly wrap the fingers around the shaft so a small portion is left exposed near the wrist.

Tip: Do not place the index finger on top of the shaft. This only hinders the natural momentum of the mallets as they rise from the bars.

Play from the wrists with a small amount of arm movement. Strike the bars near the center, rebounding up to the starting position after each note is struck. As with most percussion instruments, the bala is best played using a "circular" or flowing hand motion that is smooth and relaxed.

Note: Orff instruments feature removable bars that allow the musician to customize the instrument to facilitate learning and playing the tone patterns. Recommendations for pattern-specific bar configurations are provided in the DVD playing examples. Keep in mind that Yankadi and Macrou use different notes so it may be best to leave all the bars on for the performance.

About Mallets

Most Orff instruments come with a pair of mallets that are matched to the range and tone of the instrument. Soprano mallets are harder than alto mallets, which are harder than bass mallets. To better emulate the sound of the traditional bala from West Africa, which is usually played with hard rubber mallets, we use soprano mallets on alto xylophone and alto mallets on the bass xylophone. You may wish to do the same.

THE ROLE OF WEST AFRICAN DANCE

Traditional dance in West Africa is an extension of life's everyday activities. Dance movements often reflect aspects of daily life including fishing, hunting, and harvesting. The role of the jembe ensemble is to play music to accompany these dances. Every dance has its own unique rhythm and is performed for specific purposes. As some Guineans say, "There is no reason to drum without dance, and no reason to dance without drumming." Music and dance in Guinea are different aspects of the same expression.

Types of Rhythm and Dance

The following are the primary categories of rhythms and dances in Guinea.

Ritual or Initiation Dances

These dances are done for specific initiation rites or ritual ceremonies performed by those already initiated. These ceremonies often include the use of masks or other spiritual/sacred objects.

Nyamakala (Caste) Dances

These dances and rhythms are specifically associated with one's particular caste. They are often performed at popular festivals by caste members to identify themselves. Traditional castes include the Jeli (griots), Numu (blacksmiths), Garangé (leather workers), and Funé (mimes).

Secular and Popular Dances

These are the dances of everyday life. There are special dances for naming ceremonies, weddings, farming, and social events. Everyone in the village participates and dances at these events, and it is a time of communal gathering and great joy.

Traditional vs. Ballet Dances

Traditional dances are generally performed in a circle utilizing predefined ceremonial movements and/or individual structured improvisation. There are usually different dance steps for men and women, and the dancer dictates the solo and phrasing to be played by the lead drummer. In ballet dances, traditional steps are choreographed in a sequential order for a group to perform for an audience. In this scenario, the lead drummer signals the dance group to start, stop and change movements. The WRAP curriculum introduces students to elements of both traditional and ballet styles of dancing.

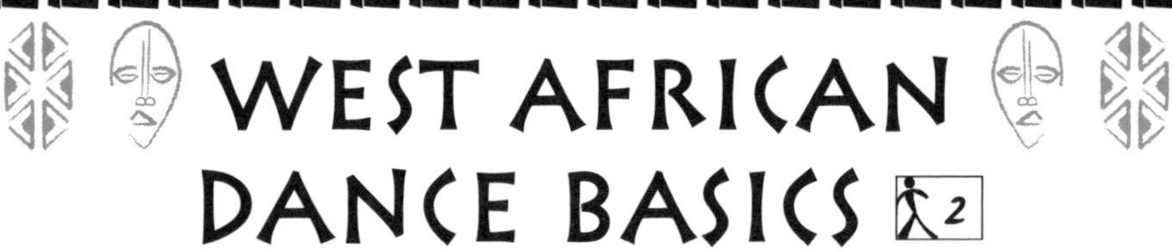

WEST AFRICAN DANCE BASICS

West African dance is a highly energetic, acrobatic, powerful, yet graceful, art form. While dance subtleties take years of practice to develop, basic movements can be performed rather quickly by students with little or no previous dance experience. The following are some brief guidelines for teaching West African dance.

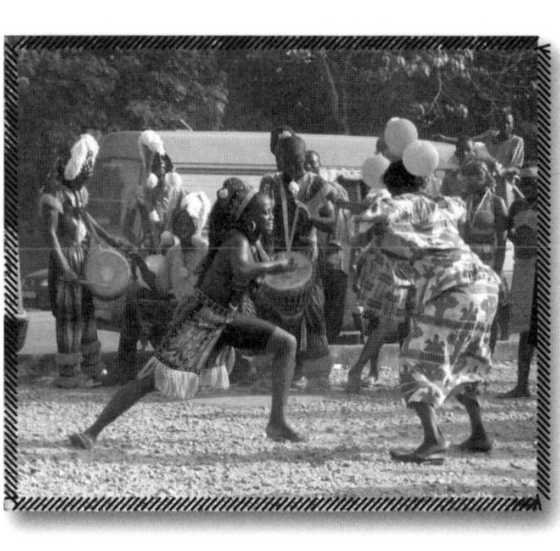

Group Formation: Introducing the Steps

- Arrange students in staggered lines behind you so everyone can see clearly. Periodically rotate students so everyone has a chance to be in front.
- Teach the steps with your back to the students. It's easier to learn the dance by shadowing than by mirroring.
- Isolate the foot patterns, then the arms, then combine the feet and arms.
- Once students are performing the feet and arm movements together, add fine points such as hands, hips, shoulders, head, and eyes.
- Always start and stop movements with the break to reinforce students' understanding of how to respond to the signal within each step. (The signal can be vocalized when teaching without music.)

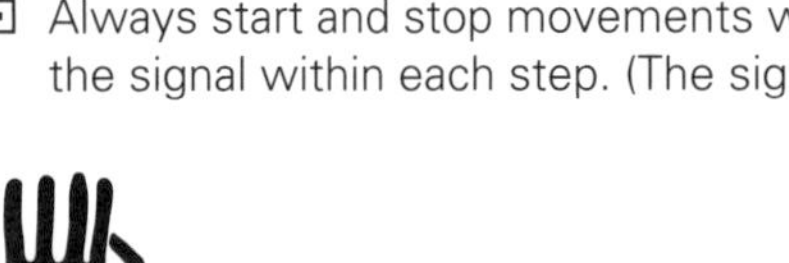

Note: In this setting, a slower (practice) tempo is common.

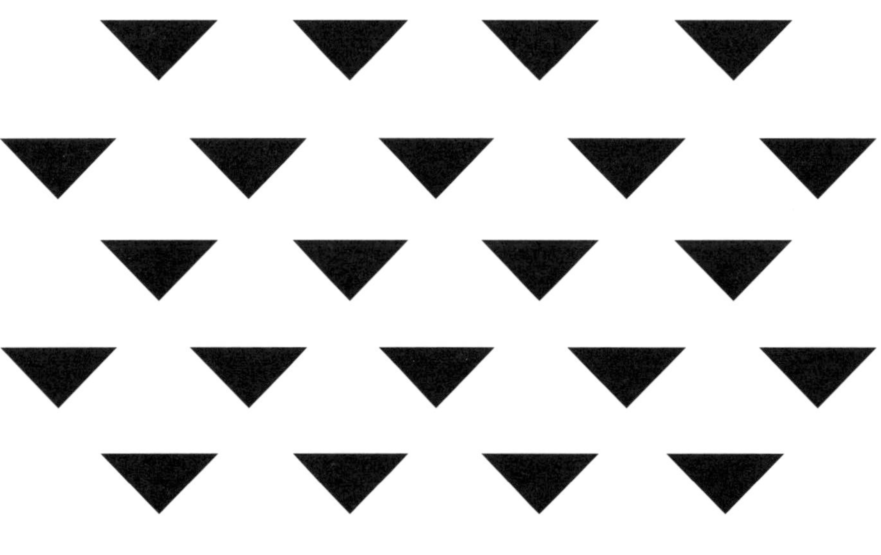

Line Formation: Practicing the Steps

- Arrange students in lines of four or five at one end of the room.
- Stand facing them at the other end of the room.
- Play the break and invite students do the first dance movement while moving towards you, one group at a time. They will need to make adjustments to keep their spacing even.
- Allow students to dance all the way to you, then play the break to cue the first line to stop, walk around the side of the room, and get in line behind the other dancers.
- Play the break to cue the next group to begin dancing towards you.
- Repeat the same format with all the dance steps.

Note: In this setting, a faster (performance) tempo is common.

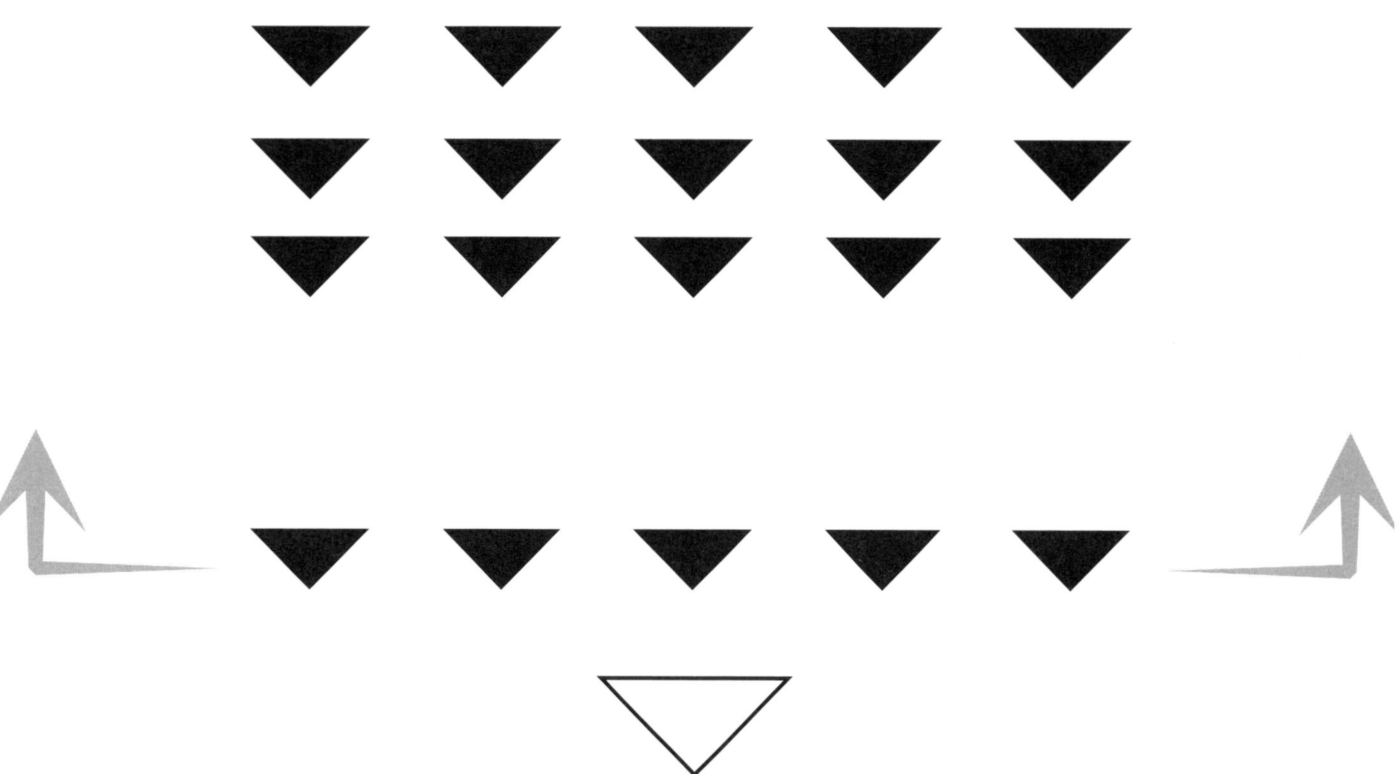

Note: This is one typical style of teaching West African dance. The goal is to isolate each movement for a period of time. Dancers benefit from being able to do several repetitions of each movement, allowing them to feel and ingrain it into their bodies. Teachers benefit from being able to observe students for a longer period of time and on an individual basis. This enables tips, corrections, and subtle changes to be shown and implemented immediately.

The dance instruction section of the DVD shows all steps from both front and back views. By using the angle button on your DVD player, you can switch your view of the dancer from front to back, allowing you to choose which view is best for you and to see all the aspects of each dance step easily.

About the Dance Notation 

Every dance step is notated using a very basic system that shows which arm and leg movements happen on which beats. While the primary method of learning the steps is from watching the DVD, the notation offers beat-by-beat precision and may help better clarify the steps. Keep in mind that African dance is a fluid art form, the scope of which extends far beyond any notation system. For this reason, the notation is best used to support what you learn from the DVD.

[7]

					[6] BREAK			
[1]	1	2	3	4	1 (5)	2 (6)	3 (7)	4 (8)
[2]	FRONT	SIDE	FRONT	SIDE	FRONT	SIDE	FRONT	CLAP
[3]		L		R		L		
[4]	STEP / BWD	STEP	STEP / BWD	STEP	STEP / BWD	STEP	STEP / BWD	JUMP
[5]	R L	R	L R	L	R L	R	L R	B

[1] Beats and/or primary beats
[2] Arm movements (see appendix G for explanations)
[3] Specifies one or both arms
[4] Foot movements (see appendix G for explanations)
[5] Specifies one or both feet
[6] Portion of the phrase where the break is played
[7] Photo of the general position

The dance notation used in this book is based on that of Phyllis Weikhart, as found in her comprehensive book Teaching Movement and Dance. *The authors would like to thank Phyllis and High/Scope Press for supporting our adaptation of her system for use in this work. While there are some differences, students of Weikhart's "Say & Do" approach will find our system easy to work with right from the start. For more about Phyllis's work and other High/Scope Press publications, visit* **highscope.org**.

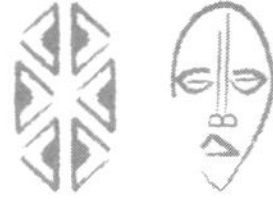 THE ROLE OF THE LEAD DRUMMER  

The lead drummer has an extremely important and diverse role in music from Guinea. This drummer always plays a jembe that is tuned to a higher pitch than the accompanying instruments. Also called the ***soloist***, the lead drummer plays different, and often improvised, patterns over the foundation provided by the accompanying parts. These improvisations involve much more than just beating a drum faster and louder than everyone else. (See sidebar, "The Lead Drummer in Guinea," on page 33) The complete depth of the soloist's role extends beyond the scope of this book; however, the basic concepts of leading a West African ensemble can easily be learned through this material and played by teachers and students.

LEAD DRUMMER QUALITIES

Before taking on the role of the lead drummer for the ensemble, teachers and students must be able to do the following:

- Perform the three basic sounds of the jembe with clear articulation.
- Demonstrate the ability to play at a louder volume than the rest of the ensemble.
- Demonstrate the ability to play in rhythm, and for extended periods of time.
- Demonstrate a thorough knowledge of all instrument patterns.
- Demonstrate a thorough knowledge of ensemble arrangements, including breaks.
- Demonstrate a thorough knowledge of all dance steps.

The lead drummer has a responsibility to both the drummers and dancers. As the leader of the musical ensemble, this person is responsible for signaling where and when to start, stop, or change rhythms or parts, and for setting the group's dynamics and tempo. As the soloists for dancers within the context of a performance, the lead drummer's most important obligation is to appropriately signal dancers to start, stop, and change movements. In order to perform these functions, two of the most important elements of a soloist's role must be mastered: the ***drum call*** (or ***break***), and the ***échauffment***.

DRUM CALL OR BREAK

The ***drum call*** (or ***break***) is one of the most vital elements in West African musical performance. The break is played by the lead drummer to signal changes in the music or dance, enabling all members of the group to respond at the same time. It is most often used at the start of the rhythm, like a drummer in a rock band pounding sticks together and shouting "1, 2, 3, 4" to signal the band to begin playing. It is also used at the end of a piece of music to indicate when the group is to stop playing, or inside the rhythm to change dance steps or choreography, like a dancer saying "5, 6, 7, 8" before going to the next movement. The break should be the loudest part of a solo so it can be clearly heard, deciphered, and responded to by both musicians and dancers.

There are many different breaks used in West African drumming. In the WRAP curriculum, students learn a few different breaks that are specific to Yankadi and Macrou. Most breaks are played on the jembe, but some are played on a whistle—an aspect that is unique to the Yankadi-Macrou celebration.

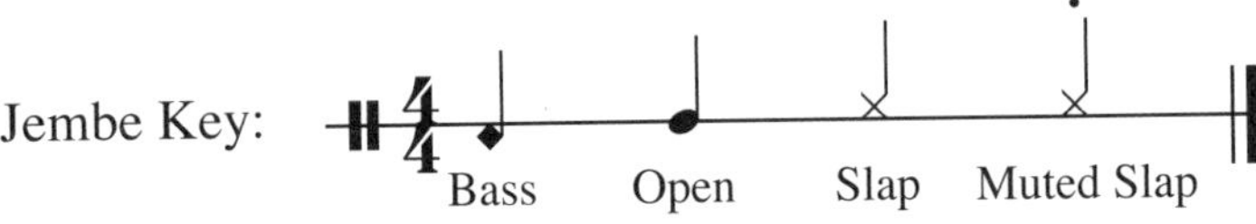

Macrou Break

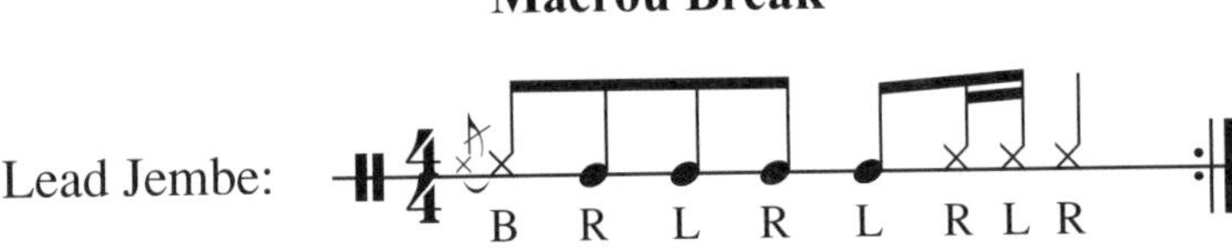

Yankadi Break

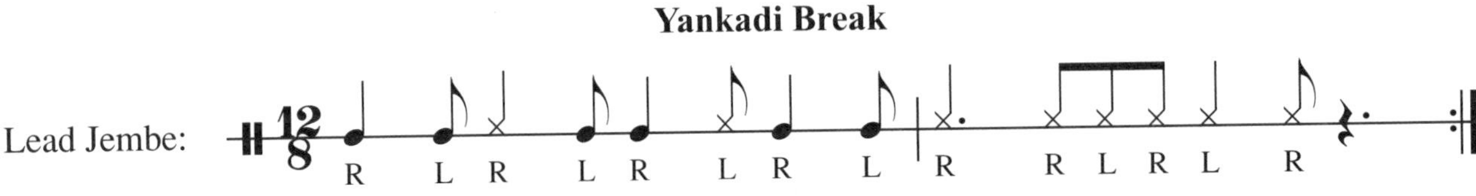

ÉCHAUFFMENT

Échauffment is a French word that means "heating up." It is commonly used in Guinea to describe a repetitive pattern played by the lead drummer to signal an upcoming break. The échauffment is commonly used to transition between slower sections of music, where songs are being sung, and faster sections of music, where dances would begin. It is also typically used at the end of certain energetic dance movements, and it is virtually always played to alert performers of the ending break. The échauffment can also be used to increase tempo and volume.

The following shows the two different échauffment patterns for Yankadi and Macrou, followed by their respective breaks.

Yankadi Échauffment and Break

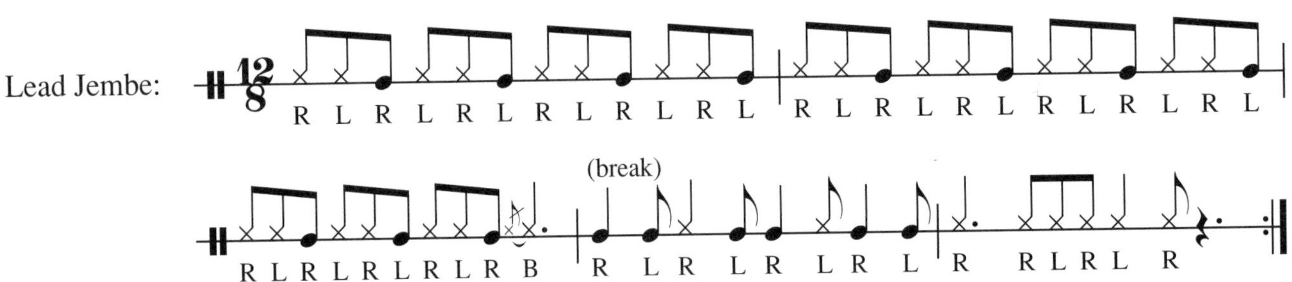

Macrou Échauffment and Break

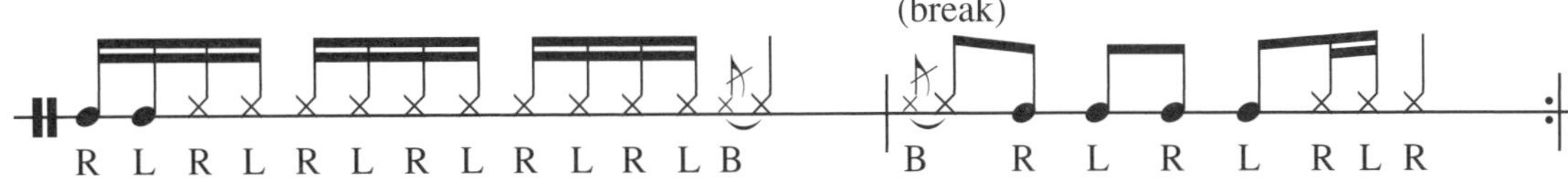

THE NEXT STEP: MARKING DANCE MOVEMENTS

The lead drummer's obligation to dancers extends well beyond playing the break in the proper place. Traditionally, the lead drummer will accent or mark the movements of the dancers by playing specific musical figures. These special musical phrases bring out the characteristics of the specific rhythm or step and add to the overall effect. While this skill takes years of practice to completely develop, teachers and more advanced students can explore some traditional solo phrasing for Yankadi and Macrou and begin using it right away.

The Lead Drummer in Guinea

In Guinea, the lead drummer is a master artist who has dedicated years of training and apprenticeship to all aspects of West African music and dance. The soloist has a thorough knowledge of all the rhythm parts, dances, and traditional solo technique that is passed down from generation to generation. The soloist is also a virtuosic player and an engaging entertainer who weaves the traditions with improvisation, demonstrating unparalleled technique, blazing speed, and knowledge of phrasing for a variety of different rhythms and solos. In most cases, the lead drummer is also the leader of the performance troupe and may also be the teacher of many of the accompanying musicians.

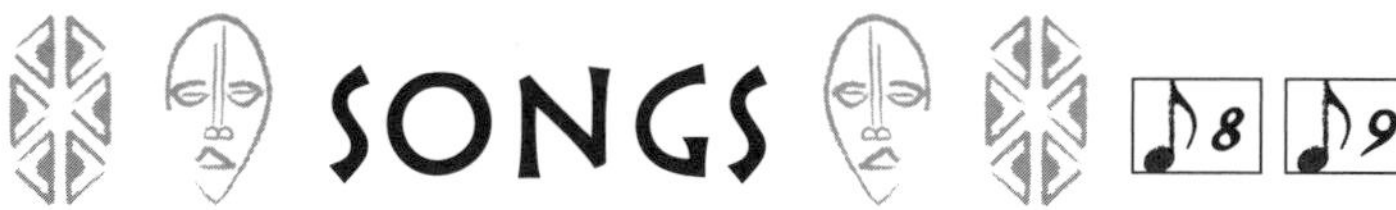

SONGS

Singing is an integral part of all traditional and ballet celebrations and performances. Songs are usually sung in a call-and-response style with a single lead voice calling a group response. Lead singers of traditional songs are usually members of the ***Jeli*** caste (see "The Role of the Jeli" on page 19) and will often improvise lyrics within the song to acknowledge or praise certain important individuals or families.

Song meanings cover a myriad of different topics and experiences of the human condition. Traditional songs about certain people, places, and events are often juxtaposed in contemporary settings against pertinent modern issues of the day, including political corruption, AIDS, and unemployment. Whether traditional or modern, the majority of lyrics continue to exalt timeless values such as love and family. Traditional rhythms can have many songs associated with them and certain songs are sung in more than one rhythm.

SUSU LANGUAGE

Just as students learn to speak the language of the jembe drum and other traditional West African instruments to help their musical communication, learning a little of the spoken languages of Guinea can help facilitate a broader cultural understanding and aid in a more well-rounded perspective of the people as a whole. While by no means a complete language course, the WRAP curriculum introduces students to the Susu language through common greetings (lessons 1–10) and a short program introduction (lessons 11–20).

Proper greetings are important Susu social customs. Greetings can last for several minutes, and it is considered very impolite not to properly greet people any time you meet or see them. Several basic greetings are learned and can be used in conversation. The performance introduction increases student vocabulary while providing a culturally unique way to introduce the Yankadi-Macrou performance to an audience. One student can introduce the performance or several students can take turns, each one saying one of the introduction sentences.

ABOUT YANKADI AND MACROU

Imagine a West African beach on a warm summer evening. The palm trees are swaying gently in the breeze. The full moon is glistening off the gentle ocean waves, and you are getting dressed in your finest ***goulahs*** and ***dugis*** (boy's and girl's clothing). Invitations have been given to young people in all the surrounding villages, and, as they arrive, the sweet smell of ***gato*** (sweet bread) fills the air. The bala begins to weave its intricate melodies, and voices fill the night air with songs of joy and happiness. "Dun-Dun, Dun-Dun." The pulsating dundun drums echo through the village and all are called to attention by the piercing jembe drum, roaring through the ***bara*** (circle) like a lion. Over the next few hours you will dance, drum, sing, see old friends and make new ones, and most of all—have FUN! For the great Yankadi-Macrou celebration has begun!

Yankadi and ***Macrou*** are two separate rhythms and dances that are almost always played together as part of the same ceremony. Often referred to as a "dance of seduction," the Yankadi and Macrou is more of a social gathering, offering the perfect environment for people to meet and get to know each other. The rhythms and dances are traditionally from the Susu ethnic group, located in the western coastal region of Guinea, and are most often played at the time of a full moon. Young people from different villages gather and participate in this social mixer. The event is exciting and fascinating. Layered rhythms, changing melodies, and intricate dance movements are all woven together in a complex, yet approachable way. Yankadi begins in a slow 12/8 swing feel, with lines of singing participants facing each other, dancing in slow, sweeping movements. With the call of a whistle and crack of the jembe drum, the music changes to a fun, up-tempo 4/4 rhythm, where high energy movements are intertwined with interactive group dances, creating a spirited and friendly environment in which to meet new friends.

As a WRAP teacher, you can choose to present the ultra-flexible Yankadi-Macrou curriculum in a variety of ways. A "ballet" type performance often starts with the slower Yankadi rhythm and then transitions into the faster, more spirited Macrou. (see DVD performance). Traditional ceremonies will often begin with Macrou, and then alternate several times with Yankadi. The rhythms and dances can also be presented independent of one another, or as individualized drumming or dancing units. We have chosen to begin our curriculum with Macrou because its meter and techniques tend to be more accessible to beginning students. We offer a slightly slower pace, allowing students to familiarize themselves with important West African musical and movement concepts and build confidence before moving to more complex rhythmical ideas.

Tip: See Chapter 20 for step-by-step examples, tips, and ideas for presenting your authentic West African Yankadi-Macrou Performance Celebration.

MACROU

LESSON 1: Welcome to Your Village

An Introduction to West African Drum, Dance and Culture

OBJECTIVES

Students will

- identify and respond appropriately to the whistle break;
- learn Macrou Dance Step 1 and perform it in a circle formation;
- identify one- and two-note cues, and respond appropriately;
- learn and perform the dundunba rhythm using proper technique;
- identify the seke-seke and perform the rhythm pattern;
- learn and perform xylophone parts 1 and 3 using proper technique;
- learn and perform part 1 of the "A Boronco" song;
- combine music and dance elements into a mini-performance.

MUSICAL SKILLS

- Rhythm patterns
- Steady beat
- Melody

LIFE SKILLS

- Group awareness
- Active listening

MOVEMENT SKILLS

- Marching
- Alternating
- Change direction

MATERIALS

- Dundunba drum with sticks
- Xylophones: BX & SX
- Seke-seke
- Whistle
- DVD player and TV
- CD player

VOCABULARY

- Dundunba
- Break
- Bala
- Susu
- Jeli
- Seke-seke

Process

LET'S SPEAK

Number

Susu/ Phonetics	English
keren *(KER-ing)*	"One"

Vocabulary/ Dialog

	Susu/ Phonetics	English
Person 1:	**I nu wali?** *(IN-nu-wa-ly)*	"How are you?"
Person 2:	**I nu wali?** *(IN-nu-wa-ly)*	"How are you?" *(Used for general greeting and appreciation.)*

➲ When speaking to more than one person, "I" is replaced with "Wo"- "Wo nu wali?"

(For additional information on the language lessons, see the "Susu Language Pronunciation Guide" in appendix H.)

LET'S MOVE

1. Arrange students in large circle facing inwards.
2. Introduce students to the break played on the whistle.

Whistle Break

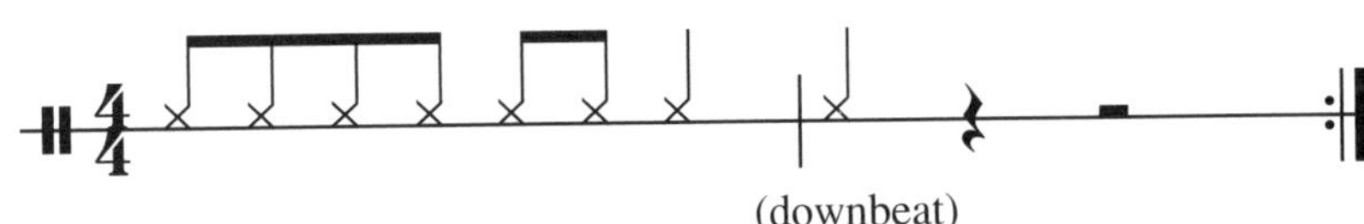

3. Encourage students to clap with you on the downbeat.
4. Invite students to stomp with the right foot on the downbeat.

Tip: Vary the tempo at which you play the break to illustrate how the break defines not only where to play or move, but also at what tempo to play or move.

5. Have students march around the circle to a steady beat. Use the break to cue students to start and stop on the downbeat.
6. Introduce the *turn step* (a quick pivot to face the opposite direction), and have students practice stopping and facing the opposite direction on the downbeat.
7. Have students march in a circle, then use the break to cue the turn step and change directions without stopping.
8. Move the turn step up to beat 4 (the last note of the break), and have students practice changing direction on beat 4, then marching on beat 1.
9. Introduce Macrou Dance Step 1 in circle formation, and highlight how it utilizes the same technique learned in the turn step.

Macrou Dance Step 1

					BREAK			
	1	2	3	4	1 (5)	2 (6)	3 (7)	4 (8)
Arms	FRONT	SIDE	FRONT	SIDE	FRONT	SIDE	FRONT	SIDE
		L		R		L		R
Feet	STEP / BWD	STEP	STEP / BWD	STEP	STEP / BWD	STEP	STEP / BWD	STEP
	R L	R	L R	L	R L	R	L R	L

Note: This step is started from the second half of beat 3 (BWD) to beat 4 (STEP) as a pickup. The rapid BWD/STEP action (beats 1 to 2 and from 3 to 4) is often called a "ball-change" and is sometimes challenging for young, beginning students. You may wish to isolate this action first, then return to learning the dance step.

1. Introduce one- and two-note cues for marching and dancing respectively.

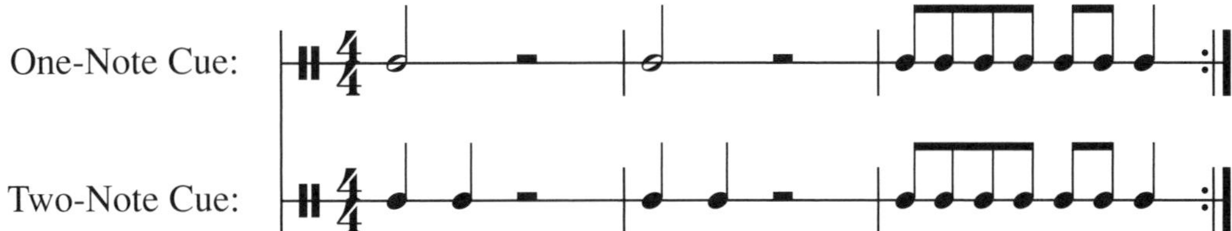

2. Explain that when students hear the one-note cue, they should MARCH around in a circle. (Choose a direction when starting.) When they hear the two-note cue, they should DANCE (Macrou Dance Step 1). When hearing the cue for the movement they are already doing, they change direction.

Accompaniment Option
Play CD track 2.

1. In a circle marching to a steady beat, introduce the dundunba rhythm using vocables or body percussion. Play all downbeats with your dominant hand. Should your students find this pattern too challenging, the simplified version may be used as an intermediate step.

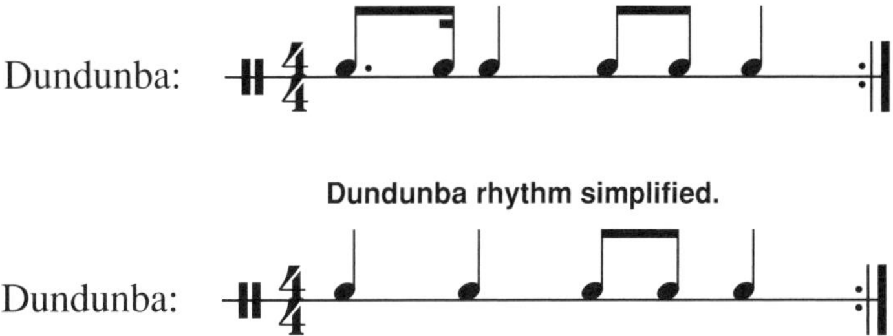

2. Invite students to match your movements.
3. Transfer the rhythm pattern to the dundunba drum demonstrating proper technique.
4. Introduce and demonstrate the seke-seke pattern and combine it with the dundunba.

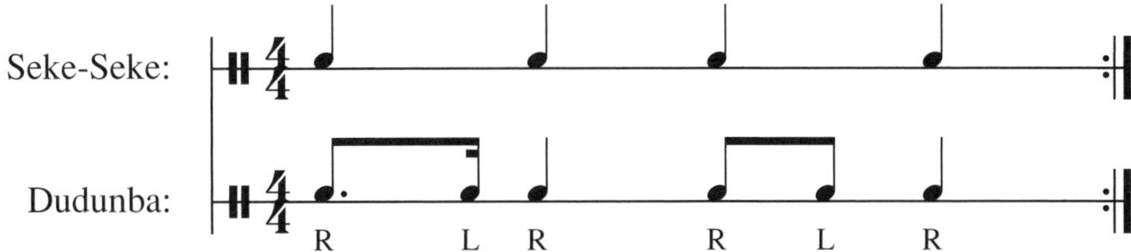

5. Introduce and demonstrate the xylophone 1 pattern. If possible, use a bass xylophone (BX).

6. Introduce and demonstrate the xylophone 3 pattern. If possible, use a soprano xylophone (SX).

7. Combine all patterns and practice playing them together.

Did you know?
*The word **xylophone** comes from the Greek words **xulon** (meaning "of wood") and **phone** (meaning "sound or voice").*

Introduce the following call-and-response portion of the song "A Boronco." For the complete lyrics and English translation, see page 50.

Tip: Divide the group into two sections, one that sings the call, and one that sings the response.

LET'S PLAY 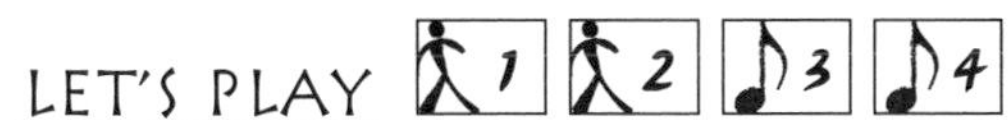

Combine the above elements of the process for mini-performance. Switch between groups of dancers and drummers. Use the whistle break to start and set the initial tempo and then to cue the instrument entrances and dance-step changes.

Let's Play Key

D=Dundunba S=Sangban K=Kenkeni J=Jembe X=Xylophone SS=Seke-seke KR=Krinyi
DS=Dance Step M=March SG=Song EM=Échauffmant

LEADER	BREAK	BREAK	1-NOTE CUE	1-NOTE CUE	2-NOTE CUE	BREAK
DRUMMERS	X1, X3 & SS	D				STOP
DANCERS	M SG (4 times)		M-CCW	M-CW	DS1	Jump/Clap

Wrap Up

- Invite students to store the instruments and straighten up the room for the next session.
- Ask students to get their Student Enrichment Books and gather for discussion.
- Review and clarify the assignment in the Student Enrichment Book for this lesson.

Evaluation 1 2 7 7 8

Were students able to

- identify and respond appropriately to the whistle break?
- learn Macrou Dance Step 1 and perform it in a circle formation? If not, try performing the step in a line (as in a conga line).
- identify one- and two-note cues and respond appropriately?
- learn and perform the dundunba rhythm using proper technique?
- learn and perform part 1 of the "A Boronco" song? If not, play the CD and have students sing along.

Discussion 4 7

- How is each break used? How does our ability to listen affect the quality of the performance?
- How does working together and being aware of those around you affect the performance?
- What are the instrument names and new vocabulary words?
- Which instrumental parts are rhythmically similar?
- Evaluate the session using P.R.I.D.E. (the WRAP core values and best practices) as discussion points.

Tip: Present a short verbal quiz by pointing to an instrument and asking students to name it.

LESSON 2: Meet the Family

Dundun Drumming as the Foundation of the Mandé Musical Orchestra

OBJECTIVES

Students will

- learn Macrou Dance Steps 2, 3, and 4 and perform them in stage formation;
- learn and perform the sangban and kenkeni rhythms using proper technique;
- combine the three dundun patterns and perform them with the seke-seke;
- review and perform part 1 of the "A Boronco" song;
- combine music and dance elements into a mini-performance.

MUSICAL SKILLS

- Rhythm patterns
- Small ensemble playing
- Dynamics

LIFE SKILLS

- Accountability
- Active listening
- Cooperation

MOVEMENT SKILLS

- Step
- Skip
- Hand coordination
- Arm swing

MATERIALS

- All dundun drums
- Xylophones: BX & SX
- Seke-seke
- Whistle
- DVD player and TV
- CD player

VOCABULARY

- Sangban
- Kenkeni
- Kenken
- Malinké
- Complementary
- Dynamics

Process

LET'S SPEAK 9

Number

	Susu/ Phonetics	English
	firin *(FIR-ing)*	"Two"

Vocabulary/ Dialog

	Susu/ Phonetics	English
Person 1:	**Arabakhadi?** *(ah-rah-BAH-kha-di)*	"What's happening?"
Person 2:	**Amurabakhi kioke.** *(ah-mur-ah-BAH-kha-KEY)*	"Nothing bad is happening."

LET'S MOVE

1. Arrange students in a large circle and review the marching step and the Macrou Dance Step 1 from lesson 1. Continue to use the one-note, two-note and break cues on the whistle to start, stop and change movements. Use the CD for accompaniment.

Tip: Slect one or more of the students' mini-performances from lesson 1 as a way to review the cues and dance steps. Discuss arranging challenges and solutions (listening, starting/ stopping, cues, movement, etc).

2. In lines of 3 to 4 students each, introduce Macrou Dance Steps 2, 3, and 4. Have students focus on the transitions between steps and how they align with the whistle break and dundunba pattern.

   Remember to use the whistle break on the correct side of the dance movement. Generally, the break is played through an even bar (4 or 8 measures) and allows the dancer to transition easily into the next movement. (See DVD.)

Tip: To facilitate learning the dance, teach the movements in line formation according to the "West African Dance Basics" section. Ultimately, the students will use both the circle and line dance choreography in the final performance.

Macrou Dance Step 2

					BREAK			
	1	2	3	4	1 (5)	2 (6)	3 (7)	4 (8)
Arms	FWD		FWD		FWD		FWD	
	R		L		L		R	
Feet	SIDE	CLOSE	SIDE	CLOSE	SIDE	CLOSE	SIDE	CLOSE
	R	L	L	R	L	R	R	L

Macrou Dance Step 3

		1	2	3	4	1 (5)	2 (6)	3 (7)	4 (8)
						BREAK			
Arms		FRONT	SIDE	FRONT	SIDE	FRONT	SIDE	FRONT	SIDE
			L		R		L		R
Feet		STEP / BWD	STEP 90° CCW	STEP / BWD	STEP 90° CCW	STEP / BWD	STEP 90° CCW	STEP / BWD	STEP 90° CCW
		R L	R	L R	L	R L	R	L R	L

Macrou Dance Step 4

		1	2	3	4	5 (9)	6 (10)	7 (11)	8 (12)
						BREAK (2nd Time)			
Arms		CROSS	OPEN	CROSS	OPEN	FRONT		SIDE	
								R	
Feet		STEP / STEP	STEP	STEP / STEP	STEP	STEP	STEP	BWD	STEP
		R L	R	L R	L	R	L	R	L
						2 Times			

Beats 1-4 *Beats 5-12*

Repeat the steps for beats 5–8 twice before returning to beat 1. Play the break during the repeat of beats 5–8.

LET'S DRUM 

1. Review the dundunba pattern from lesson 1.
2. In a circle marching to a steady beat, introduce the sangban and kenkeni rhythms using vocables and/or body percussion. (For example, tap the drum-head rhythm on their thighs and use finger snaps, or shoulder pats, in the other hand to simulate the kenken parts.)

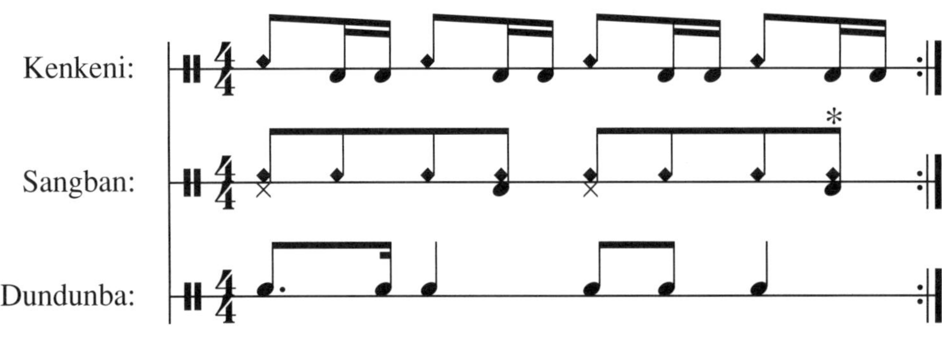

*Start here.

3. Introduce students to the sangban and kenkeni drums with the kenken (bell) attached to each. Remind students of the role that each drum plays in the dundun family and in the ensemble.
4. Create three groups and experiment with different combinations of chanting and body percussion for each of the three dundun parts.
5. Transfer all the dundun parts to their respective instruments, demonstrating proper stick and bell (kenken) technique.

Dundun Technique Tips

- Do not place the index finger on the top of the stick.
- Use a rotating motion (like turning a door knob) rather than bending the wrist.
- Allow the stick to bounce off the head for open strokes.
- Press the stick into the head without buzzing for muted strokes.
- Strike the center of the drum.

6. Perform the following dundun patterns with seke-seke. Remember to start and stop with the whistle break. This will help reinforce the students' understanding of each pattern's relationship to the break.

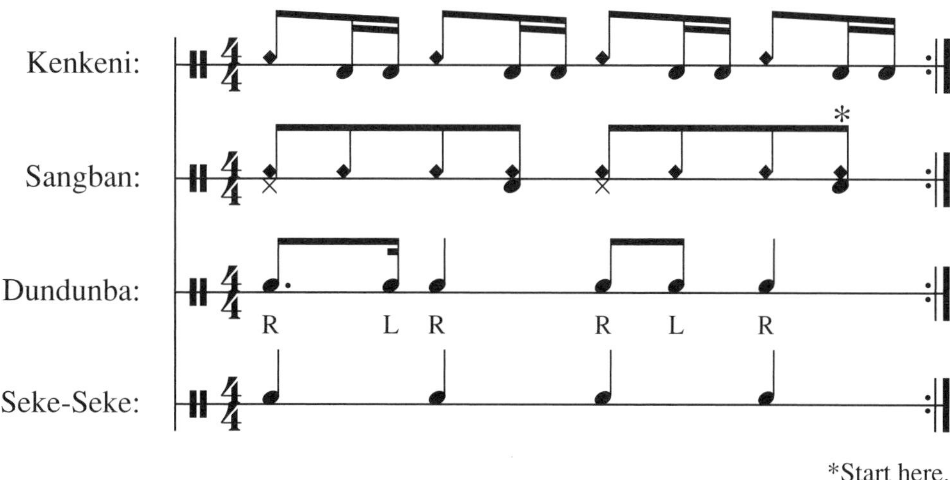

*Start here.

LET'S SING

Review the portion of the Macrou song "A Boronco" from lesson 1.

Tip: Use the xylophone parts to accompany the song. Invite or select students to lead the song from lesson 1.

LET'S PLAY

Combine the above elements of the process for mini-performance. Switch between groups of dancers and drummers. Use the whistle break to start and set the initial tempo and then to cue the instrument entrances and dance-step changes.

Let's Play Key

D=Dundunba S=Sangban K=Kenkeni J=Jembe X=Xylophone SS=Seke-seke KR=Krinyi
DS=Dance Step M=March SG=Song EM=Échauffmant

LEADER	BREAK	BREAK	BREAK	BREAK	BREAK	BREAK	BREAK	BREAK
DRUMMERS	D & SS	S	K	X1 & X3 (Drums Lower Volume)	X1 & X3 (Drums Lower Volume)	Everyone Volume Up		
DANCERS	Clap	M			SG	Stop SG DS1	DS2	DS3

LEADER	BREAK	BREAK
DRUMMERS		STOP
DANCERS	DS4	Jump/Clap

Tip: Use the whistle to signal all the breaks. Be sure to change the dance movements on an even bar (generally, every four to eight). Note the dynamic changes that occur when the xylophone and singing parts enter and when the singing ends. Repeat the mini-performance as time permits.

Wrap-Up

- Invite students to store the instruments and straighten up the room for the next session.
- Ask students to get their Student Enrichment Books and gather for discussion.
- Review and clarify the assignment in the Student Enrichment Book for this lesson.

Evaluation

Were students able to

- learn and demonstrate proper dundun technique and rhythms?
- play both the open and closed notes with the stick while striking the kenken? If not, assess and review as needed. (See the DVD.)
- keep their individual dundun parts in place while the other dunduns were playing?
- cooperate with one another and respond to the various cues as a group?
- learn Macrou Dance Steps 2–4 and perform them properly?
- combine music and dance elements into a mini-performance?

Discussion

- Why is it important to listen to each other and create the dundun melody together, and not just focus in on your own part?
- What are some strategies for supporting a healthy and dynamic group (listening, cooperation, flexibility, etc.)?
- What are some challenges you faced during the mini-performance? How did you address them?
- Evaluate the session using P.R.I.D.E. (the WRAP core values and best practices) as discussion points.

LESSON 3: Let's Dance! Let's Sing!

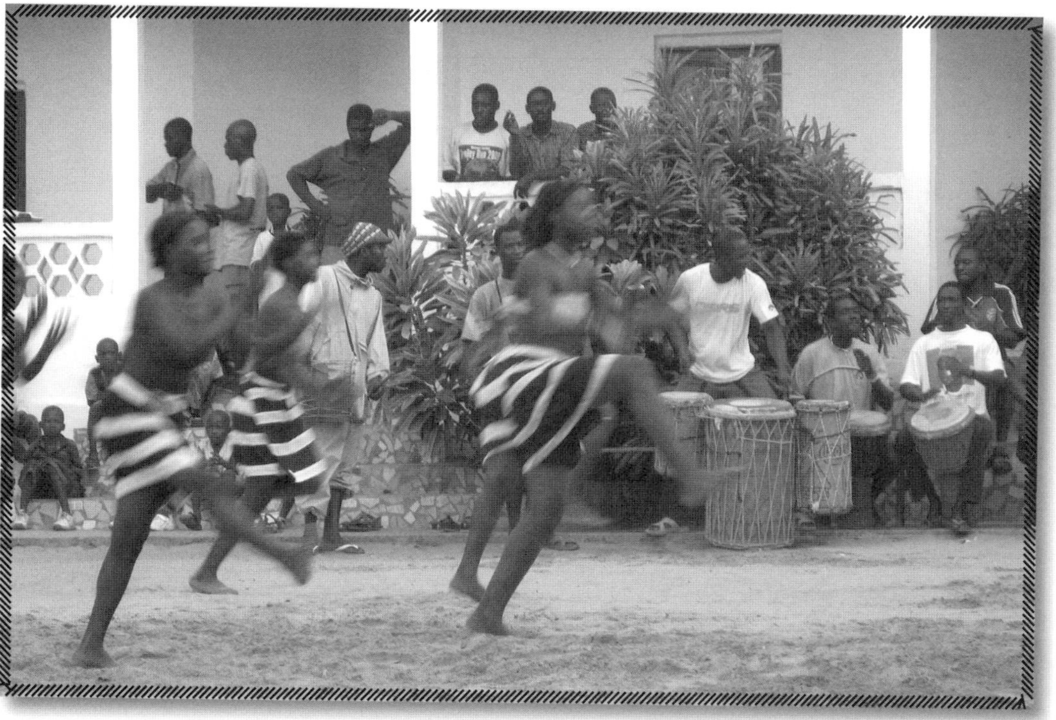

OBJECTIVES

Students will

- learn and perform Macrou Dance Steps 5, 6, and 7 in stage formation;
- review the three dundun patterns and perform them with the seke-seke;
- learn and perform the entire "A Boronco" song in a two-part format;
- combine music and dance elements into a mini-performance.

MUSICAL SKILLS

- Melody
- Small ensemble playing
- Dynamics

LIFE SKILLS

- Self awareness
- Responsibility
- Focus

MOVEMENT SKILLS

- Balance
- Contrary motion
- Restrict and expand
- Articulation of body parts
- Weight shift

MATERIALS

- All dundun drums
- Xylophones: BX & SX
- Seke-seke
- DVD player and TV
- CD player

VOCABULARY

- Faré boron *(fa-REH boh-ROHN)* - To dance
- Sigi sa *(SIH-gee sah)* - Sing!
- Guinea Ballet
- Wongai *(won-GAI)* - Let's go!
- Contrary motion
- Choreography

Process

LET'S SPEAK 9

Number

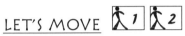

	Susu/ Phonetics	**English**
	sakhan *(SAH-xan)*	"Three"

Vocabulary/ Dialog

	Susu/ Phonetics	**English**
Person 1:	**Tana mu na?** *(TAH-na MOO nah)*	"There are no misfortunes?"
Person 2:	**Tana yo mu na.** *(TAH-na yo MOO nah)*	"Nothing bad is happening."

LET'S MOVE 1 2

1. Review Macrou Dance Steps 1–4 in group. Use the whistle-break cue to change movements while playing the CD for accompaniment. Emphasize precise articulation of body parts and the transitions between steps.
2. Introduce students to Macrou Dance Steps 5, 6, and 7. Emphasize good body balance and weight shift, and point out the contrary motion in dance step 7.

Tip: For dance patterns that are two bars in length, make sure the whistle break is played at the beginning of the second bar in the pattern, allowing dancers to complete the step and transition easily into the next one.

Macrou Dance Step 5

					BREAK			
	1	**2**	**3**	**4**	**1 (5)**	**2 (6)**	**3 (7)**	**4 (8)**
Arms	CHEST		BACK		CHEST		BACK	
	R		R		R		R	
Feet	TOUCH	BWD	HEEL	STEP	TOUCH	BWD	HEEL	STEP
	R	R	L	L	R	R	L	L

Macrou Dance Step 6

					BREAK			
	1	**2**	**3**	**4**	**1 (5)**	**2 (6)**	**3 (7)**	**4 (8)**
Arms	OUT (CIRCLE)	IN (CIRCLE)	OUT	IN	OUT	IN	OUT	IN
Feet	LEAP / STEP	STEP	LEAP / STEP	STEP	HOP	ROTATE CW	HOP	ROTATE CW
	R L	R	L R	L	L	(R)	L	(R)

Beats 1-4

Beats 5-8

Part 1

Macrou Dance Step 7: Part 1

		1	2	3	4	1 (5)	2 (6)	3 (7)	4 (8)
Arms		UP/ DOWN			UP/ DOWN	UP/ DOWN			DOWN
		R / L			L / R	(L / R)			B
Feet		STEP*	STEP*	STEP*	PIVOT (OPP)	STEP	STEP	STEP	LIFT
		R	L	R	(R)	L	R	L	(R)

***Large steps in a front-to-back rocking motion. Start facing right, then repeat on the opposite side.**

Part 2

Macrou Dance Step 7: Part 2

						BREAK			
		1	2	3	4	1 (5)	2 (6)	3 (7)	4 (8)
Arms		UP	DOWN	UP	DOWN	UP	DOWN	UP	UP/ DOWN
		B							R / L
Feet		STEP	LIFT	STEP	LIFT	STEP	LIFT	STEP	LIFT
		R	(L)	L	(R)	L	(R)	L	(R)

3. Practice the entire choreography several times with the CD, using either the slow-tempo track or performance track.

LET'S DRUM ♪2 ♪5

Review the dundunba, sangban and kenkeni rhythm patterns. Begin by practicing the vocables and body percussion exercises from lesson 2 without drums, then transfer rhythms to the instruments.

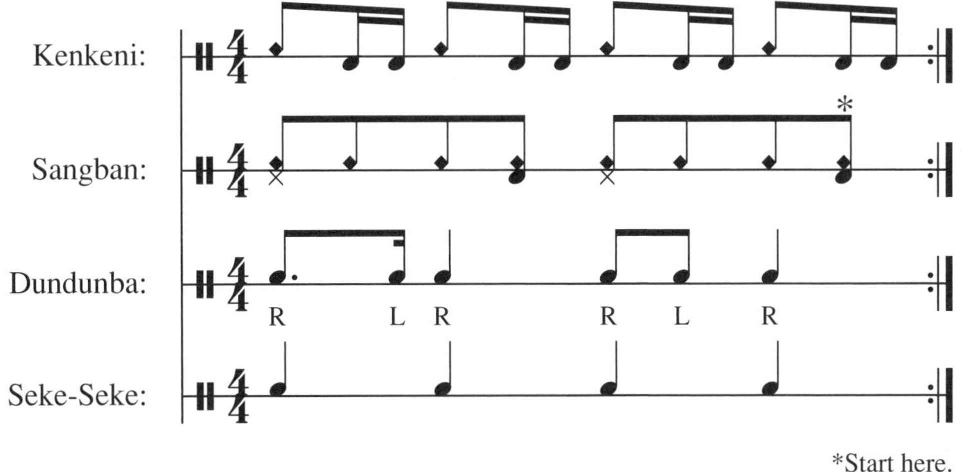

Play the seke-seke to support the steady beat.

Tip: Keep the same circle-based instrument groups from lesson 2. Have students who aren't playing a drum support their section by continuing the body percussion and/or vocables.

LET'S SING 1

1. Review the Macrou song part from lesson 1.
2. Introduce the complete Macrou song "A Boronco."

A Boronco

A Bo - ron - co Ma bo - ro - ma Eh A bo - ron - co Ma bo - ro - ma

Eh Iya - la Eh Yan - ka - di mi fa - re bo - ro - ma wa - to qui i be

3. Sing the complete song as a group, focusing on proper melody and articulation of words. Use the CD as an accompaniment, or have students play the xylophone 1 and 3 rhythm parts.
4. Introduce *call-and-response* form, and practice the song in that form.

"A Boronco" Translation

Susu	*English*
A boronco?	Do you dance?
Ma boroma.	I don't dance.
Eh Iyala.	Oh my.
Yankadi mi fare boroma wato qui i be*.	The children of the Yankadi dance here in the car*.

➲ This is the literal meaning, however, it basically translates as "dance anywhere." Any other place may be substituted, such as your city, town, school, etc. (Example: ***Oakland qui i be.***)

A Boronco

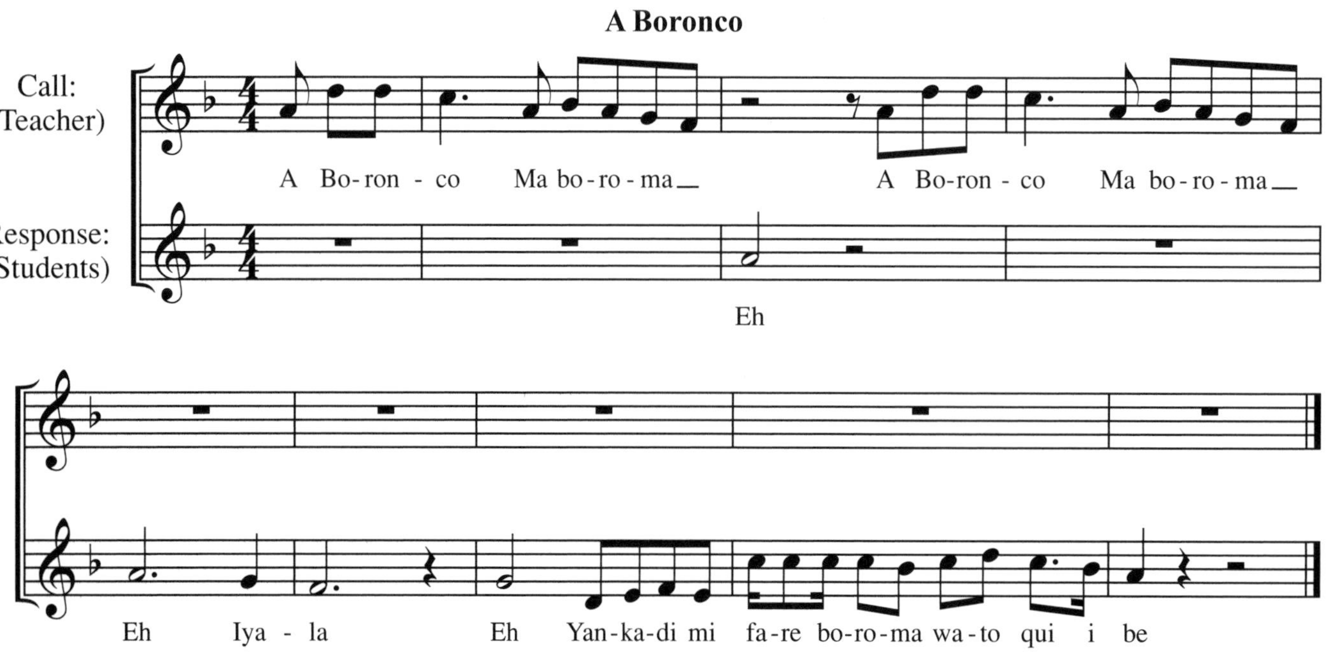
Call: (Teacher)
Response: (Students)
A Bo - ron - co Ma bo - ro - ma A Bo - ron - co Ma bo - ro - ma
Eh
Eh Iya - la Eh Yan - ka - di mi fa - re bo - ro - ma wa - to qui i be

Tip: A portion of the group can be substituted in place of the solo voice. Try experimenting with different individual students or groups performing both the call and response parts.

Continue building upon the mini-performance introduced in lesson 2. Add the additional dance steps 5–7 and the complete Macrou song.

Let's Play Key

D=Dundunba S=Sangban K=Kenkeni J=Jembe X=Xylophone SS=Seke-seke KR=Krinyi
DS=Dance Step M=March SG=Song EM=Échauffmant

TEACHER	BREAK	BREAK	BREAK	BREAK	BREAK	BREAK	BREAK	BREAK
DRUMMERS	D & SS	S	K	X1 & X3 (Drums Lower Volume)	X1 & X3 (Drums Lower Volume)	Drums Volume Up		
DANCERS	Clap				SG	Stop SG DS1	DS2	DS3

LEADER	BREAK	BREAK	BREAK	BREAK	BREAK
DRUMMERS					STOP
DANCERS	DS4	DS5	DS6	DS7	Jump/Clap

Tip: Experiment with different ways to arrange the musical and movement elements. For example, begin with the xylophones. On the next break, add the song, then kenkeni, sangban, and dance movements. Have selected students arrange the piece for the group (keep the dance steps in the same order). Make sure the musicians lower their volume any time the song is being sung, and increase volume and tempo during the dance.

Wrap-Up

- Invite students to store the instruments and straighten up the room for the next session.
- Ask students to get their Student Enrichment Books and gather for discussion.
- Review and clarify the assignment in the Student Enrichment Book for this lesson.

Evaluation

Were students able to

- learn and perform Macrou Dance Steps 5–7 with proper technique and make all the transitions?
- perform the three dundun patterns with the seke-seke?
- sing the entire "A Boronco" song?
- successfully perform the mini-performance?

Discussion

- What aspects of the movements were challenging? Suggest that students slow down the difficult movements until they can complete them with good technique.
- Are all of the students putting out their best energy and effort in the dance choreography? If not, discuss the importance of learning the dance even if they only want to drum.
- Were there difficulties in singing the melody and/or pronouncing the Susu words? Suggest that students practice saying the words broken into syllables and at a very slow tempo until they can say them comfortably.
- Evaluate the session using P.R.I.D.E. (the WRAP core values and best practices) as discussion points.

LESSON 4: Can we play, too?

An Introduction to Jembe Drumming

OBJECTIVES

Students will

- identify the jembe and learn its origins and roles in the Mandé drum and dance orchestra;
- identify and perform the three basic sounds of the jembe-drumming language (bass, tone, and slap);
- learn and perform the Macrou Jembe 1 Rhythm Pattern for Macrou;
- review Macrou Dance Steps 1–7 and combine them with musical elements into a mini-performance.

MUSICAL SKILLS

- Steady beat
- Complementary rhythmic patterns
- Small group ensemble playing

LIFE SKILLS

- Perseverance
- Motivation
- Patience

MOVEMENT SKILLS

- Balance
- Contrary motion
- Restrict and expand
- Articulation of body parts
- Weight shift

MATERIALS

- Jembe drums
- All dunduns
- Xylophones: BX & SX
- DVD player and TV
- CD player

VOCABULARY

- Jembe
- Sanbanyi
- Open tone
- Bass tone
- Slap tone
- Numu

Process

LET'S SPEAK 

Number

	Susu/ Phonetics	**English**
	naani *(NAN-nee)*	"Four"

Vocabulary/ Dialog

	Susu/ Phonetics	**English**
Person 1:	**Anyéreéfe?** *(an-yer-re-FEE)*	"How is it going?"
Person 2:	**Dondorunti, dondorunti.** *(DON-dor-un-tee)*	"It's going little by little (okay)."

LET'S MOVE 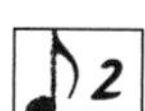 

Arrange students in lines and review Macrou Dance Steps 1–7. Emphasize the importance of performing the dance steps in time with the music and transitioning correctly from one step to the next.

- Use the CD for accompaniment.
- Use the whistle-break cue to change dance steps at the appropriate intervals.

LET'S DRUM

1. Introduce the jembe drum. Give students a general background of the origins of the instrument and define the unique and different roles it plays in the ensemble. Be sure to present information about the origins of the jembe including, but not limited to, the following:
    - The shape eminates from the mortar.
    - Primary ethnic groups are Malinké and Susu people located in and around Guinea, West Africa.
    - The first jembes are said to have been made by numu (blacksmiths).

Tip: If you or your students have no experience with jembe or world-percussion instruments, refer to appendix E, which outlines some simple, engaging activities and games designed to introduce students to the instruments in an informal and fun way. These activities will help students gain confidence and familiarity with the instruments, and they can be used to enrich any lesson or as stand-alone activities.

2. Introduce the proper technique for the production of the three basic jembe sounds (tone, slap, and bass).

About Jembe Technique

- If you have not yet mastered the skills necessary to correctly produce the three basic sounds, you may choose to have the students watch the DVD with you. Remember, proper technique is crucial to being able to clearly speak the jembe language, play the rhythm parts for the subsequent lessons, and prevent injuries. Review the section on instrument technique and the DVD as needed.
- If you do not have enough jembes for the entire class, conga drums or other hand drums can be substituted (see the instrument cross-reference chart in appendix B). Remind students, however, that the techniques they're learning are specific to the jembe drum. All the different hand drums have their own unique language and manner of being properly struck to produce the desired sounds.

Tip: Make sure your jembes and other hand drums are tuned correctly to facilitate getting the proper sound. (See appendix C.)

Track 2

3. Introduce students to the following exercises that combine the three sounds of the jembe.

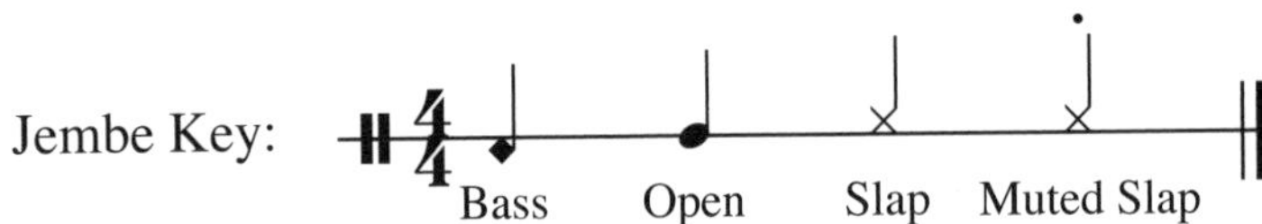

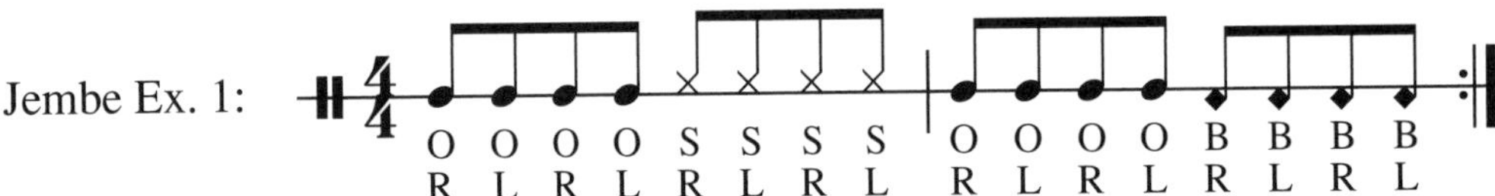

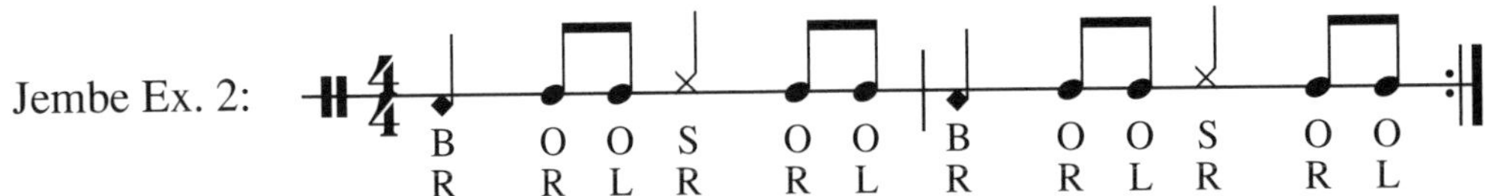

- ➲ Start at a slow tempo. Focus on maintaining proper technique and producing correct sounds.
- ➲ Use both hands equally to develop balance and coordination.
- ➲ Lead with both hands to improve dexterity. (R=L, L=R)

4. In a circle and marching to a steady beat, introduce the Jembe 1 rhythm using vocables.

Jembe 1 Rhythm Pattern

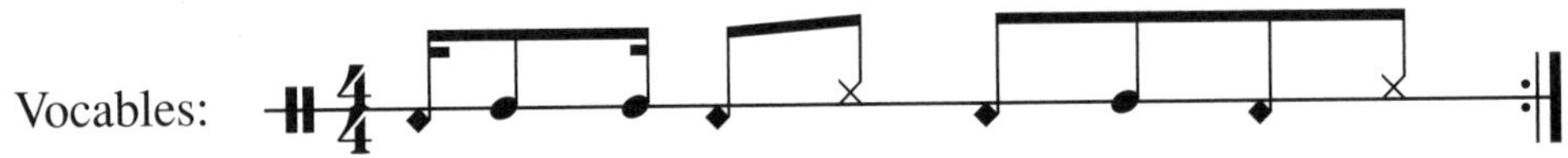

5. While still marching, play the rhythm on body percussion to approximate the bass, tone and slap sounds. Below is an example. You and your students may also enjoy creating your own.

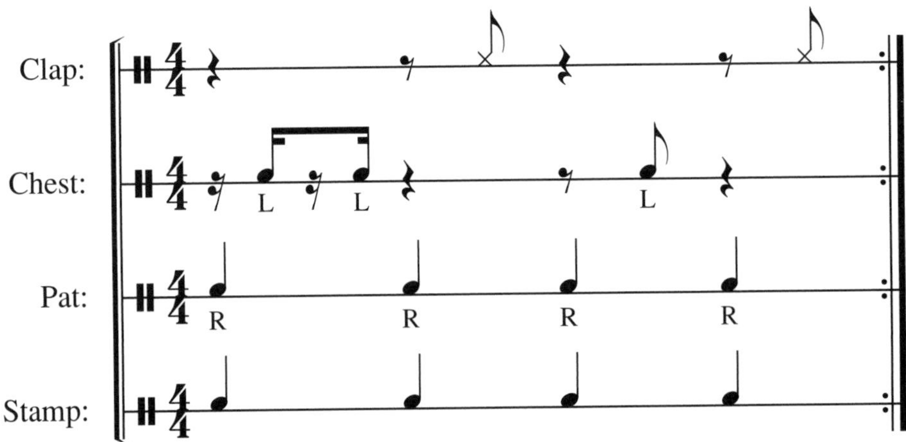

6. Combine the three jembe sounds with the vocal and body percussion examples to introduce the complete Macrou Jembe 1 Rhythm Pattern. (The following pattern construction process can be utilized to help students transfer the correct hand and rhythm patterns to the drum.) You may also use Step 1 as a simplified version for beginning groups or young children.

About the Pattern Construction Process

The jembe patterns are taught using a unique process that builds each one from its elemental foundation into the full pattern. You may find it helpful to use this approach when learning the patterns yourself and for teaching them to your students. Should you find one of the full patterns too difficult, you can use one of the simplified versions until you're ready to move on.

Complete Jembe 1 Rhythm Pattern

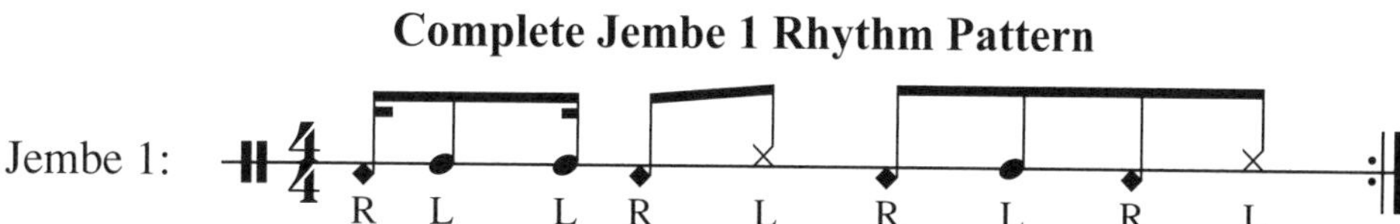

7. Invite students to play the Macrou Jembe 1 Rhythm Pattern with the dunduns and seke-seke.
   - ➲ Select students to play the dundun and seke-seke parts for accompaniment or use the CD.
   - ➲ Have students identify notes played on the jembe that align with those played on the dunduns or seke-seke. (This will help them identify how their pattern fits together with the others.)

LET'S SING
1

Review the completed Macrou song "A Boronco."

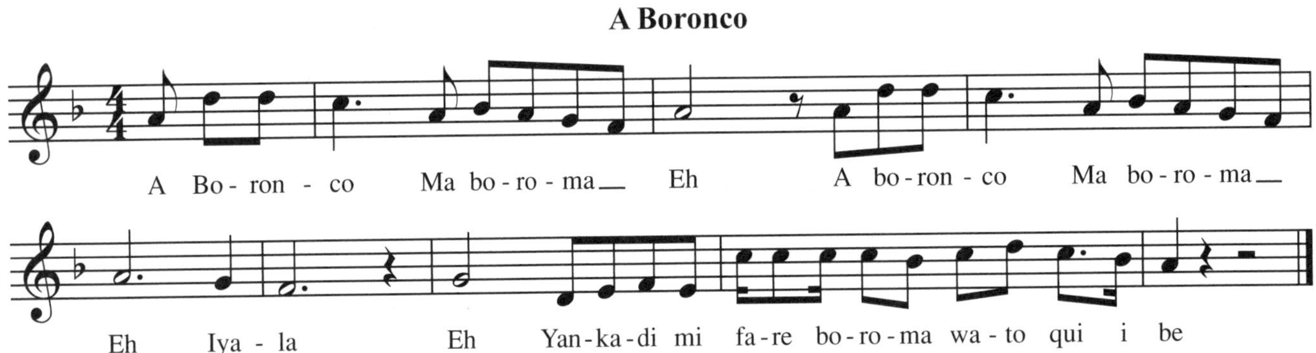
A Boronco
A Bo - ron - co Ma bo - ro - ma Eh A bo - ron - co Ma bo - ro - ma
Eh Iya - la Eh Yan - ka - di mi fa - re bo - ro - ma wa - to qui i be

- Use the CD for accompaniment, or have students play the xylophone 1 and 2 rhythm parts.
- Focus on the correct pronunciation of the words.

Tip: Experiment with different students or groups performing the call-and-response parts.

LET'S PLAY 1 2 3 4

Add the Macrou Jembe 1 Rhythm Pattern to the mini-performance, and allow students to experiment with different ways to arrange the music and movement elements.

Let's Play Key

D=Dundunba S=Sangban K=Kenkeni J=Jembe X=Xylophone SS=Seke-seke KR=Krinyi
DS=Dance Step M=March SG=Song EM=Échauffmant

LEADER	BREAK	BREAK	BREAK	BREAK	BREAK	BREAK	BREAK	BREAK
DRUMMERS	D & SS	S	K	J1	X1 & X3		Drums Lower Volume	
DANCERS	Clap					Stop SG DS1	SG (Several Rounds)	DS2

LEADER	BREAK	BREAK	BREAK	BREAK	BREAK	BREAK
DRUMMERS						STOP
DANCERS	DS3	DS4	DS5	DS6	DS7	Jump/Clap

Wrap-Up

- Invite students to store the instruments and straighten up the room for the next session.
- Ask students to get their Student Enrichment Books and gather for discussion.
- Review and clarify the assignment in the Student Enrichment Book for this lesson.

Evaluation 1 2 7 7 8

Were students able to

- identify the jembe and its origins and roles in the Mandé drum and dance orchestra?
- identify and perform the three basic sounds on the jembe (bass, tone, and slap)?
- learn and perform the Macrou Jembe 1 Rhythm Pattern?
- combine dance steps 1–7 with musical elements and complete the mini-performance?

Discussion 4 7

- Explain that producing the proper sounds takes practice. Explore strategies for learning and refining the tones without getting frustrated (allowing ample practice time each day). Let students know they will be refining these techniques throughout subsequent lessons.
- Discuss the development of good habits. "Practice doesn't make perfect, perfect practice makes perfect." —John Wooden
- What aspects of jembe playing were difficult (rhythm, hand pattern, correct sounds)? Explore ways students can improve on the jembe 1 part before the next class.
- Evaluate the session using P.R.I.D.E. (the WRAP core values and best practices) as discussion points.

LESSON 5: Are You Playing Your Jembe?

Introducing Macrou Jembe Pattern 2 and 3:2 Polyrhythm

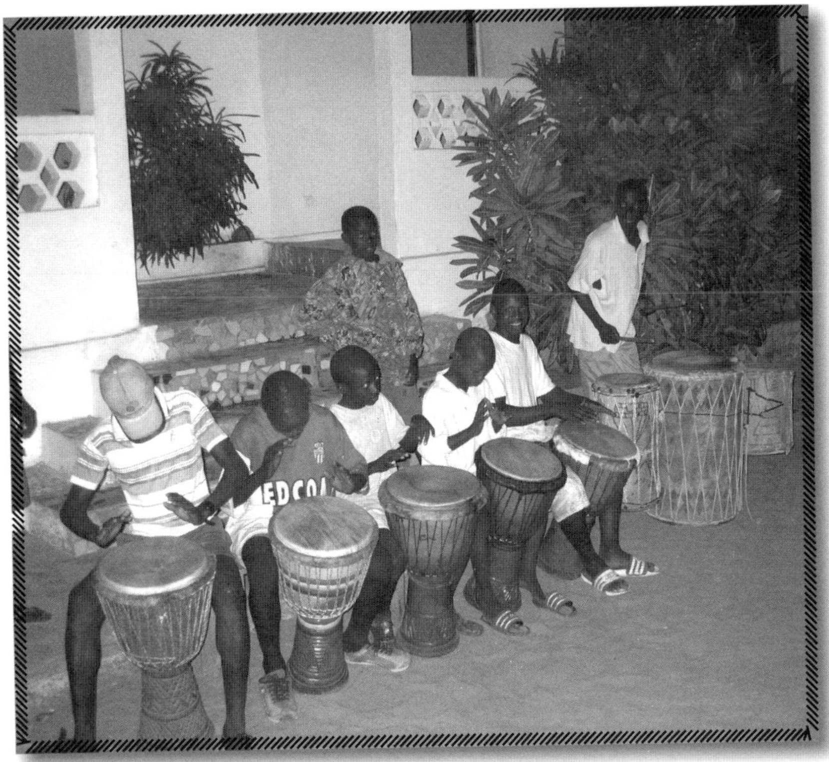

OBJECTIVES

Students will

- review and perform Macrou Dance Steps 1–7;
- learn and perform the Macrou Jembe 2 Pattern;
- perform a combination of jembe 1 & 2 with the dunduns, seke-seke, and xylophones;
- learn and perform a basic 3:2 polyrhythmic pattern.

MUSICAL SKILLS

- Steady beat
- Syncopation
- Polyrhythms

LIFE SKILLS

- Initiative
- Communication
- Courage

MOVEMENT SKILLS

- Balance
- Contrary motion
- Restrict and expand
- Articulation of body parts
- Weight shift

MATERIALS

- Jembe drums
- Dunduns
- Xylophones: BX & SX
- DVD player and TV
- CD player

VOCABULARY

- Sanbanyi (SAHN-bah-nyee)
- Polyrhythm
- Syncopation

Process

Number

	Susu/ Phonetics	**English**
	suli *(SU-ly)*	"Five"

Vocabulary/ Dialog

	Susu/ Phonetics	**English**
Person 1:	**Anyéreéfe?** *(an-yer-re-FEE)*	"How is it going?"
Person 2:	**Dondorunti, dondorunti.** *(DON-dor-un-tee)*	"It's going little by little (okay)."
Person 1: (New Dialog)	**I tan go?** *(ee taan go)*	"And you?" *(Used after a response to a question to ask the same question.)*

Review Macrou Dance Steps 1–7. Focus on the quality of the dance movements; are students fully extending arms, leaping, and maintaining proper balance? Test student memory regarding the order of dance steps and the ability to properly transition from one step to the next.

Use the dance practice track from the CD for accompaniment.

1. Review Macrou Jembe 1 Rhythm Pattern.
   - Use the vocables, body percussion and the pattern-construction process from lesson 4 to aid in remembering the patterns.
   - Concentrate on proper jembe technique and clearly producing the open, slap, and bass tones.

Jembe 1 Rhythm Pattern

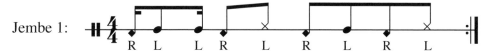

Jembe 1: R L L R L R L R L

Tip: Review the jembe technique exercises from lesson 4 to identify potential areas of improvement and concentrate on improving those skills as a group.

2. In a circle and marching to a steady beat, introduce the following rhythm and tones using vocables.

Jembe 2 Rhythm Pattern

Vocables:

3. While still marching, add the following body percussion exercise to the vocal chant. Point out the correct placement of the syncopated note (the last sixteenth note of beat 1).

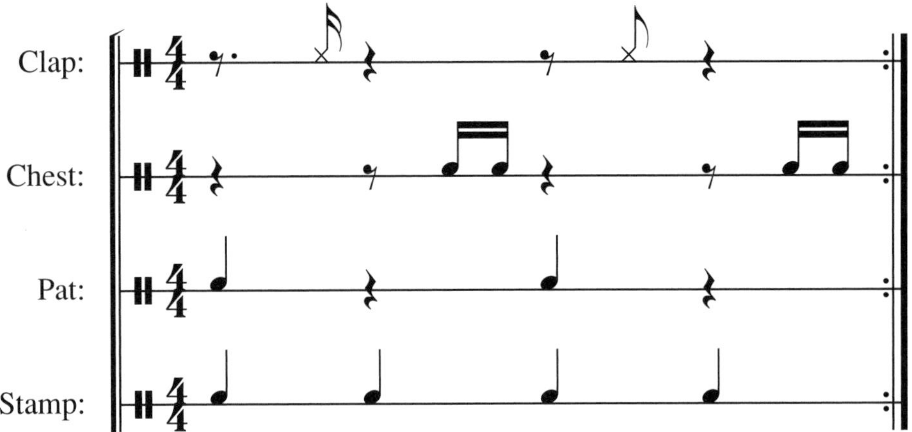

4. Invite students to transfer the vocables and body percussion to the jembe. If needed, use the following pattern-construction process.

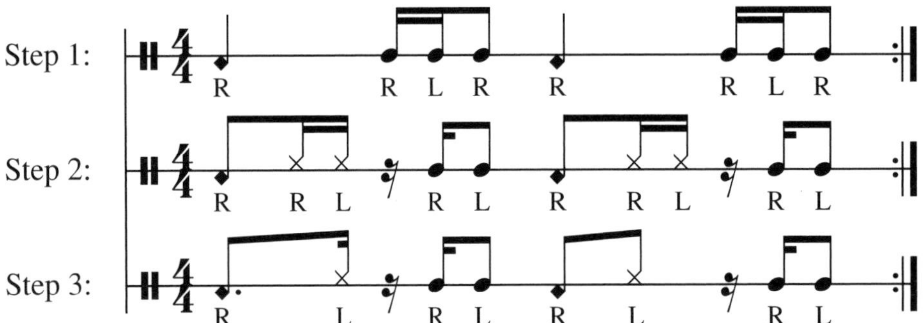

Complete Jembe 2 Rhythm Pattern

5. Once comfortable playing jembe 2 on its own, try practicing playing the jembe 2 pattern with jembe 1 pattern. Arrange students into two groups. Layer in the patterns using the whistle break as a cue. Rotate students on both patterns and have them identify which notes overlap between the patterns and which are different.

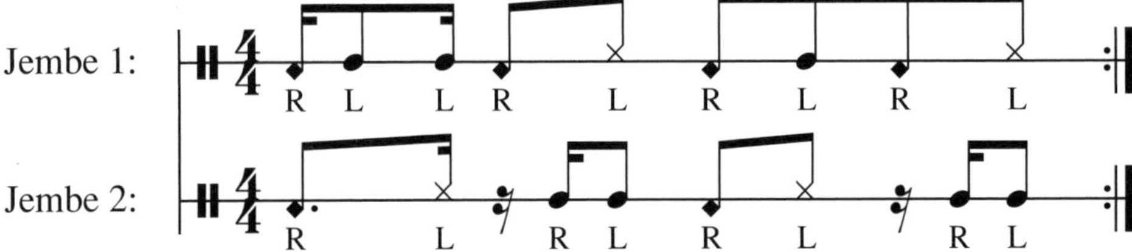

Note: There are six notes that happen at the same time. Which are they?

6. Practice playing the jembe 2 pattern with the dundun ensemble and seke-seke. When that is solid, add the jembe 1 and practice playing all the parts together.

Tip: Use the jembe 1 track from the CD while students perform pattern 2. The dundun and seke-seke tracks may also be used as accompaniment.

7. Introduce students to the concept of polyrhythms as a vital component of West African music. Use the following rhythm construction example, inviting students to join you as you model each step. Point out that this rhythm is in 3/4 time.
   - Begin with leg pats, then move to other body percussion sounds and/or instruments.
   - Play at various tempos, switching R/L hand patterns.
   - Perform the 3:2 polyrhythm in other combinations, such as hand/foot, voice/hand, and voice/drum.

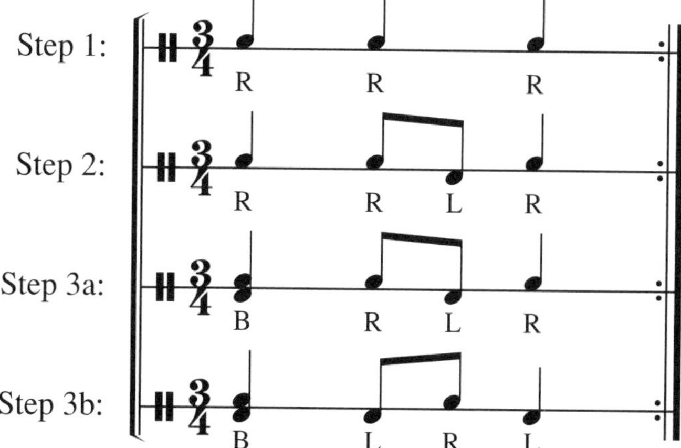

LET'S SING 1

Review the completed Macrou song "A Boronco." Use the CD for accompaniment, or have students play the xylophone parts.

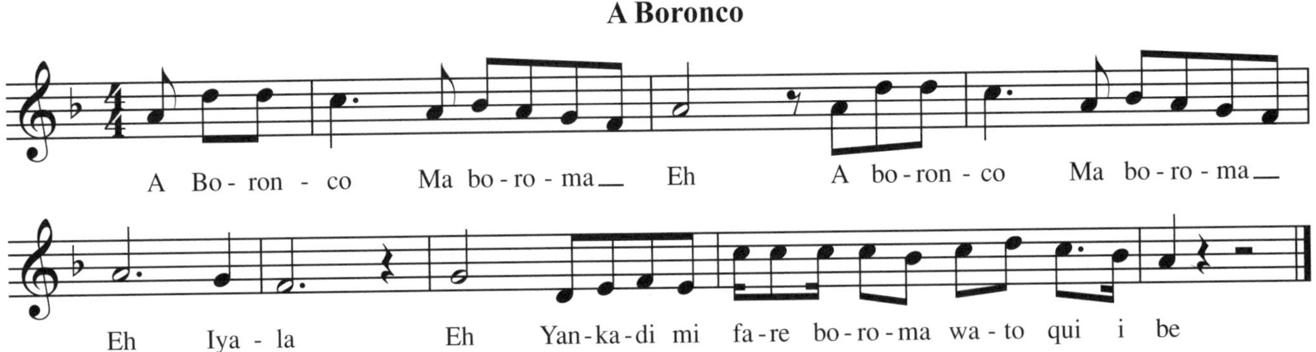
A Boronco
A Bo - ron - co Ma bo - ro - ma Eh A bo - ron - co Ma bo - ro - ma
Eh Iya - la Eh Yan - ka - di mi fa - re bo - ro - ma wa - to qui i be

> ***Did You Know?***
> *While traditional Jelis have sung the history of the families in Guinea since at least 700 A.D., the first written accounts of the region come from Arab explorers who visited the Mali Empire in the 1300s. The famous Ibn Battuta was the first to write about music and drums in the court of Mansa Souleyman in 1352–1353. The drums he spoke of are probably the precursors to the jembe and dunduns.*

LET'S PLAY 1 2 3 4

Combine all of the new musical elements in a performance. Experiment with different arrangements or layers of instruments.

Tip: Remember to only arrange the order or groupings of the musical elements, not the order of the dance steps. This will help students to practice the transitions between steps for their final performance.

Let's Play Key

D=Dundunba S=Sangban K=Kenkeni J=Jembe X=Xylophone SS=Seke-seke KR=Krinyi

DS=Dance Step M=March SG=Song EM=Échauffmant

LEADER	BREAK	BREAK	BREAK	BREAK	BREAK	BREAK	BREAK	BREAK
DRUMMERS	D & SS	S	K	J1	J2	X1 & X3	Lower Volume	Louder & Faster
DANCERS	Clap						SG	DS1

LEADER	BREAK	BREAK	BREAK	BREAK	BREAK	BREAK	BREAK
DRUMMERS							STOP
DANCERS	DS2	DS3	DS4	DS5	DS6	DS7	Clap/ Hop

Wrap-Up

- Invite students to store the instruments and straighten up the room for the next session.
- Ask students to get their Student Enrichment Books and gather for discussion.
- Review and clarify the assignment in the Student Enrichment Book for this lesson.

Evaluation 1 2 7 7 8

Were students able to

- learn and perform the Macrou Jembe 2 Rhythm Pattern?
- perform the combined jembe 1, jembe 2, dunduns, and seke-seke patterns?
- learn and perform a basic 3:2 polyrhythmic pattern?

How would you rate the quality of the students' dance movements?

1 = Poor, barely looks like dancing.

2 = Good, everyone is moving together. Some steps could be articulated more clearly.

3 = We're ready for the tour! Good extension in arms, good balance, steps and transitions are clear and precise.

Discussion 4 7

- What aspects of the dance need work to get ready for the performance? Consider showing the Village Performance section on the DVD and have students identify the qualities that make the performance interesting and fun to watch (energy, smiles, animated, big movements, costumes).
- What aspects of the jembe 2 pattern were difficult? Review the vocal chant and body percussion examples to facilitate learning the pattern.
- What makes something polyrhythmic? Explore other related terms such as ***hemiola***, and ask students to look for polyrhythmic examples in music that is familiar to them.
- Evaluate the session using P.R.I.D.E. (the WRAP core values and best practices) as discussion points.

LESSON 6: Dance To the Music

Adding the Final Dance Steps for Macrou

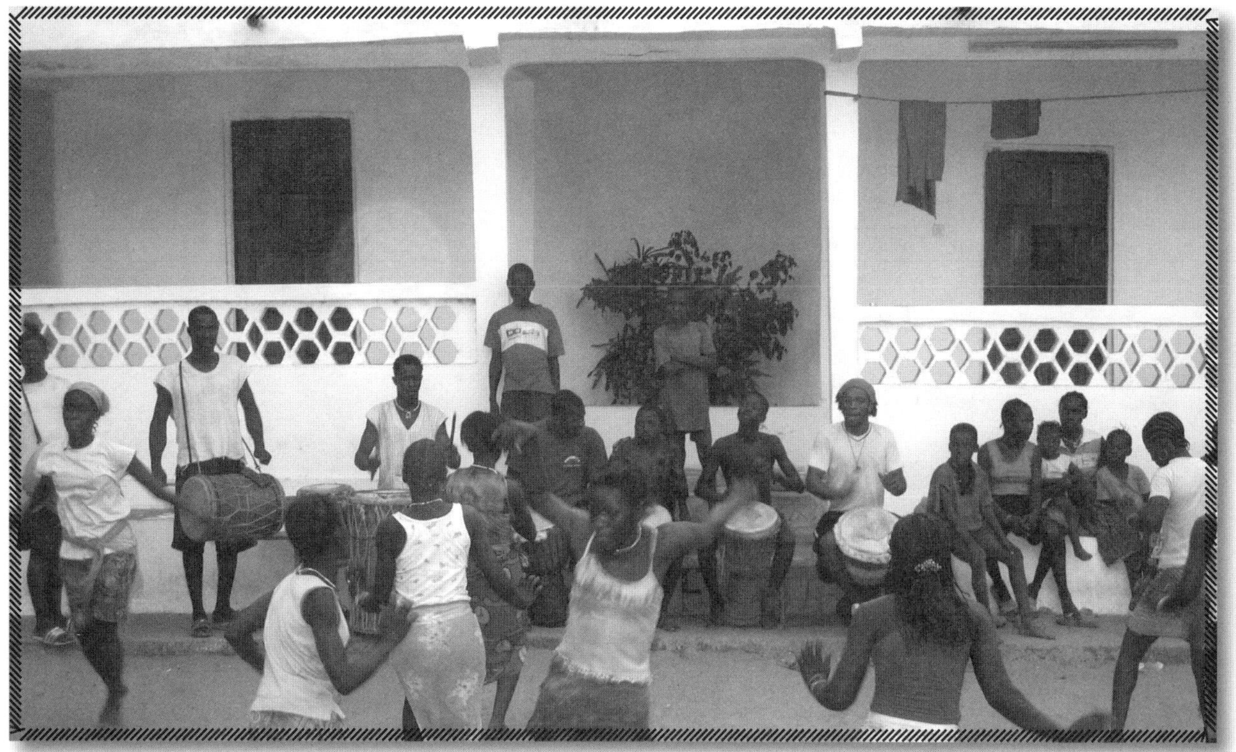

OBJECTIVES

Students will

- learn and perform Macrou Dance Steps 8 and 9;
- review jembe patterns 1 & 2 and the 2:3 syncopation;
- learn and perform the xylophone 3 pattern;
- perform a combination of musical and movement elements.

MUSICAL SKILLS

- Steady beat
- Syncopation
- Polyrhythms

LIFE SKILLS

- Resilience
- Motivation
- Group awareness
- Teamwork

MOVEMENT SKILLS

- Balance
- Contrary motion
- Restrict and expand
- Articulation of body parts
- Weight shift

MATERIALS

- Jembes
- All dunduns
- Xylophones: BX, AX & SX
- DVD player and TV
- CD player

VOCABULARY

- Jembefola – Jembe player
- Polyrhythmic
- Syncopation

Process

LET'S SPEAK ♪9

Number

	Susu/ Phonetics	**English**
	senni *(SEN-nee)*	"Six"

Review Dialog

	Susu
Person 1:	**I nu wali?**
Person 2:	**I nu wali.**
Person 1:	**Arabakhadi?**
Person 2:	**Amurabakhi kioke. I tan go, arabakhadi?**
Person 1:	**Amurabakhi kioke. Tana mu na?**
Person 2:	**Tana yo mu na. I tan go?**
Person 1:	**Tana yo mu na.**
Person 2:	**Anyéréfe?**
Person 1:	**Dondorunti, dondorunti. I tan go?**
Person 2:	**Dondorunti, dondorunti.**

LET'S MOVE 1 2

1. Review Macrou Dance Steps 1–7 using the whistle break to change steps, and the CD for accompaniment.
2. Introduce Macrou Dance Steps 8 and 9.

Macrou Dance Step 8

					BREAK			
	1	2	3	4	1 (5)	2 (6)	3 (7)	4 (8)
Arms	CIRCLE		CIRCLE		CIRCLE		CIRCLE	
	(R)		(L)		(L)		(L)	
Feet	SIDE	CLOSE	SIDE	CLOSE	SIDE	CLOSE	SIDE	CLOSE
	R	L	L	R	R	L	L	R

Macrou Dance Step 9

					BREAK			
	1	2	3	4	1 (5)	2 (6)	3 (7)	4 (8)
Arms	FWD				WAVE			
	(R)				(R)			
Feet	TOG				SHUFFLE	SHUFFLE	SHUFFLE	SHUFFLE
	B				L R	L R	L R	L R
					REPEAT UNTIL BREAK			

Note: Move backward (upstage) during the shuffle step.

3. Work on performing the complete choreography all the way through, adding the additional dance movements. Continue to change movements using the whistle-break cue. Use the CD for accompaniment, or choose students to play the dundun and jembe parts.

LET'S DRUM 

1. Review jembe parts 1 and 2.
   - Continue to emphasize proper technique and clear production of sounds.
   - Use jembe 1 and 2 vocables, body percussion and pattern-construction examples from lessons 4 and 5 to help correct any problem areas.
   - Arrange students so one half of the group is playing jembe 1 and the other jembe 2, then switch patterns on the whistle cue. Use the CD to provide dundun accompaniment or select students to play the three dundun and seke-seke parts.
2. Review the 3:2 polyrhythm construction examples from lesson 5. Invite students to experiment with different sounds and textures; for example, play the bass tone of the jembe with the right hand and the slap tone with right.

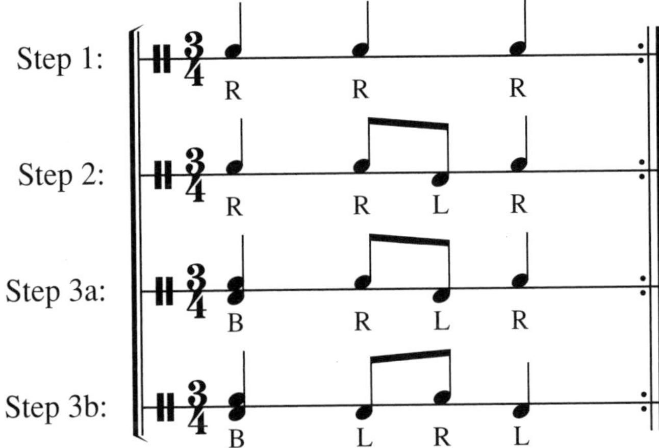

3. Add one beat to the 3:2 polyrhythm construction and have students join you in performing the following pattern.

4. Demonstrate and rehearse the xylophone 2 pattern. If possible, use an alto xylophone (AX).

5. Combine pattern 2 with patterns 1 and 3.

Xylo. 3 (SX):
R L R L R L R L R L R L R L
Xylo. 2 (AX):
L R L L R L
Xylo. 1 (BX):

6. Combine all three xylophone patterns with the dunduns and seke-seke.

The Epic of Sundiata and the Soso Bala

The ***Sundiata Epic*** *is a fascinating lore depicting the orgins of the Mali Empire. A portion of the story focuses on the instrument called the bala. The first known bala belonged to the Soso king Soumaro Kanté, who was rumoured to be able to cast spells over his enemies and defeat them by playing it. Balla Faseke Kouyate was able to endear himself to Soumaro and use the bala to help Sundiata overthrow Soumaro. The Kouyate family became the* ***griots*** *(oral historians, musicians, and preservers of tradition) for Sundiata and the Keita family, and the orginal* ***soso-bala*** *is still in possession of the Kouyate family in Niagassola, Guinea. For a time, all professional balas were rumoured to be tuned to this original.*

LET'S SING

Review the completed Macrou song "A Boronco" with all xylophones, dunduns and seke-seke.

A Boronco

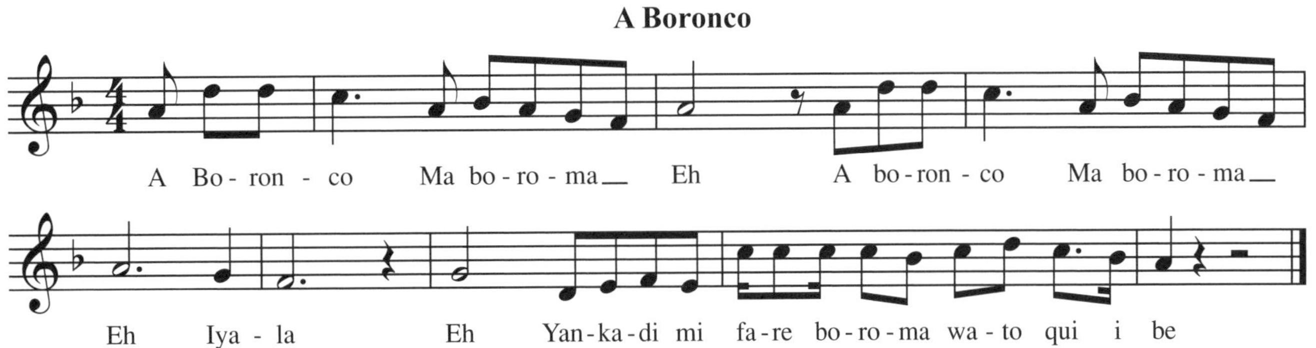
A Bo - ron - co Ma bo - ro - ma Eh A bo - ron - co Ma bo - ro - ma
Eh Iya - la Eh Yan - ka - di mi fa - re bo - ro - ma wa - to qui i be

LET'S PLAY

Add Macrou Dance Steps 8 and 9 and the xylophone 3 pattern into your mini-performance. Continue to use the whistle break to cue the drummers and dance steps.

Note: The arrangement now has all the dunduns entering together on the first break, just like they will be doing in the final performance. All members of the dundun family must feel the initial tempo and enter together from the break, as well as quickly match each other in volume.

Let's Play Key

D=Dundunba S=Sangban K=Kenkeni J=Jembe X=Xylophone SS=Seke-seke KR=Krinyi
DS=Dance Step M=March SG=Song EM=Échauffmant

LEADER	BREAK	BREAK	BREAK	BREAK	BREAK	BREAK	BREAK	BREAK
DRUMMERS	D, S, K SS	J1	J2	All X	Drums Lower Volume	Volume Up		
DANCERS	Clap				SG	Stop SG DS1	DS2	DS3

LEADER	BREAK	BREAK	BREAK	BREAK	BREAK	BREAK	BREAK
DRUMMERS							STOP
DANCERS	DS4	DS5	DS6	DS7	DS8	DS9	Jump/Clap

Wrap-Up

- Invite students to store the instruments and straighten up the room for the next session.
- Ask students to get their Student Enrichment Books and gather for discussion.
- Review and clarify the assignment in the Student Enrichment Book for this lesson.

Evaluation

Were students able to

- learn the final two dance movements?
- improve the quality of the dance from the last lesson?
- perform the xylophone 3 pattern?

How would you rate the quality of the student's dance movements?

1 = Needs improvement! Student's hands are all over the place. They are not pulling the sound out of the drum.
2 = It's coming! Bass tones and hand placement are good. Still no clear differentiation between the tone and slap.
3 = We're all jembefolas! Hand placement is perfect and there is a noticeable difference between the three sounds.

Discussion

- What areas of the dance could use improvement? Make a note to focus on those areas during the next lesson.
- Explain that playing the jembe is like playing any other classical instrument. It takes time and practice to make the proper sounds. Consider showing the jembe technique section of the DVD to help students refine their skills.
- What role does persistence play in developing good technique?
- Do you need to use a xylophone to practice the rhythm patterns? (No!) Discuss ways for students to practice between lessons without instruments.
- Evaluate the session using P.R.I.D.E. (the WRAP core values and best practices) as discussion points.

LESSON 7: A Voice From the Forest

Adding the Third Macrou Jembe Pattern and Krinyi

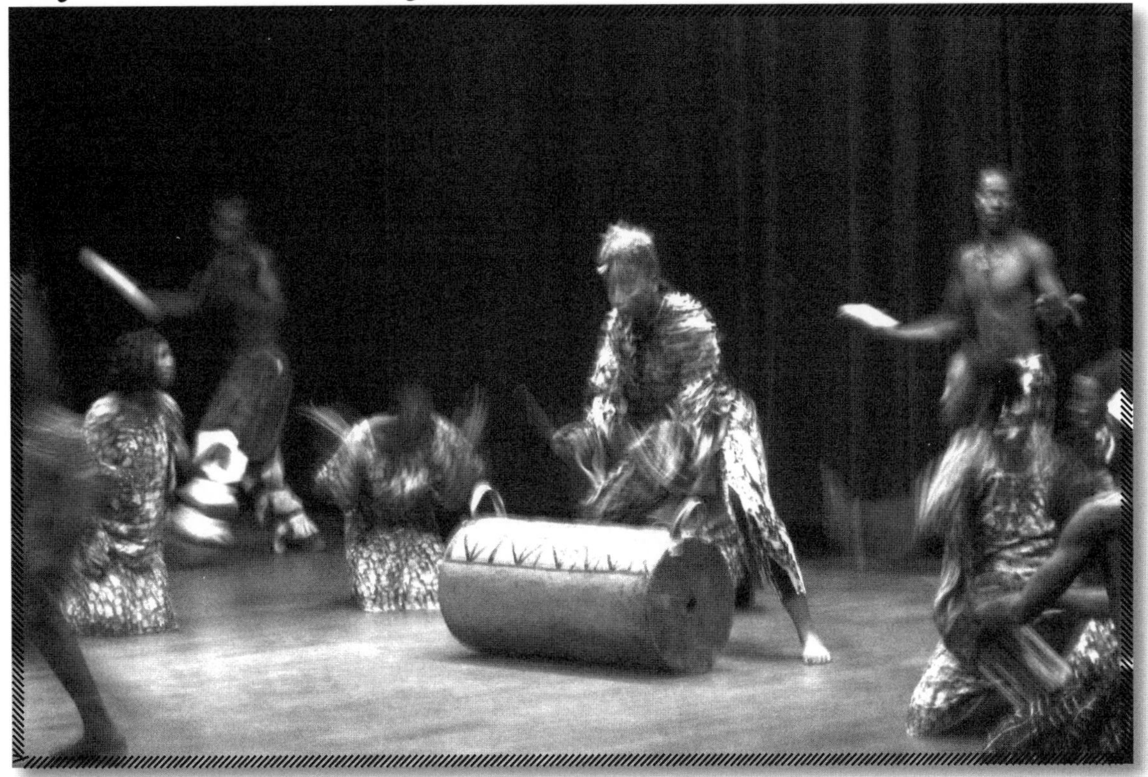

OBJECTIVES

Students will

- learn and perform the jembe 3 pattern;
- identify the krinyi and perform the rhythm pattern;
- combine all musical and movement elements in a group mini- performance.

MUSICAL SKILLS

- Steady beat
- Syncopation
- Polyrhythms

LIFE SKILLS

- Resilience
- Motivation
- Group awareness

MOVEMENT SKILLS

- Balance
- Contrary motion
- Restrict and expand
- Articulation of body parts
- Weight shift

MATERIALS

- All Drums
- Xylophones
- Krinyi
- DVD player and TV
- CD player

VOCABULARY

- Krinyi *(KREEN-yee)*
- Polyrhythm
- Syncopation

Process

LET'S SPEAK 9

Number

	Susu/ Phonetics	English
	solo feren *(SO-lo FIR-ring)*	"Seven"

Vocabulary/ Dialog

	Susu/ Phonetics	English
Person 1:	**I khili di?** *(EE KHI-lee dee)*	"What is your name?"
Person 2:	**N'khili** __________. *(n KHI-lee)*	"My name is __________."

Review the complete Macrou dance choreography. Play the CD for accompaniment and use the whistle-break cue to change steps while all students practice the dance.

LET'S DRUM

1. Review the jembe 1 and 2 patterns in groups, allowing each student to play both parts. Use the CD for dundun and seke-seke accompaniment, or have a third group play the parts on the drums.
2. In a circle and marching to a steady beat, introduce the following jembe 3 rhythm using vocables.

Jembe 3 Rhythm Pattern

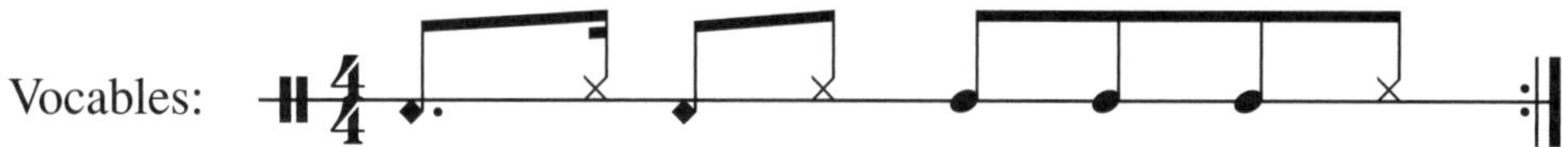

3. While still marching, add the following body percussion exercise to the vocal chant.

4. Invite students to transfer the vocables and body percussion to the jembes. You may find it helpful to utilize the following pattern-construction process to ensure proper hand patterning and tone placement, or to use as a simplified version.

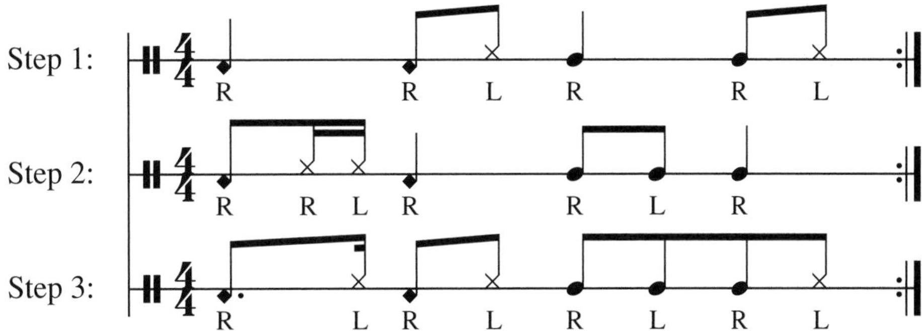

Complete Jembe 3 Rhythm Pattern

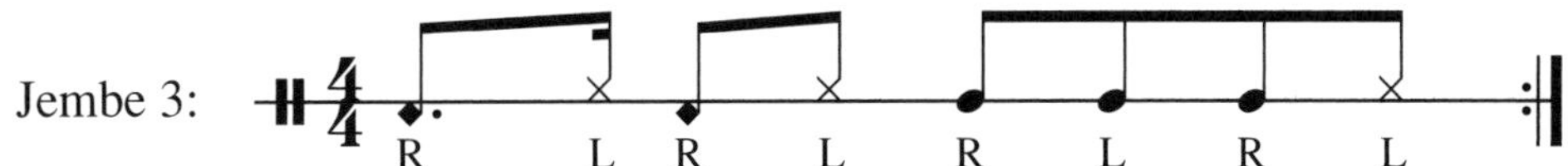

5. Once comfortable performing the jembe 3 pattern, combine it with the jembe 1 and 2 patterns.
   - ➲ Arrange the group in a semi-circle around you and designate portions of the group to play one of the three parts on drums or body percussion. Rotate the patterns between groups.
   - ➲ Use the CD for accompaniment, or have students play the dundun and seke-seke parts.

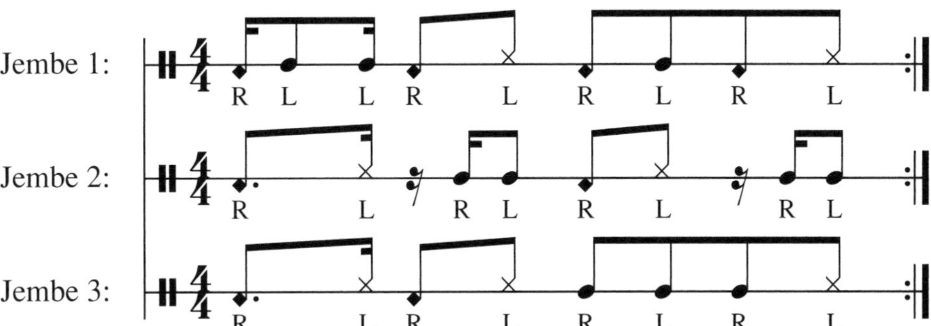

Tip: You can begin by using just the vocables and/or body percussion, and layer in each instrument group using the whistle cue. Experiment with cuing the groups in different orders so students hear how all the parts fit together. If practicing a-cappella (vocal only) versions, try vocalizing the whistle cue as well.

6. In a circle and marching to a steady beat, introduce the following rhythm using vocables.

7. While still marching, add the following body-percussion pattern to the vocal chant.

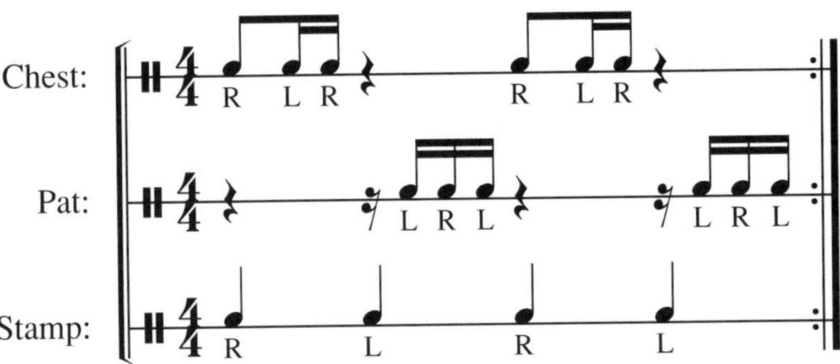

8. Introduce the krinyi (log drum) live or with the DVD, and re-enforce its role in the ensemble. (Refer to the "Instrument Guide," if necessary.)

9. Transfer the vocables and body percussion to the krinyi, and add it to the rest of the drum and percussion parts.

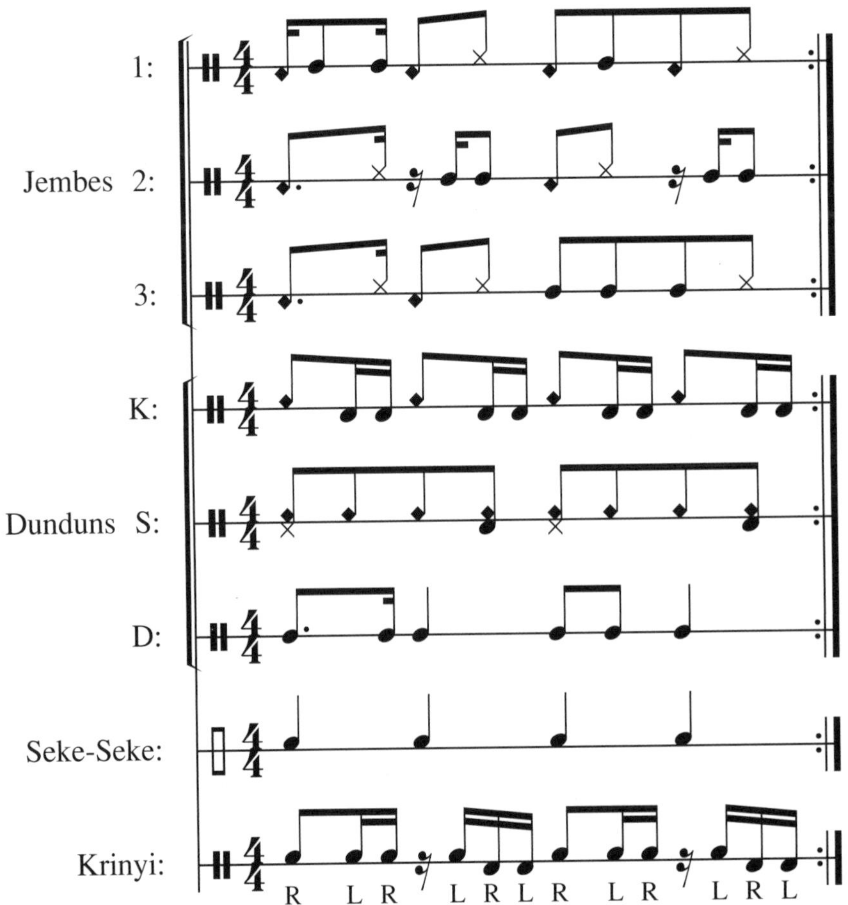

10. Rotate students playing the krinyi part with the rest of the ensemble.

LET'S SING
1

Review the completed Macrou song "A Boronco" with all xylophones and seke-seke. Ask for student volunteers to be the lead singer.

A Boronco
A Bo-ron - co Ma bo-ro - ma Eh A bo-ron - co Ma bo-ro - ma
Eh Iya - la Eh Yan-ka-di mi fa-re bo-ro-ma wa-to qui i be

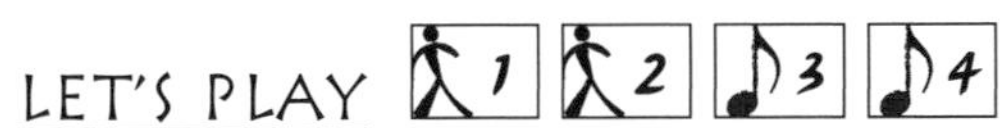
LET'S PLAY
1
2
3
4

Add the jembe 3 and krinyi patterns to the mini-performance, layering in only the new parts separately. Focus on playing and dancing together as a group. Pay close attention to the dynamic cues as you work on dancing with accuracy and energy.

Let's Play Key

D=Dundunba S=Sangban K=Kenkeni J=Jembe X=Xylophone SS=Seke-seke KR=Krinyi
DS=Dance Step M=March SG=Song EM=Échauffmant

LEADER	BREAK	BREAK	1-Note Cue	EM	BREAK	BREAK	BREAK	BREAK
DRUMMERS	D, S, K, SS	J1, J2	J3	KR	All X	Drums Lower Volume	Volume Up	
DANCERS	Clap					SG (Several)	DS1	DS2
LEADER	BREAK	BREAK	BREAK	EM	BREAK	EM	BREAK	BREAK
DRUMMERS								
DANCERS	DS3	DS4	DS5	DS6	DS7	DS8	DS9	(DS9)
LEADER	BREAK	BREAK	BREAK	BREAK	BREAK	BREAK	EM	
DRUMMERS	STOP							
DANCERS	Jump/Clap							

Wrap-Up

- Invite students to store the instruments and straighten up the room for the next session.
- Ask students to get their Student Enrichment Books and gather for discussion.
- Review and clarify the assignment in the Student Enrichment Book for this lesson.

Evaluation

Are students able to

- perform the jembe 3 pattern?
- identify and perform the krinyi with proper technique and rhythm?
- perform all musical and movement elements together?

Discussion

- Which students need a little extra skill-building help? Discuss ways to have students co-mentor each other to make the entire ensemble stronger.
- What areas of the performance need work? Are there group members who are willing to take a leadership role and organize practice time before the next class?
- How is the WRAP ensemble like a sports team? What are the roles and responsibilities?
- Compare and contrast the WRAP ensemble with a touring music/dance group.
- Evaluate the session using P.R.I.D.E. (the WRAP core values and best practices) as discussion points.

Tip: Remind students that drums are only necessary when working on technique. The rhythmic aspects can be practiced with body percussion or on virtually any surface.

LESSON 8: Breakin' It Down

Adding the Macrou Break on the Jembe

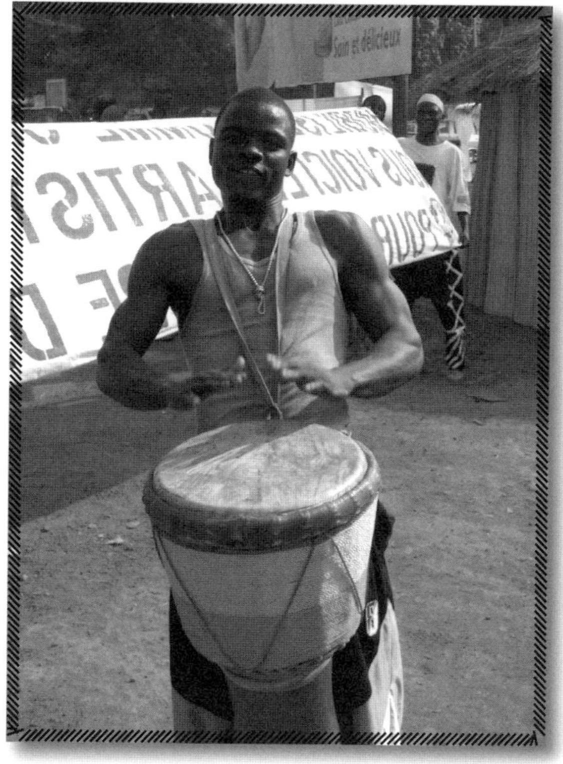

OBJECTIVES

Students will

- demonstrate an understanding of the role of the lead drummer in traditional West African music;
- learn and perform the Macrou échauffment and jembe break;
- demonstrate individual and group awareness, confidence and performing skills.

MUSICAL SKILLS

- Pattern recognition
- Phrasing
- Form

LIFE SKILLS

- Active listening
- Accountability
- Group awareness

MOVEMENT SKILLS

- Balance
- Contrary motion
- Restrict and expand
- Articulation of body parts
- Weight shift

MATERIALS

- Jembes
- Dunduns
- Xylophones
- Krinyi
- Seke-seke
- DVD player and TV
- CD player

VOCABULARY

- Lead or solo jembe
- Flam
- Échauffment (eh-shawf-mah)

Process

LET'S SPEAK 9

Number

	Susu/ Phonetics	**English**
	solo masakhan *(SO-lo MAS-sah-khan)*	"Eight"

Vocabulary/ Dialog

	Susu/ Phonetics	**English**
Person 1:	**I kelikhi minden?** *(EE KE-la khee MIN-de)*	"Where do you come from?"
Person 2:	**N'kelakhi** ________. *(n KE-la-khee)*	"I come from ________."

Use the CD to review the complete Macrou dance choreography using the whistle break to cue dance steps. Ask students to dance as if they were performing for a large audience.

Tip: Remind the students that the movements need to be twice as big to translate for the audience; for example, arms must be completely outstretched and knees brought up high. Also remind them that dancing in West Africa is a time of celebration and joy. Ask the students to describe expressions of celebration and joy and translate those qualities into their dance (SMILES and ENERGY).

LET'S DRUM

1. Review the jembe 1 and 2 patterns in groups, allowing each student to play both parts. Use the CD for dundun and seke-seke accompaniment, or have a third group play the parts on the drums.
   - ➲ Use vocables, body percussion, and rhythm-construction process as needed.
   - ➲ Continue to emphasize proper technique and clear differentiation between the jembe sounds.
2. Introduce students to the following break played on the jembe. Note that it serves the same function as the whistle cue and takes up the same amount of space in the measure.

Macrou Jembe Break

Note: Discuss the function of breaks in the ensemble and how the Macrou whistle break is a unique component of the Macrou traditional celebration. While dancing ballet choreography, the break cue is always played on the lead or solo jembe drum. Briefly explain the function of the lead jembe in the ensemble and how it is responsible for not only playing the breaks, but also for marking or accenting the dancers' movements.

The Flam

The Macrou jembe break begins with a flam on beat 1. A flam is a rhythmic figure where one note is played slightly ahead of the other.

3. Practice using the Macrou jembe break to start and stop each of the jembe, dundun, xylophone, seke-sek and krinyi patterns.
   - ➲ Note that the break is played only by the lead drum.
   - ➲ Remind students to play through the entire break figure and end on the "one" or downbeat of the next measure.

4. Introduce the échauffment pattern and define its role in the ensemble, which is to get ready for the cue. Note that there is a flam on beat 4 of the third measure. You may have to leave out the note just before it in order to play this figure. If the flam is too difficult, play a single note.
5. Practice playing the échauffment and break together with the students so everyone has a chance to play it.

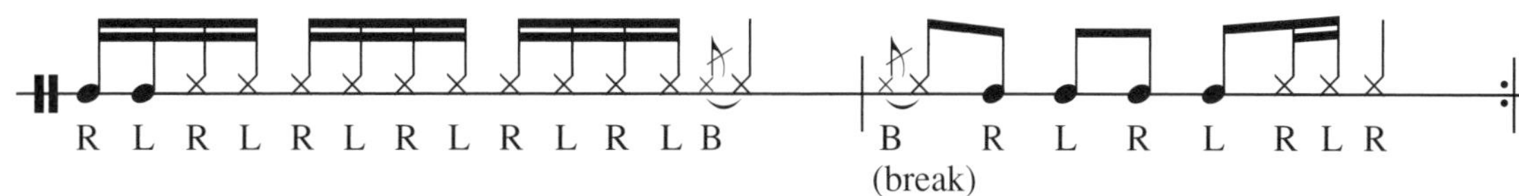

Tip: Use alternating hand patterns. Emphasize the final quarter note (beat 4 of measure 3) with a loud slap flam before giving the break. Try to make your break the loudest part you play.

6. Arrange students in a semi-circle around you, and designate groups to each instrument part. Rotate playing all the instrumental parts through the different groups. Try layering in each group using the jembe break.
7. After the ensemble has played together for a while, play the échauffment and jembe break to stop. Make sure everyone continues playing through the break and ends with a slap flam on the downbeat of the next bar. If time allows, invite students to try leading the group by playing the échauffment and break.

Review the Macrou song with the xylophone accompaniment. Focus on clearly articulating all of the words and projecting with the voice. Perform several rounds of call-and-response.

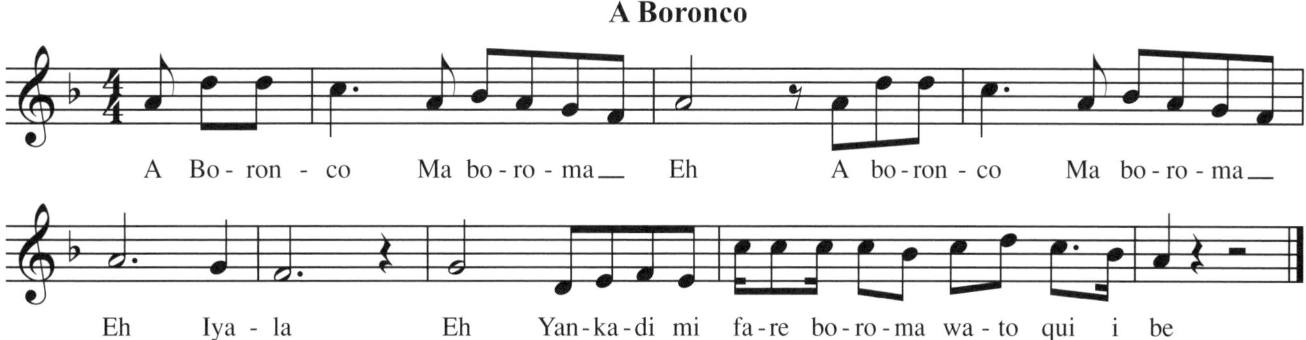

Did You Know?

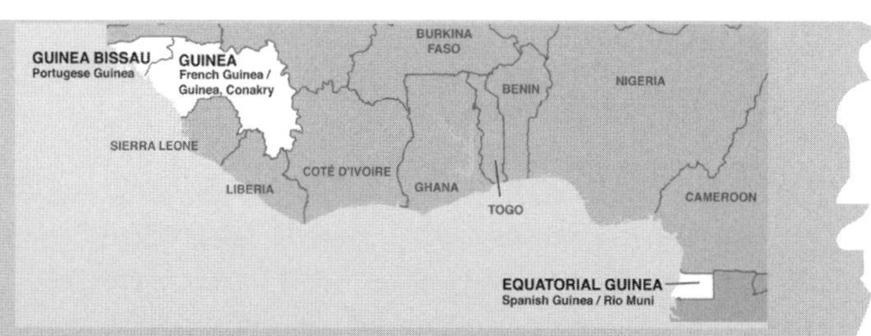

The name "Guinea" most likely originates from a word in the Berber language that, loosely translated, means "Land of the Blacks." In the Susu language, the word Guinè (gi-NAY) means "woman." While possible, its unlikely that the country derived its name from this meaning since the term "Guinea" has been used for centuries to describe the West African region that extends south of the Sahara desert and north of what is still called the Gulf of Guinea, a region well-larger than the Susu have ever inhabited. (The Gulf of Guinea contains the geographic center of the earth—where the equator and the prime meridian meet!) When Europeans colonized the region, three different countries became known as "Guinea." After acquiring independence, they changed their respective names slightly to differentiate themselves. The three countries are the Republic of Equatorial Guinea (formerly Spanish Guinea or Rio Muni), the Republic of Guinea Bissau (named from the capital city of Bissau and formerly known as Portuguese Guinea), and the Republic of Guinea (formerly French Guinea and sometimes referred to as Guinea, Conakry, after the capital city). To further complicate matters, the island country of Papua New Guinea (located in the Pacific Ocean, just north of Australia) received part of its name from the Spanish explorer Ynigo Ortiz de Retez, who, in 1545, renamed the island "Nueva (New) Guinea" because he thought the people resembled those he had encountered earlier while exploring the Gulf of Guinea. (The people have no actual blood relations.)

LET'S PLAY 

The following arrangement includes all the elements of the final Macrou performance. If ready, allow students to try playing the breaks and échauffment.

Tip: Make sure students are playing the break on the correct side of the dance movement as outlined earlier. You can help by playing the whistle cue along with them to give more confidence and volume.

Let's Play Key

D=Dundunba S=Sangban K=Kenkeni J=Jembe X=Xylophone SS=Seke-seke KR=Krinyi

DS=Dance Step M=March SG=Song EM=Échauffmant

LEADER	BREAK	BREAK	BREAK	BREAK	BREAK	BREAK	BREAK	BREAK
DRUMMERS	All	Volume Down	Volume & Tempo Up					
DANCERS	Clap	SG (Several)	DS1	DS2	DS3	DS4	DS5	DS6

LEADER	BREAK	BREAK	BREAK	EM	BREAK
DRUMMERS					STOP
DANCERS	DS7	DS8	DS9		Jump/Clap

Wrap-Up

- Invite students to store the instruments and straighten up the room for the next session.
- Ask students to get their Student Enrichment Books and gather for discussion.
- Review and clarify the assignment in the Student Enrichment Book for this lesson.

Evaluation 1 2 7 7 8

Were students able to

- transfer the whistle-break cue onto the jembe, and play and respond to the break in the proper time? If not, try practicing the whistle break and jembe break together.
- understand the échauffment and the function of the lead drummer in the ensemble? If not, consider playing the Yankadi-Macrou performance track from the CD and have them actively listen and identify all instances of the échauffment and break combinations.
- demonstrate the ability to perform their role within the structure of the music and dance? In other words, are they able to play their drumming pattern consistently, even when all the other patterns are added?
- match relative volume and tempo? If not, discuss balance and the importance of active listening.
- move together and respond to the breaks in unison?

Discussion 4 7

- How can the students work together to refine their drumming and dance skills, both individually and as a group, by co-mentoring each other?
- What skills and knowledge does the lead drummer need to have in order to be effective? How is the lead drummer like an orchestra conductor or a record producer?
- Evaluate the session using P.R.I.D.E. (the WRAP core values and best practices) as discussion points.

LESSON 9: The Big Finish

Adding the Macrou Performance Arrangement

OBJECTIVES

Students will

- review, refine, and perform the Macrou dance choreography;
- review, refine and perform all Macrou drum, xylophone, and song elements;
- learn, perform, and add an ensemble-ending arrangement.

MUSICAL SKILLS

- Arranging
- Ensemble playing
- Leading/conducting

LIFE SKILLS

- Active listening
- Accountability
- Group awareness
- Follow through

MOVEMENT SKILLS

- Group awareness
- Articulation

MATERIALS

- Jembes
- Dunduns
- Xylophones
- Krinyi
- DVD player and TV
- CD player

VOCABULARY

- Coda
- Finale

Process

LET'S SPEAK ♪9

Number

	Susu/ Phonetics	**English**
	solo manani *(SO-lo MAN-na-nee)*	"Nine"

Vocabulary/ Dialog

	Susu/ Phonetics	**English**
Person 1:	**Won na temui.** *(won na TEM-we)*	"See you later."
Person 2:	**Awa, won na temui.** *(AH-wa won na TEM-we)*	"Okay, see you later."

LET'S MOVE

1. Review the entire Macrou choreography, focusing on the quality of movements, unison response to the breaks, and high energy. Use the CD for accompaniment.
2. Introduce the ending dance arrangement for Macrou. Emphasize the precise timing of the movements, group synchronization, and spatial awareness.

   Practice transitioning from Macrou Dance Step 9 into the arrangement using your voice to call the jembe break without accompaniment.

Macrou Ending Dance Sequence

	8	1	2	3	4	1 (5)	2 (6)	3 (7)	4 (8)	1
Arms	DOWN	UP	DOWN	UP	DOWN	FWD	FWD	FWD	KNEES	FWD
		(R)				(R)	(L)	(R)	B	**
Feet	LIFT	STEP	LIFT	STEP	LIFT	FWD	FWD	FWD	TOG	
	(R)	R	(L)	L	(R)	R	L	R	B	

Beats 8-4

Beats 5-7

Heads up and hands forward. Smile!

Beats 8-1

3. Practice the entire Macrou choreography, including the ending arrangement, with the CD.

LET'S DRUM 2 5

1. Review the Macrou dundun, seke-seke, jembe, krinyi, and xylophone patterns.
2. Review the Macrou jembe break and the échauffment patterns. Select students to lead the ensemble using the jembe break to begin and the échauffment/break combination to end. Ensure that all students play through the break and end on "one" (the downbeat) of the final bar.
3. Review the jembe 1 and 2 patterns in groups, allowing each student to play both parts. Use the CD for dundun and seke-seke accompaniment, or have a third group play the parts on the drums.
   - ➲ Focus first on the dunduns, krinyi, and seke-seke, then add the jembes and xylophones.
   - ➲ Once comfortable with the arrangement, start the group from the break and play the Macrou rhythm. Have all parts enter at the same time and play for several bars. Next, begin the échauffment and transition into the arrangement using the Macrou jembe break.
   - ➲ Have students perform the role of the lead drummer.

Macrou Ending Arrangement

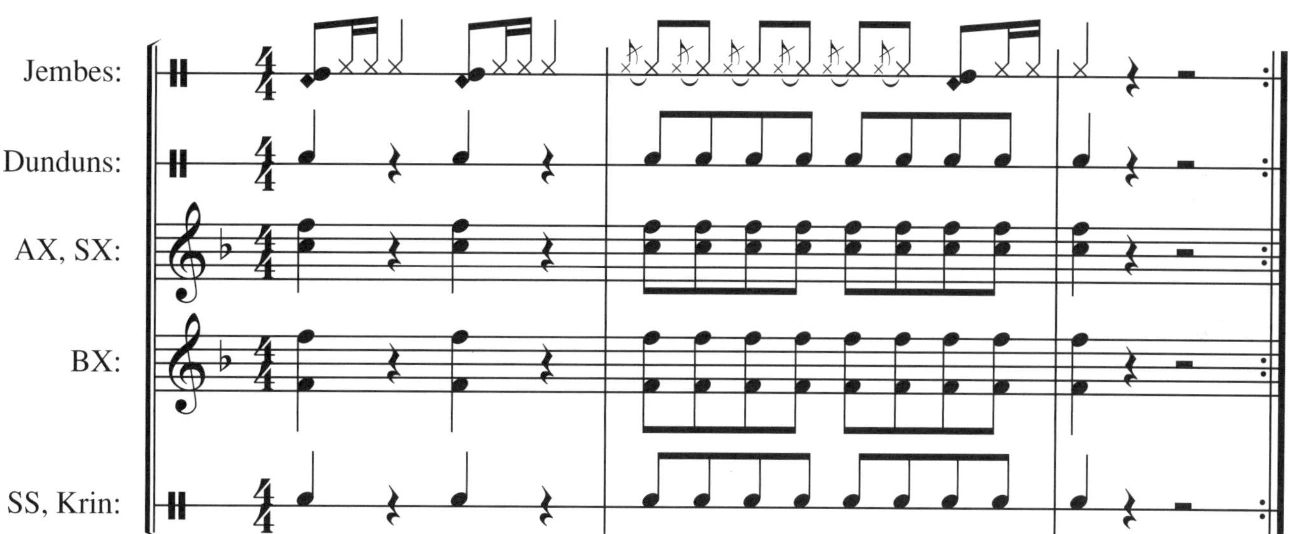
Jembes:
Dunduns:
AX, SX:
BX:
SS, Krin:

Note: The Macrou Ending Arrangement introduces a bass/tone flam on the jembes (beats 1 and 3 of bar 1, and beat 4 of bar 2. Review and demonstrate the flam technique in lesson 8.

LET'S SING
1

Review the Macrou song using the xylophones and seke-seke as accompaniment.

A Boronco

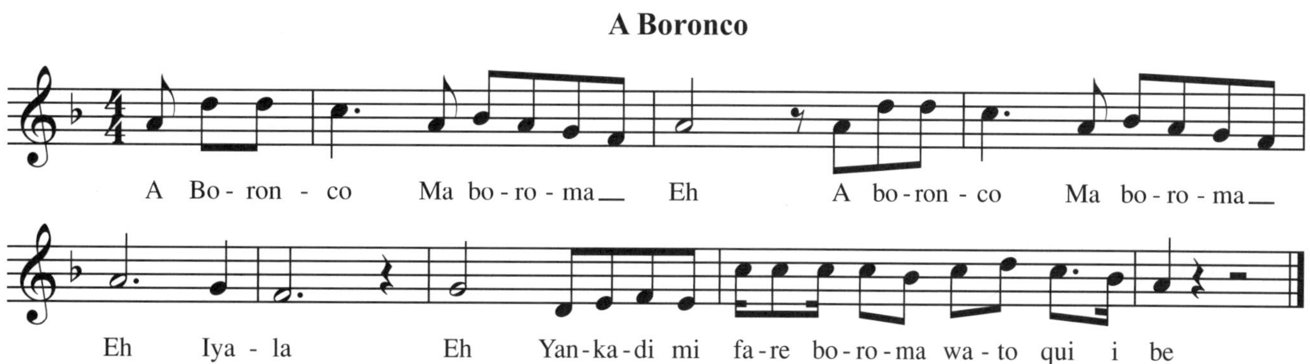
A Bo-ron-co Ma bo-ro-ma Eh A bo-ron-co Ma bo-ro-ma
Eh Iya-la Eh Yan-ka-di mi fa-re bo-ro-ma wa-to qui i be

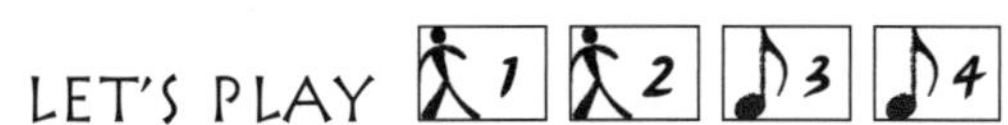

Incorporate the new Macrou Ending Arrangement into the mini-performance. Play the lead-drummer cues, or select advanced students to perform the function of the lead drummer by calling the break as well as the break/échauffment combination.

Note: Dance Step 1 is now beginning on the first break and being performed while singing the song. This reflects how the dance will be used when combined with Yankadi in the performance choreography. Also note the échauffment/break-cue combination as a way to transition in tempo and volume from the song portion to the dance portion of the arrangement.

Let's Play Key

D=Dundunba S=Sangban K=Kenkeni J=Jembe X=Xylophone SS=Seke-seke KR=Krinyi
DS=Dance Step M=March SG=Song EM=Échauffmant

LEADER	BREAK	BREAK	EM	BREAK	BREAK	BREAK	BREAK	BREAK
DRUMMERS	All Enter	Volume Down	Volume & Tempo Up					
DANCERS	DS1	SG	Stop SG	DS2	DS3	DS4	DS5	DS6

LEADER	BREAK	BREAK	BREAK	EM	BREAK
DRUMMERS					Ending Arrangement
DANCERS	DS7	DS8	DS9	(DS9)	Ending Arrangement

Wrap Up

- Invite students to store the instruments and straighten up the room for the next session.
- Ask students to get their Student Enrichment Books and gather for discussion.
- Review and clarify the assignment in the Student Enrichment Book for this lesson.

Evaluation

Were students able to

- perform the ending Macrou dance arrangement? If not, have students identify and review challenging sections.
- perform the ending Macrou arrangements on the instruments? If not, try having students listen to the performance on the CD and invite them to silently play along by air drumming.
- demonstrate an ability to perform the drum and dance arrangement together during the mini-performance? If not, have students watch the arrangement from the performance on the DVD or review it verbally.

Discussion

- What is the primary purpose of West African drumming? (To accompany dance.)
- Why is it important to perform both the musical and movement elements together? What factors determine how well that happens?
- What aspects of the program do students need to work on to reach their performance goal? Who is ready to take a leadership role and be responsible for helping the group achieve that goal?
- Evaluate the session using P.R.I.D.E. (the WRAP core values and best practices) as discussion points.

LESSON 10: The Macrou Review

Reviewing the Macrou Rhythm and Dance

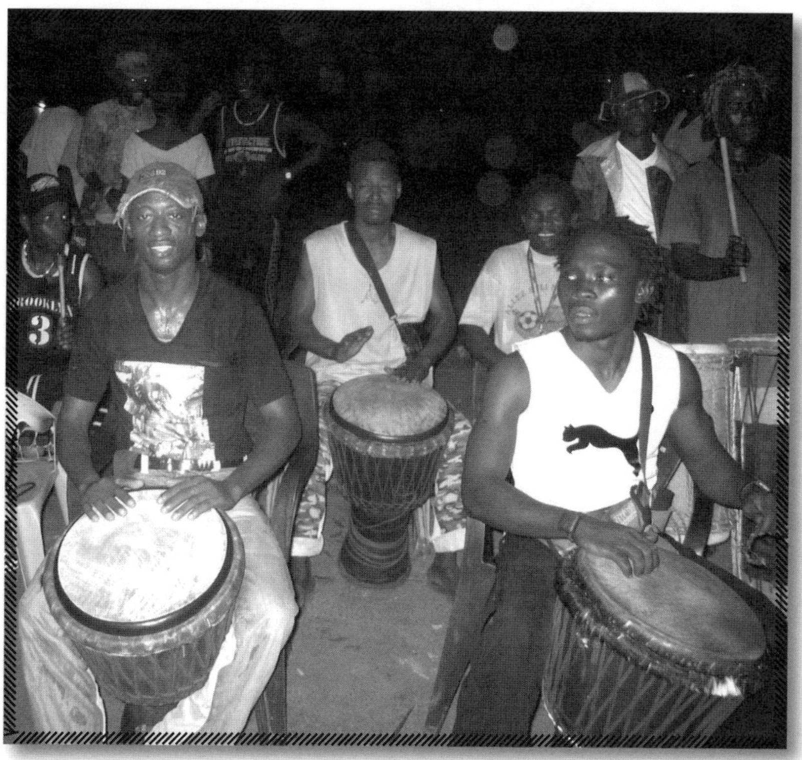

OBJECTIVES

Students will

- review, refine and perform individual components of the Macrou dance, rhythm patterns, and song;
- combine all elements of the Macrou celebration into an ensemble performance;
- enhance group awareness, active listening and individual responsibility through a mini-performance of Macrou.

MUSICAL SKILLS

- Performing
- Arranging
- Texture (layering)

LIFE SKILLS

- Active listening
- Accountability
- Group awareness
- Teamwork

MOVEMENT SKILLS

- Group awareness
- Balance
- Staging

MATERIALS

- Jembes
- Dunduns
- Xylophones
- Seke-seke
- Krinyi
- DVD player and TV
- CD player

VOCABULARY

- Upstage
- Downstage

Process

LET'S SPEAK 9

Number

	Susu/ Phonetics	**English**
	fuu *(foo)*	"Ten"

Dialog Review

	Susu
Person 1:	**I nu wali?**
Person 2:	**I nu wali.**
Person 1:	**Arabakhadi?**
Person 2:	**Amurabakhi kioke. I tan go, arabakhadi?**
Person 1:	**Amurabakhi kioke. Tana mu na?**
Person 2:	**Tana yo mu na. I tan go?**
Person 1:	**Tana yo mu na.**
Person 2:	**Anyéréfe?**
Person 1:	**Dondorunti, dondorunti. I tan go?**
Person 2:	**Dondorunti, dondorunti.**
Person 1:	**I khili di?**
Person 2:	**N'khili _________. I tan go?**
Person 1:	**N'khili _________**
Person 2:	**I kela khee minden?**
Person 1:	**N'kela khee _________. I tan go?**
Person 2:	**N'kela khee _________.**
Person 1:	**N'khili _________. I tan go?**
Person 2:	**Awa, won na temui.**

LET'S MOVE 1 2

Briefly review all of the Macrou dance movements including the ending arrangement.

- Emphasize making big movements (fully extending arms, bringing knees high), proper body balance, and performing with energy. Stress having fun while dancing!
- Make sure students are transitioning between dance steps in tempo and are hearing and responding to the breaks.
- Use the CD as accompaniment and encourage everyone to dance.

LET'S DRUM 2 5

1. Briefly review the Macrou dundun, seke-seke, jembe, krinyi, and xylophone patterns.
   - If needed, use vocables and body percussion to help recall parts.
   - Ensure that students are demonstrating proper playing technique and the ability to perform each rhythm pattern.
2. Combine all of the Macrou drum and xylophone patterns and practice playing the rhythm as an ensemble. Include the Macrou ending break each time the rhythm is stopped.
   - Select advanced students to lead the ensemble by playing the Macrou jembe break to start the rhythm, and the échauffment/break combination to lead into the ending arrangement.
   - Focus on steady tempo, the individual responsibility of holding one's pattern, and everyone's responsibility to keep the tempo steady while matching relative volume.

LET'S SING

Briefly review the Macrou song using xylophone accompaniment.

LET'S PLAY 1 2 3 4

Arrange students in a performance environment according to the following Performance Staging Diagram. Note how the dancers are now facing downstage (towards the audience). This arrangement reflects the stage setup for the final performance and the major difference between traditional West African ceremonies and West African ballet performances: the participants face the musicians in traditional West African ceremonies, and West African ballet performances are staged for an audience.

Note: This format introduces many new challenges for dancers. Dancers must actively listen to the break being given by the lead drummer and cannot rely on any type of visual cues. The lead drummer must perform the jembe-break cues clearly and at a louder volume so dancers can properly interpret them and respond on time.

Performance Stage Diagram

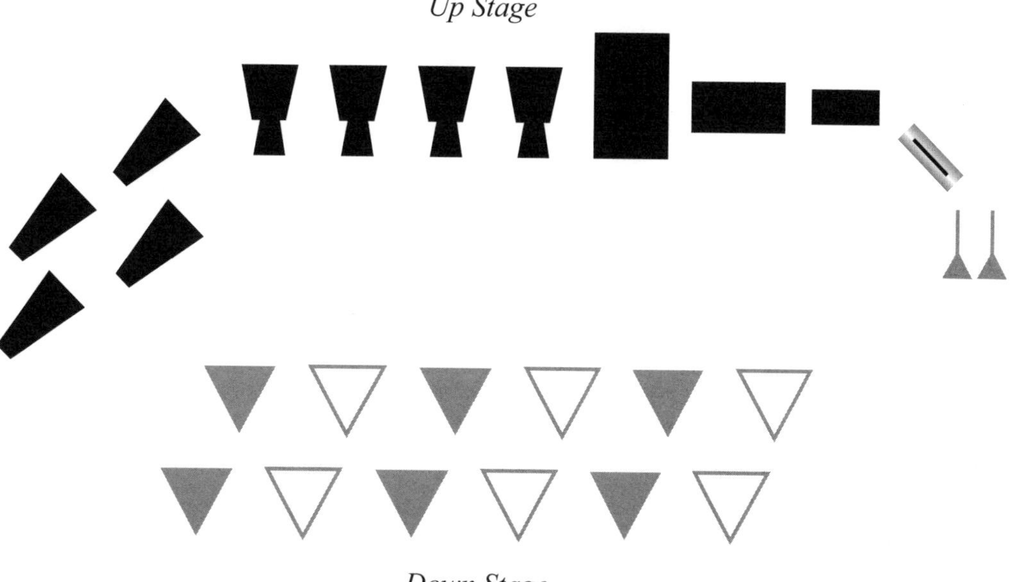

- Have students perform the rhythm and dance as if this were a real performance. Dancers should be energetic, smiling and exaggerating their movements. Drummers should be watching the dancers, ready to respond to any subtle changes in dynamics and tempo.
- Discuss group dynamics: "drumming for the dancers" and "dancing for the drummers." Remind students of the interconnectedness of all musical and movement elements, and how they must constantly be responsible for their own pattern or movement as well as for how their pattern or movement is interacting with all the others, and how it contributes to the ensemble as a whole.
- Ask musicians to pay special attention to the dynamic cues.

Let's Play Key

D=Dundunba S=Sangban K=Kenkeni J=Jembe X=Xylophone SS=Seke-seke KR=Krinyi
DS=Dance Step M=March SG=Song EM=Échauffmant

LEADER	BREAK	BREAK	EM	BREAK	BREAK	BREAK	BREAK	BREAK
DRUMMERS	All Enter	Volume Down	Volume & Tempo Up					
DANCERS	DS1	SG	Stop SG	DS2	DS3	DS4	DS5	DS6

LEADER	BREAK	BREAK	BREAK	EM	BREAK
DRUMMERS					Ending Arrangement
DANCERS	DS7	DS8	DS9	(DS9)	Ending Arrangement

Tip: Play the whistle along with the jembe to reinforce the break and to help dancers hear the cue. To use this method, blow the whistle on quarter notes for one bar to signal the jembe player to give the break. For advanced students who can easily perform the échauffment and break cues, you may wish to introduce some of the patterns found in appendix A, "Lead Jembe Patterns."

Wrap-Up

- Invite students to store the instruments and straighten up the room for the next session.
- Ask students to get their Student Enrichment Books and gather for discussion.
- Review and clarify the assignment in the Student Enrichment Book for this lesson.

Evaluation 1 2 7 7 8

Are students able to

- demonstrate a thorough knowledge and ability to perform all the Macrou rhythm, dance, and song components?
- work together as a performance group?

Rate the group on a scale from 1-3 on performance skills:

1 = Needs a lot of improvement. (Consider reviewing previous lessons.)
2 = Pretty good, could use some small refinement. (Call some extra rehearsal time.)
3 = We got it nailed. (Party time!)

Identify where extra help may be needed in the next performance section.

- Are the dancers moving together? If not, consider practicing in front of mirrors or in a circular formation that allows everyone to see each other.
- Are the dancers smiling and performing the movements and song with energy?
- Are drummers responding to breaks and dynamic cues together?
- Are the drummers playing together and watching/responding to the dance movements?
- Are the xylophone and song parts clear and understandable?
- Is the lead drummer playing the breaks and échauffment patterns clearly and in the proper places?

Discussion 4 7

- Survey students for issues and concerns, and work with them to develop strategies to address them.
- Take some time to acknowledge what is working. Talk about what students like about the program and how much everyone has learned so far. Enjoy being in the process!
- Ask each student to point out something they like about how another student is working in, and contributing to, the ensemble.
- Evaluate the session using P.R.I.D.E. (the WRAP core values and best practices) as discussion points.

YANKADI

LESSON 11 : SOCIAL SKILLS

Introducing Yankadi

OBJECTIVES

Students will

- learn the structure and function of the Yankadi rhythm and dance within the Yankadi-Macrou village celebration;
- learn and play rhythms in 12/8 meter;
- learn the Yankadi Jembe Break and how to respond musically and physically;
- incorporate elements of the traditional Yankadi dance, drum, song and xylophone into a mini-performance.

MUSICAL SKILLS

- Rhythm patterns
- Steady beat
- Melody
- 12/8 meter

LIFE SKILLS

- Group awareness
- Active listening
- Socializing

MOVEMENT SKILLS

- Marching
- Alternating
- Change direction

MATERIALS

- Dundunba and sangban
- Bass xylophone: BX
- Seke-seke
- DVD player and TV
- CD player

VOCABULARY

- Dundunba
- Break
- Sangban

Process

LET'S SPEAK

Number

	Susu/ Phonetics	**English**
	fuu anun keren *(foo ah-NOON KER-ring)*	"Eleven"

Vocabulary: Learning to Introduce Yankadi and Macrou

	Susu	**English**
	Guiné nun khamé wo nusanén fa fera mukhukha Yankadi-Macrou.	"Ladies and gentlemen, welcome to our Yankadi-Macrou celebration."

LET'S MOVE

1. Arrange students in large circle facing inwards.
2. Introduce students to the Yankadi jembe break using vocables.

   Sing the break and have the group respond by clapping on the downbeat to gain a better understanding of the underlying pulse. Do this at several different tempos to reinforce how the break sets the tempo of the music, as well as when to start, stop, or change a pattern or movement.

Yankadi Jembe Break

3. Set up for group dance rehearsal, and introduce the Yankadi Dance Steps 1 and 2.
   - Sing the Yankadi break to signal starting, changing, and stopping the movements. Practice switching back and forth between the movements.
   - Use the CD for accompaniment.

Note: Each column (1, 2, 3, 4, etc.) represents the dotted quarter-note (♩.) pulse. The numbers 1-8 encompass a two-bar phrase.

Yankadi Dance Step 1

					BREAK			
	1	2	3	4	5	6	7	8 (Start)
Arms	SWING			OPEN	SWING			OPEN
							R	
Feet	STEP*	STEP	STEP	TURN (Close)	STEP	STEP	STEP	TURN (Close)
	R	L	R	(R)	L	R	L	(L)

***This step is performed first facing to the right, then to the left. Steps are non-locomotor (weight shifts only). Arms swing as if walking.**

Yankadi Dance Step 2

		1	2	3	4	5	6	7	8 (Start)
						BREAK			
Arms		SWING			OPEN	SWING			OPEN
Feet		FWD	FWD	FWD	TURN (Close)	FWD	FWD	FWD	TURN (Close)
		R	L	R	(R)	L	R	L	(L)

Step 2 is virtually the same as step 1, but with forward movement to the right, then left.

Beats 1-4

Beats 5-8

Note: Remember that the break must be given in the correct place within the dance movements to create smooth transitions from one to another. In the first two Yankadi dance movements, give the break so the students start and stop in the same place. Also, note that both dance steps start on beat 8.

LET'S DRUM 

1. Introduce the following body-percussion exercise to help students feel the 12/8 pulse. Have students pat their thighs on the downbeats, then strike the back of one hand on beats 2, 5, 8, and 11. For example, to begin the pattern, pat your thigh with the right hand, then slap your right hand with your left as it rises, then pat your thigh again with the right hand. Ensure students are using an alternating hand pattern.

× = Slap back of other hand.

2. In a circle and marching to a steady beat, introduce the Yankadi dundunba pattern using vocables. (You can also use vocables with the above body percussion pattern as a foundation.)

*Start here.

3. Add thigh pats to the vocable rhythm.

4. Stop the dundunba pattern and demonstrate the sangban pattern with the kenken in a similar fashion.

Sangban:

5. Have students transfer the vocables to body percussion. Use chest taps for the kenken and thigh pats for the drum.
6. Split the circle and have groups perform the dundunba and sangban patterns.
7. Transfer the vocables and body percussion to the dundunba and sangban drums. Have a student play the seke-seke pattern as accompaniment.

Seke-Seke:

Tip: If students are struggling with the left/right-hand coordination necessary to play the kenken pattern, separate the kenken and drum patterns between two different students.

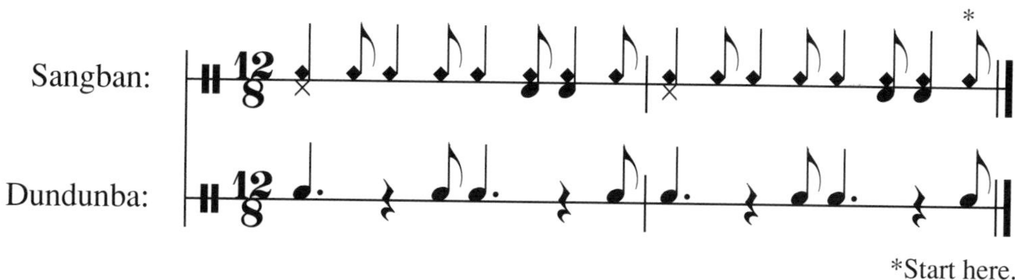
Sangban:
Dundunba:
*
*Start here.

8. Introduce the following xylophone 1 pattern and add it to the dunduns and seke-seke.

Xylo. 1 (BX):
L R L R L R L R

LET'S SING

Introduce the first verse to the Yankadi song "Bere Mu Sorbè." Use the xylophone 1 pattern as accompaniment. For the complete lyrics and English translation, see page 102.

Bere Mu Sorbè
Be - re mu sor - bè ka - na fo - ry ah eh
Be - re mu sor - bè ka - na fo - ry eh

Note: The first note of the melody is given in the second note of the xylophone 1 pattern.

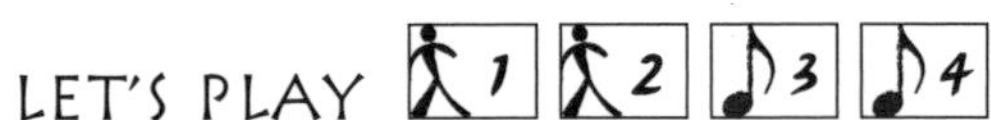

Combine the above elements for a mini-performance. Play the Yankadi Jembe Break on the jembe to start, stop, and change movements.

Let's Play Key

D=Dundunba S=Sangban K=Kenkeni J=Jembe X=Xylophone SS=Seke-seke KR=Krinyi
DS=Dance Step M=March SG=Song EM=Échauffmant

LEADER	BREAK	BREAK	BREAK	BREAK	BREAK	BREAK	BREAK
DRUMMERS	D & SS	S	X1	Volume Down	Volume & Tempo Up		STOP
DANCERS	Clap			SG (Several Rounds)	DS1	DS1	Jump/Clap

Wrap-Up

- Invite students to store the instruments and straighten up the room for the next session.
- Ask students to get their Student Enrichment Books and gather for discussion.
- Review and clarify the assignment in the Student Enrichment Book for this lesson.

Evaluation

Were students able to

- respond appropriately to the Yankadi break?
- switch dance movements on time?
- start and stop the rhythm parts correctly? If not, review the break with the vocables and clapping on the pulse so students get a better feel for the patterns.
- understand the difference in meter between Yankadi and Macrou? If not, review 4/4 and 12/8 time signatures.
- perform the dundunba and sangban patterns correctly? If not, what aspects were difficult? Review dundun and kenken technique before the next lesson.
- understand the "swing feel" of Yankadi and express that aspect in the rhythm patterns and dance movements?

Discussion

- What makes something "swing"? Have students identify popular songs that incorporate the same feel.
- What are some events that young people in the West participate in that have the same function as the Yankadi-Macrou celebration (parties, dances, sports, etc.)?
- Evaluate the session using P.R.I.D.E. (the WRAP core values and best practices) as discussion points.

LESSON 12: THAT SWINGIN' FEELING

Adding the Kenkeni and Xylophone 2

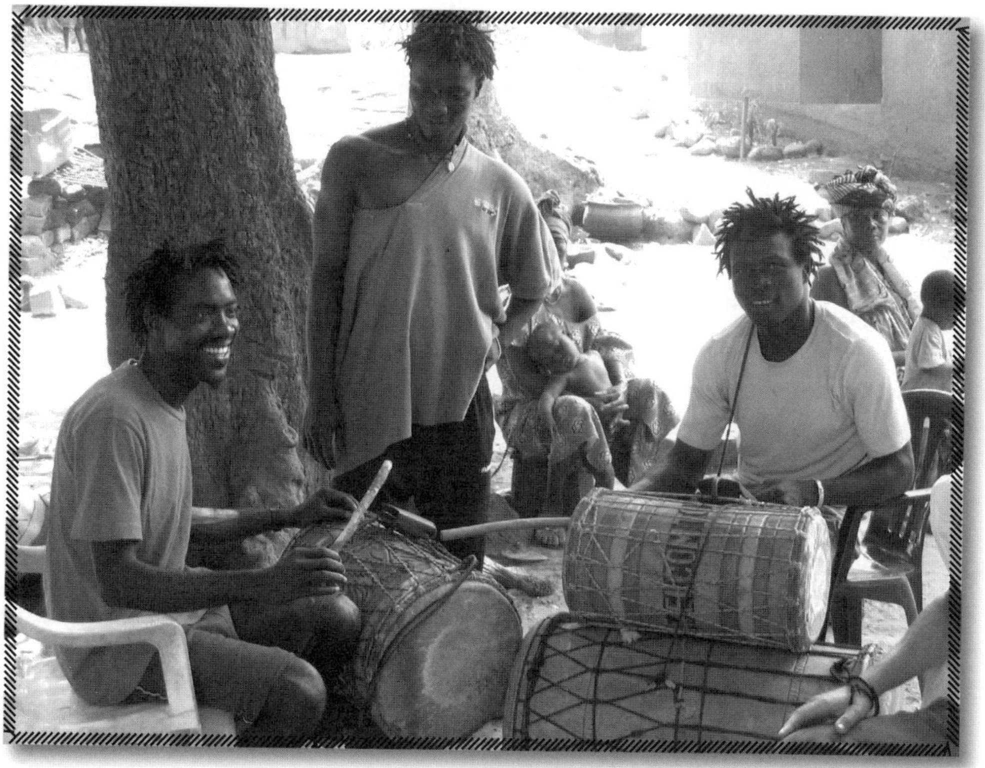

OBJECTIVES

Students will

- learn the structure and function of the Yankadi rhythm and dance within the Yankadi-Macrou village celebration;
- learn and play rhythms in 12/8 meter;
- learn the Yankadi Jembe Break and how to respond musically and physically;
- incorporate elements of the traditional Yankadi dance, drum, song and xylophone into a mini-performance.

MUSICAL SKILLS

- Rhythm pattern identification
- Ensemble playing
- Melody recognition

LIFE SKILLS

- Group awareness
- Active listening

MOVEMENT SKILLS

- Contrary motion
- Reverse direction

MATERIALS

- All dunduns
- Xylophones: BX & AX
- Seke-seke
- DVD player and TV
- CD player

VOCABULARY

- Kenkeni
- Bala
- Jeli

Process

LET'S SPEAK ♪9

Number

Susu/ Phonetics	**English**
fuu anun firin *(foo ah-NOON FIR-ring)*	"Twelve"

Vocabulary

Susu	**English**
Khulunyi, fare nun sigui nakui khakhili na ara (koé, yanyi, gésségé) kelifera Guinée, West Africa.	"The music, dance and song that you will experience (tonight, day, morning) comes from Guinea, West Africa."

LET'S MOVE

1. Review Yankadi dance movements in *group formation.*
   - ➲ Sing or play the Yankadi break on the jembe drum to cue starting, changing, and stopping.
   - ➲ Use the CD for accompaniment, or select student to play the dundunba, sangban and seke-seke patterns.
2. Introduce Yankadi Dance Steps 3 and 4. Make sure students are responding to the break, starting, stopping and performing the movements at the proper tempo.

Yankadi Dance Step 3

	1	2	3	4	5	6	7	8 (Start)
Arms	FWD	SWING	SWING	FWD	FWD	SWING	SWING	FWD
	(R)			(R)	(L)			(L)
Feet	SIDE	BACK	SIDE	TOUCH (BWD)	SIDE	BACK	SIDE	TOUCH (BWD)
	L	R	L	(R)	R	L	R	(L)

Use the last position (beat 8) as a transition from Yankadi Dance Step 2 to begin this pattern.

Yankadi Dance Step 3 Transition

					BREAK			
	1	2	3	4	5	6	7	8 (Start)
Arms	FWD	SWING	SWING	FWD	FWD	SWING	SWING	FWD
	(R)			(R)	(L)			(L)
Feet	SIDE	BACK	SIDE	TOUCH (BWD)	SIDE	BACK	SIDE	STEP
	L	R	L	(R)	R	L	R	L

On the break, complete this sequence with a LEFT STEP (feet are together). This will allow a smooth transition into step 4.

Yankadi Dance Step 4 : Part 1

		1	2	3	4	1 (5)	2 (6)	3 (7)	4 (8)
Arms		CIRCLE							
		(R)							
Feet		SIDE	TOUCH	SIDE	TOUCH	SIDE	TOUCH	SIDE	UP
		R	L	L	(R)	R	L	L	(R)

Arms circle forward, alternating. Beat 8 (UP) acts as a transition to part 2.

Yankadi Dance Step 4: Part 2

	BREAK							
	1	2	3	4	1 (5)	2 (6)	3 (7)	4 (8)
Arms	UP	DOWN	UP	DOWN	UP	DOWN	UP (High)	DOWN
Feet	STEP	UP	STEP	UP	STEP	UP	STEP	UP
	R	(L)	L	(R)	R	(L)	L	(R)

Tip: Remind students to "dance to the dunduns." This will help them get the proper feel and stay in the right time. Encourage large movements—stretch!

Time permitting, rehearse all four steps in **line formation** to focus on each step.

LET'S DRUM 2 5

1. Review the dundunba and sangban patterns for Yankadi.
   - Use the vocables and body percussion from the lesson as needed.
   - Make sure students are exhibiting proper dundun and kenkeni techniques.
2. In a circle and marching to a steady beat, introduce the kenkeni pattern using vocables, then add body percussion (chest for bell, snap for muted stroke and pat for open stroke).

Kenkeni:

3. Divide the circle into three even sections and have each one perform one of the dundun patterns using chant and/or body percussion. Experiment with different combinations of the vocables and body percussion so students clearly hear and feel each part.

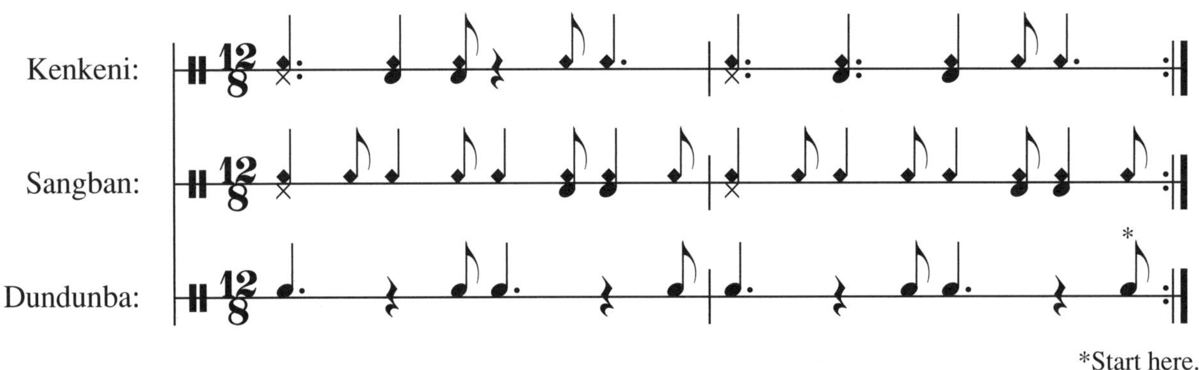

4. Keep the same grouping and transfer the three dundun patterns to the appropriate drums, using the break to bring in each one (D, S, then K).

   - Ensure that students are stopping and starting their patterns at the correct time in relation to the break.
   - Use the seke-seke to provide a steady beat.

5. Introduce students to the xylophone 2 pattern.

6. Add the xylophone 1 and 2 patterns to the ensemble and rotate students on each part.

Review the Yankadi song part from lesson 11, accompanied by the xylophone 1 and 2 patterns. Focus on singing the correct pitches, and stress the correct pronunciation and articulation of the words.

Now you're ready to combine all elements into a mini-performance. Use the jembe to play the break. Make sure students are responding in the proper place and time with each break cue and observing the changes in dynamics and tempo.

Note: The song is now being sung while performing dance step 1. This reflects how the parts will be combined in the final performance.

Let's Play Key

D=Dundunba S=Sangban K=Kenkeni J=Jembe X=Xylophone SS=Seke-seke KR=Krinyi
DS=Dance Step M=March SG=Song EM=Échauffmant

LEADER	BREAK	BREAK	EM	BREAK	BREAK	BREAK	BREAK	BREAK
DRUMMERS	D & SS	S	K	X1 & X2	Lower Volume	Volume & Tempo Up		
DANCERS	Clap				SG DS1	End SG DS2	DS3	DS4

LEADER	BREAK
DRUMMERS	STOP
DANCERS	Jump/Clap

Wrap-Up

- Invite students to store the instruments and straighten up the room for the next session.
- Ask students to get their Student Enrichment Books and gather for discussion.
- Review and clarify the assignment in the Student Enrichment Book for this lesson.

Evaluation 1 2 7 7 8

Were students able to

- correctly perform the kenkeni pattern? If not, review the kenkeni vocal chant and body-percussion exercises.
- demonstrate active listening and group awareness skills in the dundun ensemble?
- match the tempo from the break and play together in rhythm?
- play at the same relative volume?
- perform all aspects of the mini-performance?

Discussion 4 7

- Review the roles of the dundun instruments in the ensemble and ask students how they can fulfill these roles to the best of their abilities. Identify specific strategies.
- Why does Yankadi seem to feel slower than Macrou, even though it's at the same tempo?
- Identify problem areas and work with your students to address them before the next class session.
- Evaluate the session using P.R.I.D.E. (the WRAP core values and best practices) as discussion points.

LESSON 13: CALLING ALL JEMBEFOLAS

Introducing the Yankadi Jembe 1 Rhythm Pattern

OBJECTIVES

Students will

- learn and perform jembe drumming exercises in 12/8 meter;
- transfer their experience of hearing and responding to the Yankadi break to playing the cue on the jembe;
- learn and perform the Yankadi Jembe 1 Rhythm Pattern;
- learn and perform the Yankadi song "Bere Mu Sorbè."

MUSICAL SKILLS

- Responding to cues
- Melody recognition
- Transfer of patterns

LIFE SKILLS

- Group awareness
- Public speaking

MOVEMENT SKILLS

- Body percussion
- Change direction

MATERIALS

- Jembe
- Dunduns
- Xylophones: BX & AX
- Seke-seke
- DVD player and TV
- CD player

VOCABULARY

- Jembe
- Swing feel
- Susu

Process

LET'S SPEAK

Number

Susu/ Phonetics	English
fuu anun sakhan *(foo ah-NOON SAH-khan)*	"Thirteen"

Vocabulary

Susu	English
Guiné nun khamé wo nusanén fa fera mukhukha Yankadi-Macrou. Khulunyi, fare nun sigui nakui khakhili na ara (koé, yanyi, gésségé) kelifera Guinée, West Africa.	"Ladies and gentelmen, welcome to our Yankadi-Macrou celebration. The music, dance and song that you will experience (tonight, day, morning) comes from Guinea, West Africa."

LET'S MOVE

In **group** or **line formation**, review Yankadi Dance Steps 1–4.

- ➲ Use the CD for accompaniment, or rotate students through the dundun and seke-seke parts.
- ➲ Continue to play the break for the students on jembe, and make sure they are responding to the break at the proper tempo.

LET'S DRUM

1. Review all three Yankadi dundun patterns in a small group ensemble.
   - ➲ Use the vocables and body percussion from the lesson as needed.
   - ➲ Make sure students are exhibiting proper dundun and kenkeni techniques.
2. Review proper jembe technique and introduce the following technique and skill-building exercises.
   - ➲ Make sure students use alternating hand movements.
   - ➲ Focus on trying to make the sound as consistent as possible, both from note-to-note and hand-to-hand.

Jembe Technique Exercises

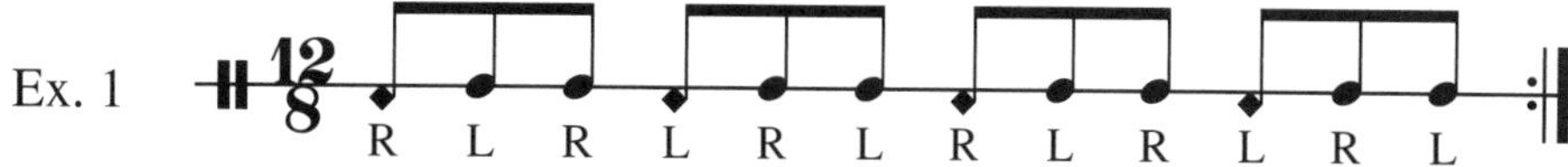

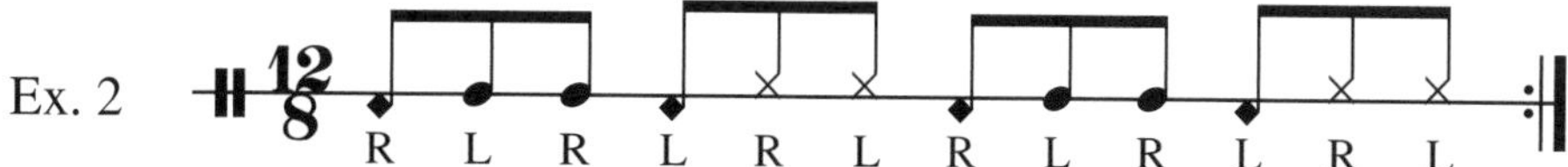

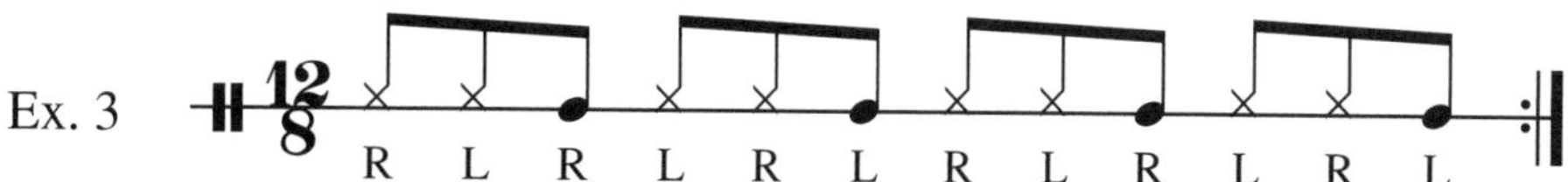

Tip: Most of us have a dominant or strong hand, and another that often needs help! Jembe players want the sounds emanating from both hands to be identical. Encourage students to spend time playing all of the jembe exercises with a reversed hand pattern. For example, if they are right-handed, all the notes played in the right hand should now be played in the left. This will help develop the weaker hand, and soon they'll have two strong hands.

3. Review the Yankadi break and have students match you in playing it on the jembe drums. Students who don't have a drum vocalize the jembe sounds until it's their turn.

The Yankadi Break

4. In a circle and marching to a steady beat, introduce the Yankadi Jembe 1 Rhythm Pattern using vocables.

Yankadi Jembe 1 Rhythm Pattern

5. While still marching, model the following body percussion example (or make up your own).

Jembe 1 (Body Percussion)

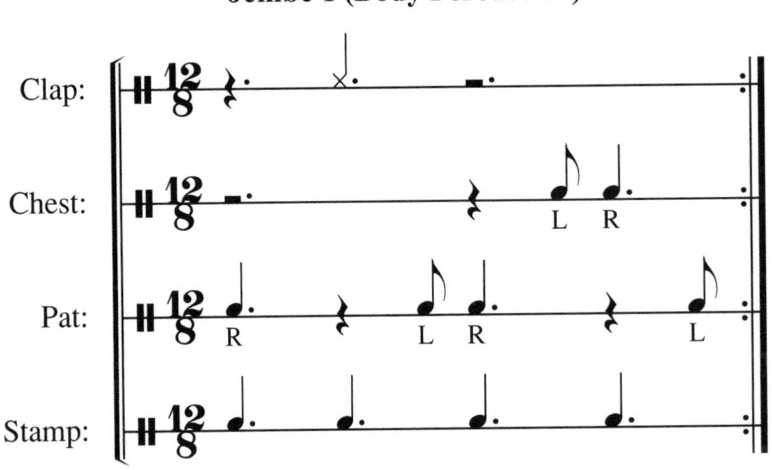

6. Once comfortable with the pattern, transfer it to the jembe drums. Students who aren't playing a drum can continue support by singing and playing the chants and body percussion.

Jembe 1 Rhythm Pattern

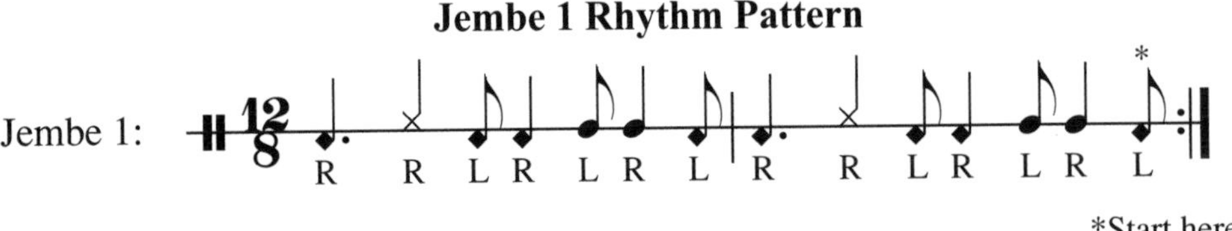

7. Add the jembe 1 pattern to the dundun ensemble and seke-seke patterns, and have students practice performing all of the parts together. Have students play the Yankadi break to bring in the dunduns and seke-seke, then play another break to bring in the jembe 1 pattern. Always begin and end with the break.

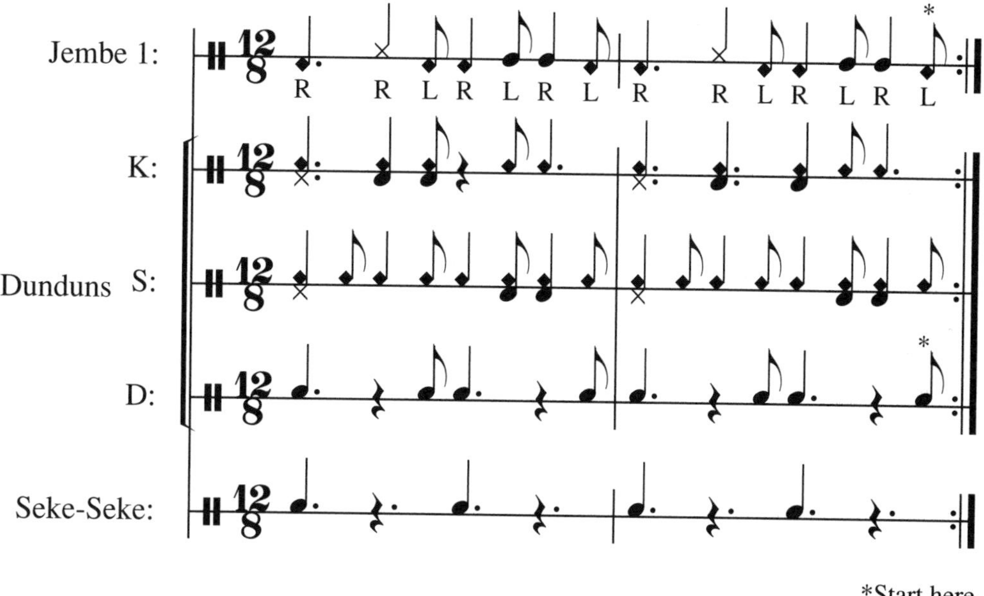

Tip: Show students that the bass and tone notes of the jembe 1 pattern are mimicking the combined dundunba and sangban patterns.

LET'S SING

1. Review the first part to the Yankadi song "Bere Mu Sorbè."
2. Add the remainder of the song, focusing on the correct melody and proper pronunciation. Practice singing the song utilizing the two xylophone accompaniment parts from lessons 11 and 12.

"Bere Mu Sorbè" Translation

SUSU	ENGLISH
Bere mu sorbè	Playing doesn't your seriousness
Kana fory* ah eh	Break old people say *(Asking an elder person)*
Bere mu sorbè	Playing doesn't your seriousness
Kana fory eh	Break an old person says *(an elder person replying)*
Eh-woiyoh	*(expressive—no translation)*
Awayire	It's the truth.

This is a very old proverb that means

"Wise people say there is a time for work and a time for play. It's the truth"

(*Fory means "old" but it really is a respectful term more like "wise.")

LET'S PLAY

Combine the new jembe pattern and complete song into the following mini-performance. Select different students to play the beginning break on the jembe and, for more advanced students, the breaks to change dance steps.

Let's Play Key

D=Dundunba S=Sangban K=Kenkeni J=Jembe X=Xylophone SS=Seke-seke KR=Krinyi
DS=Dance Step M=March SG=Song EM=Échauffmant

LEADER	BREAK	BREAK	BREAK	BREAK	BREAK	BREAK	BREAK
DRUMMERS	D & SS	S	K	J1	X1 & X2	Volume Down	Volume Up
DANCERS	Clap					SG DS1	Stop SG DS2

LEADER	BREAK	BREAK	BREAK
DRUMMERS			STOP
DANCERS	DS3	DS4	Jump/Clap

Wrap-Up

- Invite students to store the instruments and straighten up the room for the next session.
- Ask students to get their Student Enrichment Books and gather for discussion.
- Review and clarify the assignment in the Student Enrichment Book for this lesson.

Evaluation 1 2 7 7 8

Were students able to

- perform the jembe exercises and the jembe 1 pattern?
- play the Yankadi jembe break?
- sing the Yankadi song with the correct melody and proper pronunciation?

Discussion 4 7

- What challenges did students face with jembe technique? If the entire group is struggling, review the jembe technique section on the DVD.

Tip: Consider spending five minutes after school or at lunch with each student over the next week. One-on-one attention can really help improve technique.

- What would help students learn, perform, and respond to the break? In a circle, try having each student verbally "play" (say) the break in rhythm.
- Encourage students to work on the song at home.
- Evaluate the session using P.R.I.D.E. (the WRAP core values and best practices) as discussion points.

LESSON 14: DANCE, DANCE, DANCE

Adding Yankadi Dance Steps 5 and 6

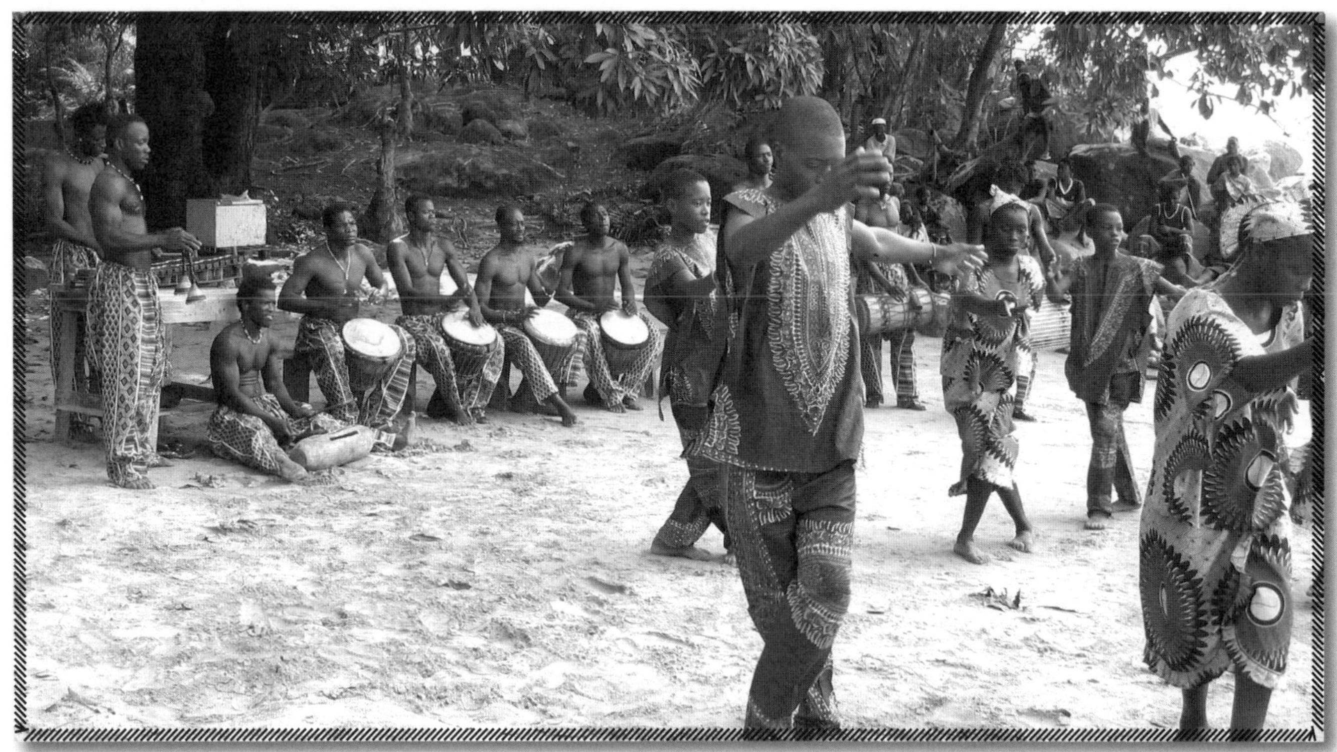

OBJECTIVES

Students will

- learn and perform Yankadi Dance Steps 5 and 6;
- learn and perform the Yankadi Jembe 2 Rhythm Pattern;
- review the song "Bere Mu Sorbè";
- combine all musical and movement elements into a mini- performance.

MUSICAL SKILLS

- Combing Rhythms
- Feeling the steady beat

LIFE SKILLS

- Initiative
- Teamwork

MOVEMENT SKILLS

- Spin
- Twist

MATERIALS

- Jembes
- Dunduns
- Xylophones: BX & AX
- Seke-seke
- DVD player and TV
- CD player

VOCABULARY

- Contrary motion
- The Charleston

Process

LET'S SPEAK ♪9

Number

	Susu/ Phonetics	**English**
Vocabulary	**fuu anun naani** *(foo ah-NOON NA-nee)*	"Fourteen"

Susu	**English**
La Guinée na kui na makhasé nun fare abara findi baloe ra n'de bé.	"In Guinea there are special rhythms and dances for almost every event in life."

LET'S MOVE 1 2

1. Review Yankadi Dance Steps 1–4 with the CD.
   - ➲ Play the breaks on the jembe drum.
   - ➲ Focus on full extensions of the movements, staying in time, and dancing together.
2. Introduce Yankadi Dance Steps 5 and 6.

Yankadi Dance Step 5: Part 1 (Transition)

	1	2	3	4	5	6	7	8
Arms	CHEST/ BWD							DOWN
	L/R							
Feet	BWD				Turn 120° CCW	Turn 120° CCW	Turn 120° CCW	UP
	L							(R)

On the break, perform Part 1 one time, then move to Part 2. Continue Part 2 until the next break.

Yankadi Dance Step 5: Part 2

	BREAK							
	1	**2**	**3**	**4**	**5**	**6**	**7**	**8**
Arms	UP	DOWN	UP	DOWN	UP	DOWN	UP (High)	DOWN
Feet	STEP	UP	STEP	UP	STEP	UP	STEP	UP
	R	(L)	L	(R)	R	(L)	L	(R)

On the break, move backwards.

Yankadi Dance Step 6: Transition (1X)

	1	2	3	4	5	6	7	8
Arms	SWING		SWING		SWING		SWING	
Feet	FWD		FWD		FWD		FWD	
	R		L		R		L	

Walk forward eight beats.

Yankadi Dance Step 6: Part 1a

	1	2	3	4	5	6	7	8
Arms	CLAP	SWING	SWING	SWING	RIGHT	LEFT	RIGHT	OPEN
					**	**	**	
Feet	KICK	BWD	TOUCH (BWD)	STEP (Turn CCW)	CROSS	TOUCH	CROSS	STEP
	R	R	L	L	R	R	R	R

****The head turns to follow the hands.**

Yankadi Dance Step 6: Part 1b

	1	2	3	4	5 (BREAK)	6 (BREAK)	7 (BREAK)	8 (BREAK)
Arms	CLAP	SWING	SWING	SWING	RIGHT	LEFT	RIGHT	OPEN
					**	**	**	
Feet	KICK	BWD	TOUCH (BWD)	STEP (Turn CW)	CROSS	TOUCH	CROSS	STEP
	L	L	R	R	L	L	L	L

Alternate between Parts 1a and 1b until the break.
Note the similarity between this step and the popular dance called the Charleston.

Tip: Dance step 6 is longer and more challenging than some of the others. Consider teaching the movement in three sections: the walk forward, right cross-over, and left cross-over. Make sure to signal the break on the left side (Part 1b). See the DVD for details.

3. Combine dance steps 5 and 6 with the rest of the choreography, and practice the dance in **group formation**. If time permits, use **line formation** to isolate each step.

LET'S DRUM 2 5

1. Review the Yankadi Jembe 1 Rhythm Pattern. In a circle and stepping to a steady beat, introduce the Yankadi Jembe 2 Rhythm Pattern using vocables.

Jembe 2 Rhythm Pattern

*Start here.

2. While still stepping in place, consider applying this body-percussion pattern.

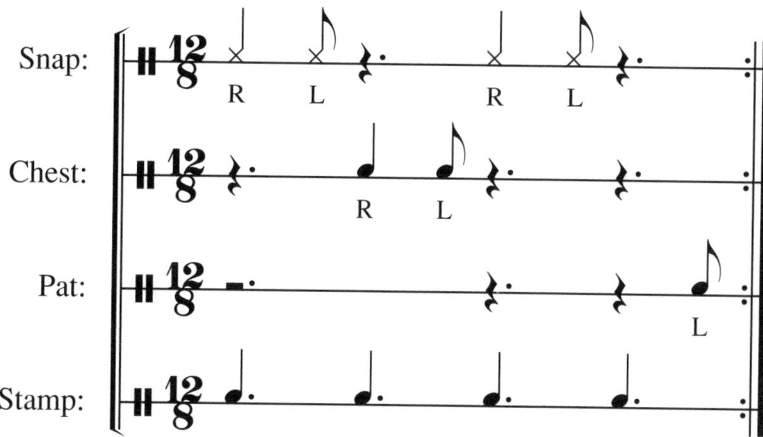

3. Invite students to perform the Yankadi jembe 2 pattern on the drums.

Jembe 2 Rhythm Pattern

*Start here.

4. Combine Yankadi jembe patterns 1 and 2.

*Start here.

- Point out how the two rhythms align and complement each other.
- Use the break to start and stop both jembe patterns, separately and together.
- Add dundun accompaniment or use the CD.

5. Practice playing both jembe patterns with the full dundun ensemble and seke-seke. Layer in all parts one at a time. Start and stop using the break. Repeat.

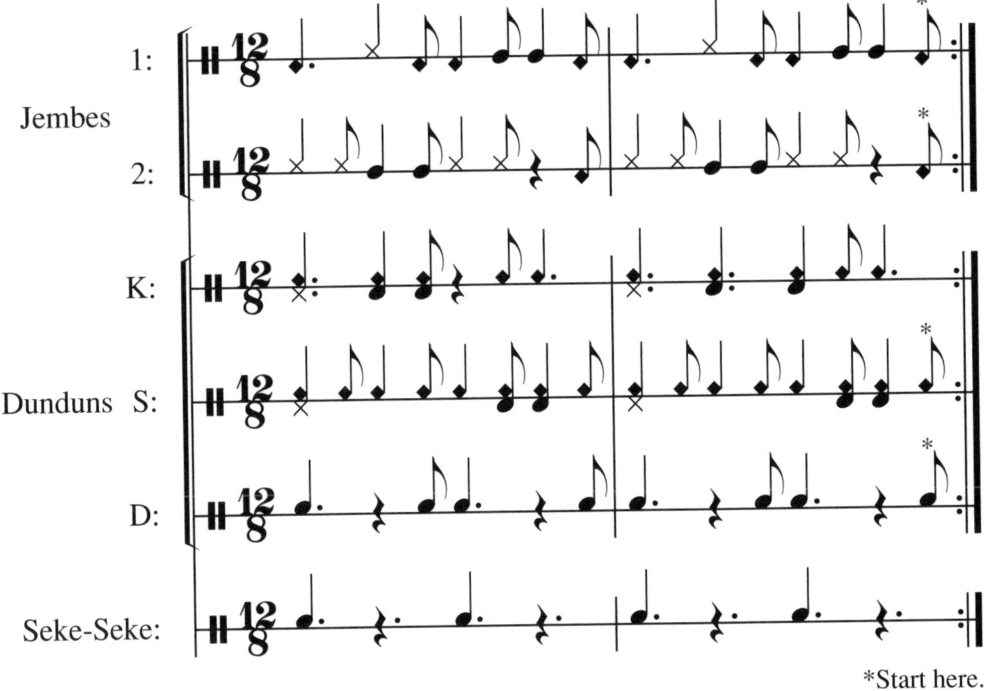
Jembes
1:
2:
K:
Dunduns S:
D:
Seke-Seke:
*Start here.

LET'S SING

1. Review the complete Yankadi song "Bere Mu Sorbè."
2. Introduce the call-and-response (chorus) sections of the song.
   - Use the xylophone patterns for accompaniment.
   - Add the seke-seke to mark the steady beat.
   - Rotate students through the lead and chorus sections.

Bere Mu Sorbè
Lead:
Chorus:
Be - re mu sor - bè ka - na fo - ry ah eh
Be - re mu sor - bè ka - na fo-ry eh
Eh - - - woi - yoh
Eh - - - woi - yoh
Be - re mu sor - bè ka - na fo-ry ah eh A - wa - yi - re
Be - re mu sor - bè ka - na fo-ry ah eh A - wa - yi - re

Combine the completed Yankadi choreography, the jembe 2 pattern, and xylophone 3 pattern into the ensemble, following the mini-performance below. Allow advanced students to call the breaks for the group using the Yankadi jembe break

Let's Play Key

D=Dundunba S=Sangban K=Kenkeni J=Jembe X=Xylophone SS=Seke-seke KR=Krinyi
DS=Dance Step M=March SG=Song EM=Échauffmant

LEADER	BREAK	BREAK	BREAK	BREAK	BREAK	BREAK	BREAK	BREAK
DRUMMERS	D & SS	S	K	J1	J2	X1 & X2	Drums Lower Volume	Volume & Tempo Up
DANCERS	Clap						SG & DS1	Stop SG DS2

LEADER	BREAK	BREAK	BREAK	BREAK	BREAK
DRUMMERS					STOP
DANCERS	DS3	DS4	DS5	DS6	Jump/Clap

Wrap-Up

- Invite students to store the instruments and straighten up the room for the next session.
- Ask students to get their Student Enrichment Books and gather for discussion.
- Review and clarify the assignment in the Student Enrichment Book for this lesson.

Evaluation 1 2 7 7 8

Were students able to

- learn and perform Yankadi Dance Steps 5 and 6?
- learn and perform the Yankadi Jembe 2 Rhythm Pattern?
- learn and perform xylophone pattern 3?
- perform the song "Bere Mu Sorbè"?

Discussion 4 7

- What role does active listening and cooperation play in allowing all instruments in the ensemble to be heard?
- Why is it important to know how to play all the rhythm patterns in the ensemble and how they fit together?
- What should you do if you get lost or fall out of rhythm? How do you know when you're out of sync with the group?
- Evaluate the session using P.R.I.D.E. (the WRAP core values and best practices) as discussion points.

LESSON 15: THE RETURN OF THE JELI

Adding the Jembe 3 and Xylophone 3 Patterns

OBJECTIVES

Students will

- learn and perform the Yankadi Jembe 3 Rhythm Pattern;
- learn and perform xylophone pattern 3 and combine it with patterns 1 & 2;
- combine all musical and movement elements into a mini-performance.

MUSICAL SKILLS

- Flam
- Muted slap

LIFE SKILLS

- Mutual support
- Diversity

MOVEMENT SKILLS

- Sequencing

MATERIALS

- Jembes
- Dunduns
- Xylophones
- Seke-seke
- DVD player and TV
- CD player

VOCABULARY

- Balafola (Bala player)
- Numu

Process

LET'S SPEAK

Number

Susu/ Phonetics	**English**
fuu anun suli *(foo ah-NOON SU-ly)*	"Fifteen"

Vocabulary

Susu	**English**
Na makhase munsema, di nu bari, khili safe, futi khiri, wali a nun fe gbétée.	"There are rhythms for birth, naming, weddings, working, and more."

LET'S MOVE

Review the entire Yankadi dance choreography. Pay special attention to step 6, introduced in lesson 13.

- Use the CD for accompaniment so all students can practice together.
- Focus attention on articulating each movement, making them as full and energetic as possible.
- Say or play the break to cue each dance step.

LET'S DRUM

1. Review the jembe 1 and 2 patterns.
   - Start with voice, then body percussion, moving finally to the drums.
   - Play each pattern separately, then together.
2. In a circle and stepping to a steady beat, introduce the Yankadi Jembe 3 Rhythm Pattern using vocables.

Jembe 3 Rhythm Pattern

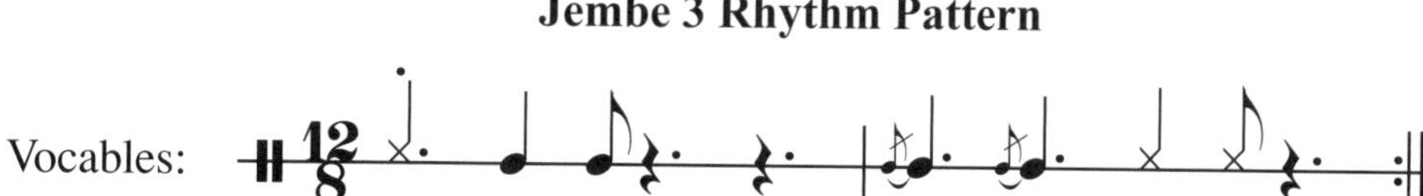

3. While still stepping, add body percussion.

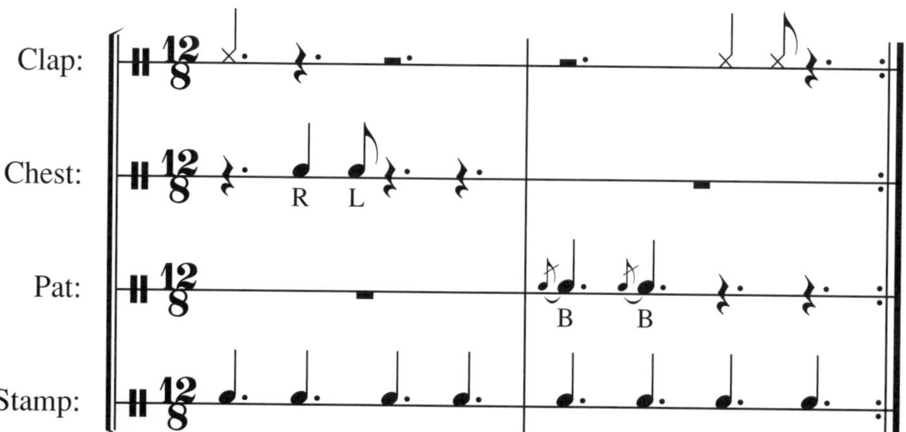

4. Have students join you in performing the jembe 3 pattern on the drums.

   Pay special attention to the new muted slap tone on beat 1 of the pattern. Make sure students are not hitting the bass tone and producing an extra note as they hold the skin. (See the jembe technique section, or watch the DVD for examples and explanation.)

Jembe 3 Rhythm Pattern

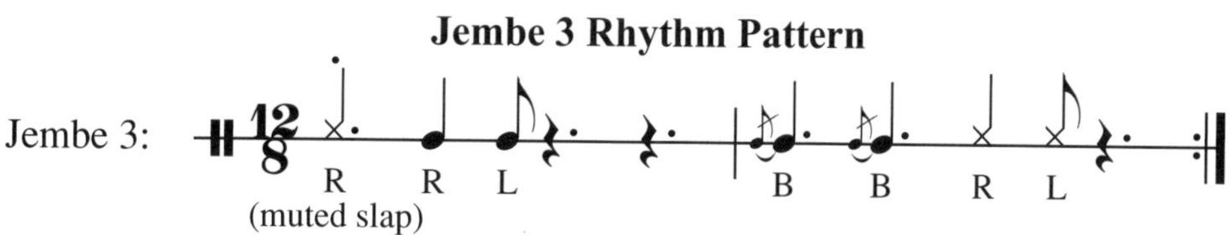

5. Combine jembe patterns 1, 2, and 3. Rotate students through each.

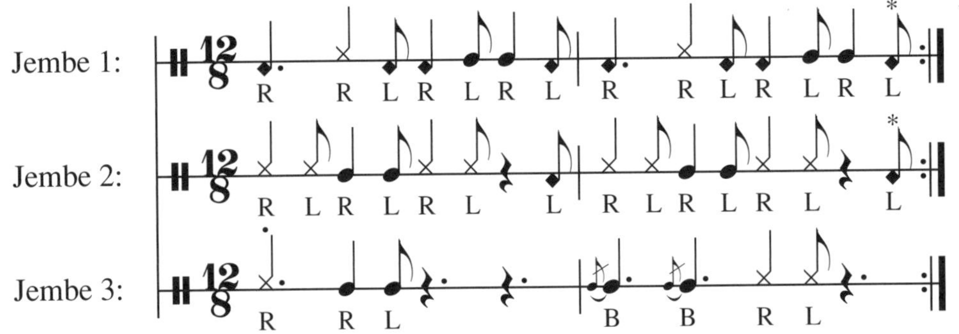

6. Introduce xylophone pattern 3.

7. Combine xylophone 3 with patterns 1 and 2. Rotate students so they can perform all three of the parts.

Tip: Take time to remind students of the origins of the bala, what it looks like, and the special caste of musicians that play it.

LET'S SING

Review the Yankadi song "Bere Mu Sorbè."

- ➲ Add the seke-seke to mark the steady beat.
- ➲ Rotate students through the lead and chorus sections.

Bere Mu Sorbè
Lead:
Chorus:
Be - re mu sor - bè ka - na fo - ry ah eh
Be - re mu sor - bè ka - na fo - ry eh
Eh - - - woi - yoh
Eh - - - woi - yoh
Be - re mu sor - bè ka - na fo - ry ah eh A - wa - yi - re
Be - re mu sor - bè ka - na fo - ry ah eh A - wa - yi - re

LET'S PLAY

Combine all of the complete Yankadi musical and dance elements into a mini-performance.

Let's Play Key

D=Dundunba S=Sangban K=Kenkeni J=Jembe X=Xylophone SS=Seke-seke KR=Krinyi
DS=Dance Step M=March SG=Song EM=Échauffmant

LEADER	BREAK	BREAK	BREAK	BREAK	BREAK	BREAK	BREAK	BREAK
DRUMMERS	D & SS	S	K	J1	J2	J3	X1, X2, X3	Volume Down
DANCERS	Clap							SG + DS1

LEADER	BREAK	BREAK	BREAK	BREAK	BREAK	BREAK
DRUMMERS	Volume & Tempo Up					STOP
DANCERS	Stop SG DS2	DS3	DS4	DS5	DS6	Jump/Clap

Guinea Music Today 7 8

While West Africa as a whole is famous for percussion, perhaps no other country in the region has produced more internationally recognized virtuoso percussionists as Guinea. It is said that, in Guinea, "Everything is said with music." Guinea ballet companies have won numerous international awards and have appeared in the 1984 Los Angeles Olympic Games and in several television specials including ***Heritage*** *in 1992. Famous Guinean drummers like Mamady Keita (originally with the National Ballet Djoliba) and Famadou Konate (original soloist for Les Ballets Africains) have helped to open the door for many Guinea percussionists and groups including Les Percussions de Guinee, Wofa, Wassa, and renowned artists/dancer/choreographer Kemoko Sano's Les Merveilles de Guinee. Famous dancers from these ballet troupes, including Bangally Bangoura and Yamoussa Soumah, were named as two of the 50 greatest dancers in the world at the 1994 Academy Awards show. Traditional music and dance performed in the context of ballet continues to be extremely popular. In 2005, the Franco-Guinean Cultural Center held a ballet competition in Conakry, in which 35 private ballets performed.*

The first modern groups that combined instruments like drumset, guitar, bass, and piano with African music helped usher in the area of African jazz in the 1960s and were spearheaded by Guinean groups like Bembaya Jazz, Kaluoum Star, and (later) famous saxophonists Maitre Barry, Momo Wandel, and Keleigui Traore. Jeli musicians playing kora and bala have made a name for themselves on the popular music scene. Artists such as M'Bady Kouyate and Prince Diabate have redefined modern kora playing, and famous popular singers like Mory Kante, Sekouba Bambino, Ibro Diabate, and Macire Sylla are starting to become well known in Europe and the U.S. Currently in Guinea, artists combining traditional instruments with modern songs and melodies, like Les Etoile de Bulibinet and Les Espoire de Coronthie, are hugely popular, and reggae artists such as Alpha Wess and hip-hop rappers like Bill de Sam, Deggy Force 3, and Legitime Defense are putting a Guinea spin on other popular art forms.

Wrap-Up

- Invite students to store the instruments and straighten up the room for the next session.
- Ask students to get their Student Enrichment Books and gather for discussion.
- Review and clarify the assignment in the Student Enrichment Book for this lesson.

Evaluation 1 2 7 7 8

Are students able to

- play all three xylophone patterns? If not, provide opportunities for review.
- sing the melody of the song and pronounce the words correctly? If not, review the words and pronunciation. Use the CD as a sing-along track.
- demonstrate competency on all three jembe and dundun patterns and place them in a musical context?

Discussion 4 7

- Where are the weak areas of the performance and how can the group work together to address them?
- Why is it important to work together as a musical family?
- What tools does one need to make a bala? (What tasks are involved?) What tools might be available in the village? How are they used? (Demonstrate the basic action.)
- Why is no single part more important than the music that's being created by the entire group?
- Evaluate the session using P.R.I.D.E. (the WRAP core values and best practices) as discussion points.

LESSON 16: HEAT IT UP!

The Yankadi Échauffment

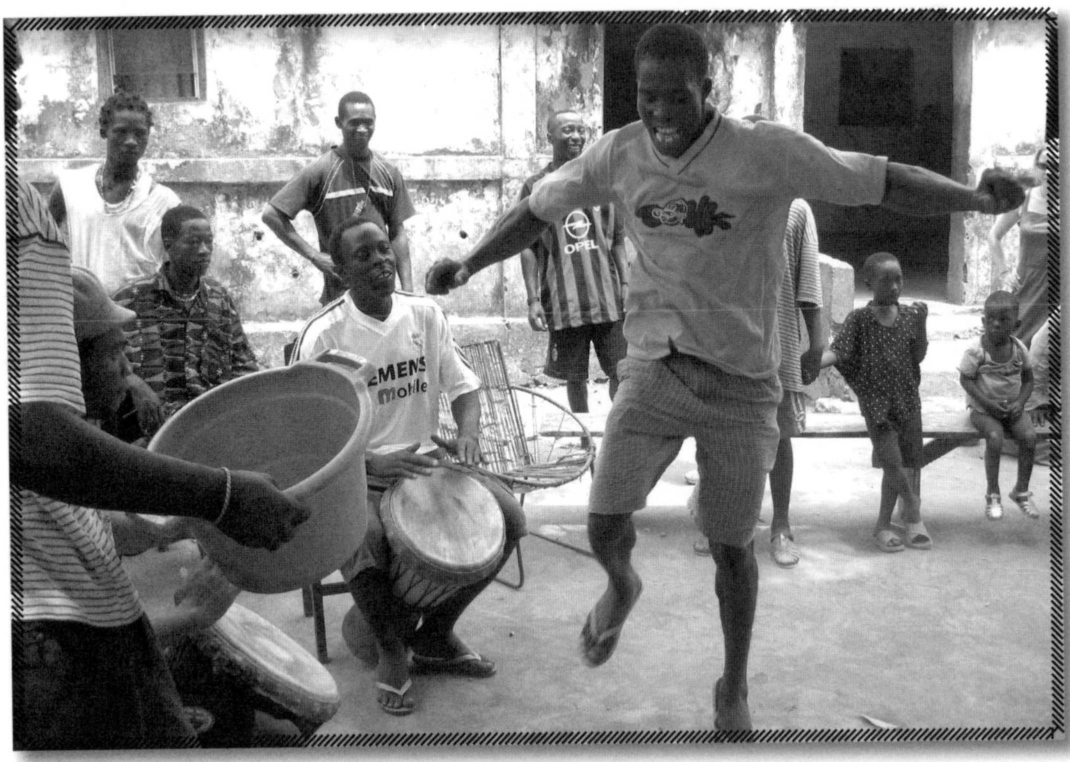

OBJECTIVES

Students will

- review the Yankadi dance steps and choreography, refining technique and articulation of movement;
- review Yankadi jembe and xylophone patterns;
- learn and perform the Yankadi échauffment pattern on jembe and add it to the mini-performance arrangement.

MUSICAL SKILLS

- Playing for dance
- Arranging
- Singing
- Feeling long phrases

LIFE SKILLS

- Cooperation
- Active listening

MOVEMENT SKILLS

- Coordination of group movement
- Attention to hand and head position
- Shadowing

MATERIALS

- Jembes
- Dunduns
- Xylophones
- Seke-seke
- DVD player and TV
- CD player

VOCABULARY

- Échauffment

Process

LET'S SPEAK

Number

	Susu/ Phonetics	**English**
	fuu anun senni *(foo ah-NOON SEN-ee)*	"Sixteen"

Vocabulary

	Susu	**English**
	La Guinée na kui na makhasé nun fare abara findi baloe ra n'de bé. Na makhase munsema, di nu bari, khili safe, futi khiri, wali a nun fe gbétée.	"In Guinea there are special rhythms and dances for almost every event in life. There are rhythms for birth, naming, weddings, working, and more."

LET'S MOVE

1. Review the Yankadi dance steps. Use both **group** and **line formations** to rehearse dance steps 1–6.
2. After all six steps have been reviewed, assemble students in their performance lines and practice them in sequence. Play the CD for accompaniment to give students a chance to respond to the breaks.

LET'S DRUM 2 5

1. Review the Yankadi dundun, xylophone, seke-seke, and jembe patterns. Select students to take the lead-drummer role and play the beginning and ending breaks.

Yankadi Instrumental Score

2. Demonstrate the Yankadi échauffment pattern leading into the break, and invite the students to play it along with you.
   - ➲ Remind students of the role of the échauffment pattern. (Preparing for the break.)
   - ➲ Make sure students are alternating hands and, if possible, playing the flam on the tenth note (beat 4) of the measure before the break.

Yankadi Échauffment Pattern

Lead Jembe:
R L R L R L R L R L R L R L R L R L R L R L R L
R L R L R L R L R B R L R L R L R L R R L R L R

3. Select students to start and stop the group using the break and échauffment/break combinations.
4. Review the xylophone patterns for Yankadi.

LET'S SING

Review the Yankadi song using the xylophone patterns as accompaniment.

Bere Mu Sorbè

Lead:
Chorus:
Be - re mu sor - bè ka - na fo - ry ah eh
Be - re mu sor - bè ka - na fo - ry eh
Eh - - - woi - yoh
Eh - - - woi - yoh
Be - re mu sor - bè ka - na fo - ry ah eh A - wa - yi - re
Be - re mu sor - bè ka - na fo - ry ah eh A - wa - yi - re

LET'S PLAY

Combine all of the Yankadi elements for the Yankadi mini-performance. As the lead drummer, play the whole arrangement first to show students how to properly use the échauffment and break, then select students to perform the lead part. Note how all the drums and dance step 1 are now combined at the beginning of the arrangement. This reflects how these patterns will enter in final performance.

Let's Play Key

D=Dundunba S=Sangban K=Kenkeni J=Jembe X=Xylophone SS=Seke-seke KR=Krinyi
DS=Dance Step M=March SG=Song EM=Échauffmant

LEADER	BREAK	BREAK	BREAK	BREAK	BREAK	BREAK	BREAK	BREAK
DRUMMERS	All	Drums Volume Down	Volume & Tempo Up					STOP
DANCERS	DS1	DS1 + SG	Stop SG DS2	DS3	DS4	DS5	DS6	Jump/Clap

Wrap-Up

- Invite students to store the instruments and straighten up the room for the next session.
- Ask students to get their Student Enrichment Books and gather for discussion.
- Review and clarify the assignment in the Student Enrichment Book for this lesson.

Evaluation

Are students able to

- display a clear understanding of all the dance movements?
- dance through the choreography unassisted? If not, consider making a room available for students to practice the dance to the CD at lunch or after school.
- play the échauffment pattern for Yankadi and put the break in the proper place? If not, review the échauffment pattern and have students listen to how it is used on the CD.
- play through the entire Yankadi mini-performance?

Discussion

- What aspects of the performance were difficult?
- What are the strong areas of the ensemble?
- What is the function of the échauffment within the ensemble?
- Evaluate the session using P.R.I.D.E. (the WRAP core values and best practices) as discussion points.

LESSON 17: FINISHING TOUCHES

The Yankadi Performance Arrangement

OBJECTIVES

Students will

- review and refine Yankadi dance choreography;
- review Yankadi drum, xylophone and song elements;
- learn and demonstrate an understanding of the Yankadi ending arrangement;
- perform the complete Yankadi drumming and dance arrangement.

MUSICAL SKILLS

- Connecting drumming and dance
- Arranging

LIFE SKILLS

- Group awareness
- Active listening

MOVEMENT SKILLS

- Balanace
- Moving in unison

MATERIALS

- Jembes
- Dunduns
- Xylophones
- Seke-seke
- DVD player and TV
- CD player

VOCABULARY

- Coda
- Synchronization

Process

LET'S SPEAK

Number

Susu/ Phonetics	English
fuu nun solo feren *(foo ah-NOON SO-lo FI-ring)*	"Seventeen"

Vocabulary

Susu	English
Yankadi-Macrou makhase nun fare a ma senkhiné won n'tan nyama néné khana na ralan nun won kha bore compininya nyi takhun.	"Yankadi-Mcrou is a special rhythm and dance for meeting new people and sharing with friends."

LET'S MOVE 

1. Review the Yankadi dance choreography, focusing on proper techniques and dancing with energy and joy. Use the CD so all students are able to practice the dance together.
2. Introduce the ending dance arrangement for Yankadi. Focus on precise timing, body balance, group synchronization, and awareness of self and others. Practice calling the break with your voice beginning with Yankadi Dance Step 6 and transitioning into the arrangement without accompaniment.

Tip: Use the Macrou whistle to provide the cadence during the arrangement. (Listen to the CD.)

Yankadi Ending Arrangement: Part 1a

	1	2	3	4	5	6	7	8
Arms	CLAP			HIGH/ LOW				HIGH/ LOW
				L / R				R / L
Feet	JUMP			STEP / STEP	STEP			UP
	R			L R	L			R L

Yankadi Ending Arrangement: Part 1b

	1	2	3	4	5	6	7	8
Arms				HIGH/ LOW				DOWN
				L / R				
Feet	STEP			STEP / STEP	STEP			UP
	R			L R	L			(R)

Yankadi Ending Arrangement: Part 2

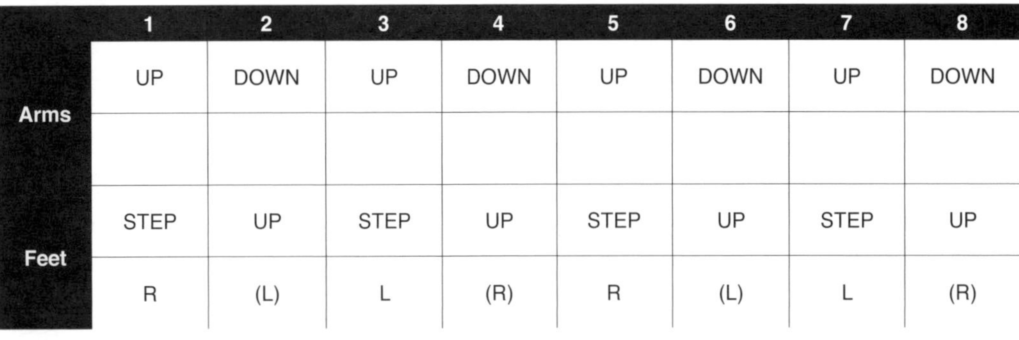

	1	2	3	4	5	6	7	8
Arms	UP	DOWN	UP	DOWN	UP	DOWN	UP	DOWN
Feet	STEP	UP	STEP	UP	STEP	UP	STEP	UP
	R	(L)	L	(R)	R	(L)	L	(R)

Yankadi Ending Arrangement: Part 3

	1	2	3	4	1
Arms	Circle BWD				CLAP
	(R)	(L)	(R)	(L)	
Feet	BWD	BWD	BWD	BWD	JUMP
	R	L	R	B	B

3. Practice the entire ending sequence using the CD for accompaniment, and add it to the arrangement.

Note: The Yankadi ending arrangement is also used as the transition between Yankadi and Macrou in the final performance, hence the meter change from 12/8 to 4/4 and the introduction of the whistle. The whistle part can also be played on the jembe, as shown in the final performance and demonstrated on the CD. Students should be able to respond to either the whistle or jembe cue.

LET'S DRUM 2 5

1. Review all drum, xylophone and percussion parts.
2. Review the échauffment and break. Select students to lead the ensemble using the break to start and the échauffment/ break combination to end. Ensure that all students play through the break and end on "one" (the downbeat) of the next bar.
3. Introduce the Yankadi Ending Arrangement.
   - Rehearse the dunduns and seke-seke, then add the jembes and xylophone patterns.
   - Once comfortable with the arrangement, start the Yankadi rhythm from the break. Bring in the rest of the instruments with the break and play for several bars.
   - Begin the échauffment, and transition into the arrangement using the Yankadi break. Use the whistle cues or jembe cues to keep the rhythm moving through the arrangement.
   - Have selected students perform the role of the lead drummer.

Yankadi Ending Arrangement

Note: The Whistle, lead jembe, or both may be used to play the cues.

Tip: To ensure students have a complete understanding of the time, try playing through the arrangements using no lead jembe or whistle cues. Remind students that the lead patterns are improvised parts and they should not rely on the lead drum or whistle to provide the tempo or phrasing.

LET'S SING
1

Review the Yankadi song using the xylophone patterns as accompaniment. Have different combinations of individual students or groups sing the lead and response parts.

Bere Mu Sorbè
Lead:
Chorus:
Be - re mu sor - bè ka - na fo - ry ah eh
Be - re mu sor - bè ka - na fo - ry eh
Eh - - - woi - yoh
Eh - - - woi - yoh
Be - re mu sor - bè ka - na fo - ry ah eh A - wa - yi - re
Be - re mu sor - bè ka - na fo - ry ah eh A - wa - yi - re

LET'S PLAY 1 2 3 4

Incorporate the new Yankadi Ending Arrangement into the mini-performance. Play the lead pattern and/or select advanced students to perform the breaks. Make sure all dance breaks are called in the appropriate places.

Let's Play Key

D=Dundunba S=Sangban K=Kenkeni J=Jembe X=Xylophone SS=Seke-seke KR=Krinyi
DS=Dance Step M=March SG=Song EM=Échauffmant

LEADER	BREAK	BREAK	BREAK	BREAK	BREAK	BREAK	BREAK	EM/ BREAK
DRUMMERS	All	Volume Down	Volume & Tempo Up					Yankadi Ending Arrangement
DANCERS	DS1	DS1 + SG	Stop SG DS2	DS3	DS4	DS5	DS6	Yankadi Ending Arrangement

Wrap-Up

- ☐ Invite students to store the instruments and straighten up the room for the next session.
- ☐ Ask students to get their Student Enrichment Books and gather for discussion.
- ☐ Review and clarify the assignment in the Student Enrichment Book for this lesson.

Evaluation 1 2 7 7 8

Were students able to

- learn the new Yankadi transition arrangement and perform it in the proper tempo? If not, review the meter-change segue from Macrou and any other areas that need refinement.
- play the Yankadi arrangement on the instruments in the proper tempo? If not, have students listen to the performance on the CD. Ask them to consider the associated dance movements as they practice the arrangement.
- demonstrate the ability to perform the drum and dance arrangement together? If not, have students watch the arrangement from the performance on the DVD and discuss the primary purpose of West African drumming (to accompany the dance).

Discussion 4 7

- What is the form of the ending arrangement? (AAAABBC)
- How does the energy level change during the transition arrangement?
- Does the tempo change or just the feel? Why does it feel faster in 4/4 than in 12/8?
- Evaluate the session using P.R.I.D.E. (the WRAP core values and best practices) as discussion points.

LESSON 18: THE YANKADI REVIEW

Reviewing the Yankadi Rhythm and Dance

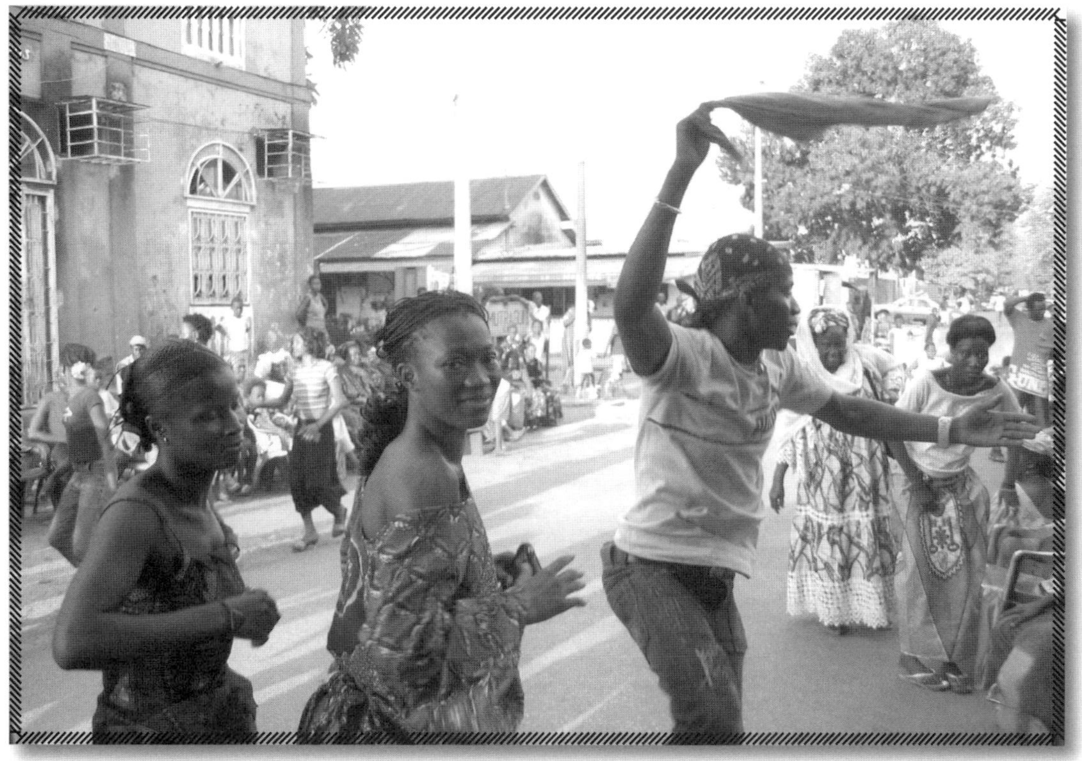

OBJECTIVES

Students will

- review and perform all components of the Yankadi program;
- combine all elements of Yankadi celebration into the complete performance;
- discuss and review performance goals, addressing critical areas.

MUSICAL SKILLS

- Refining a performance
- Production

LIFE SKILLS

- Group awareness
- Problem solving

MOVEMENT SKILLS

- Spatial awareness
- Group patterning
- Preparation

MATERIALS

- Jembes
- Dunduns
- Xylophones
- Seke-seke
- DVD player and TV
- CD player

VOCABULARY

- Choreography

Process

LET'S SPEAK

Number

Susu/ Phonetics	**English**
fuu anun solo masakhan *(foo ah-NOON SO-lo MAS-sah-xan)*	"Eighteen"

Vocabulary

Susu	**English**
Mu kha kolon wo ma nyakha mané mukha makhase nun fare ra.	"We hope you enjoy our music and dance."

LET'S MOVE

Briefly review the Yankadi choreography and arrangement.

- Focus on making the movements as "big" as possible.
- Use the Yankadi performance track for accompaniment.

LET'S DRUM

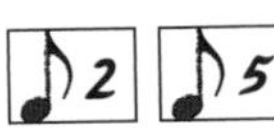

1. Briefly review the Yankadi drum and xylophone patterns (appendix P). Warm up with vocables and/or body percussion.
2. Combine all the components, and practice playing the Yankadi rhythm as an ensemble. Include the full Yankadi ending arrangement. Have selected students perform the role of the lead jembe by calling the beginning break, the ending échauffment/break combination, and arrangement cues.

LET'S SING

Briefly review the Yankadi song using the xylophones and seke-seke as accompaniment.

LET'S PLAY

Arrange the group for performance. See the following diagram.

Performance Staging Diagram

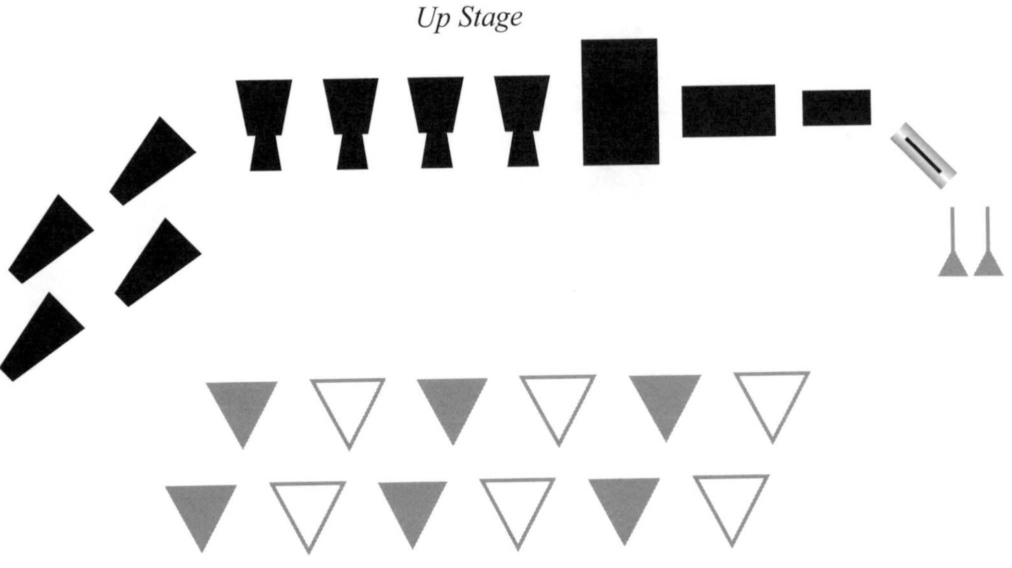

Note: The dancers are now facing the audience and not the musicians. This encourages active listening, rather than relying on visual cues. This arrangement also places added responsibility on the lead drummer to make the break cues as clear as possible, allowing dancers to hear them easily and respond.

- Have students perform the Yankadi rhythm as if they were playing for a large audience. Dancers should be energetic, smiling, and exaggerating their movements. Drummers should be watching the dancers and ready to respond to subtle tempo changes and ending arrangement cues.
- Focus the group on "drumming for the dancers" and "dancing for the drummers." Remind students of the interconnectedness of all musical and movement elements, and how they must be responsible not only for their own pattern or movement, but also for how their pattern or movement is integrated with and contributing to the entire ensemble.
- Emphasize dynamics and balance.

Let's Play Key

D=Dundunba S=Sangban K=Kenkeni J=Jembe X=Xylophone SS=Seke-seke KR=Krinyi
DS=Dance Step M=March SG=Song EM=Échauffmant

LEADER	BREAK	BREAK	BREAK	BREAK	BREAK	BREAK	BREAK	EM/ BREAK
DRUMMERS	All	Volume Down	Volume & Tempo Up					Yankadi Ending Arrangement
DANCERS	DS1	DS1 + SG	Stop SG DS2	DS3	DS4	DS5	DS6	Yankadi Ending Arrangement

Wrap-Up

- Invite students to store the instruments and straighten up the room for the next session.
- Ask students to get their Student Enrichment Books and gather for discussion.
- Review and clarify the assignment in the Student Enrichment Book for this lesson.

Evaluation 1 2 7 7 8

Were students able to

- demonstrate a thorough knowledge of, and ability to perform, all the Yankadi rhythm, dance and song components? If not, have students identify areas that could use improvement and practice those parts before the next class session.
- work together as a performance group? Rate their performance skills on a scale from 1–5 (1 = needs a lot of improvement; 5 = we got it nailed!).

Use your answers to identify growth areas. Some questions to consider when assessing your group include the following:

- Are the dancers moving together in sync?
- Are the dancers smiling and performing the movements and song with energy?
- Are drummers responding to breaks and dynamic cues together?
- Are the drummers playing together and balancing their relative volume?
- Are the xylophones in sync with each other and the drummers?
- Is the song clear and understandable?
- Is the lead drummer playing the breaks

Discussion 4 7

- What was difficult about the performance arrangement?
- How can we work together to make sure everyone is where they need to be at every stage of the performance?

  Some questions to consider might include the following:
  - → Where and when do the dancers enter?
  - → Where do you need to be at each part of the performance?
  - → How will you make sure you are ready for the next part of the performance?
  - → What will you do if you make a mistake or something unexpected happens?
- What special tasks are needed to ensure the best possible outcomes? Who is willing to take on those roles?
- Evaluate the session using P.R.I.D.E. (the WRAP core values and best practices) as discussion points.

LESSON 19: PUTTING IT ALL TOGETHER

Combining the Yankadi and Macrou Rhythms and Dances

OBJECTIVES

Students will

- combine the Yankadi and Macrou performances into a full West African ballet presentation;
- enhance performance skills by creating and rehearsing in a performance environment.

MUSICAL SKILLS

- Performance
- Production
- Presentation

LIFE SKILLS

- Teamwork
- Improvisation

MOVEMENT SKILLS

- Awareness of self and others
- Group flow and organization

MATERIALS

- Jembes
- Dunduns
- Xylophones
- Seke-seke
- Krinyi
- DVD player and TV
- CD player

VOCABULARY

- West African Ballet

Process

LET'S SPEAK 9

Number

Susu/ Phonetics	**English**
fuu anun solo manani *(foo ah-NOON SO-lo MAN-na-nee)*	"Nineteen"

Vocabulary

Susu	**English**
Yankadi-Macrou makhase nun fare a ma senkhiné won n'tan nyama néné na na ralan nun won kha bore compininya nyi takhun. Mu kha kolon wo ma nyakha mané mukha makhase nun fare ra.	"Yankadi-Macrou is a special rhythm and dance for meeting new people and sharing with friends. We hope you enjoy our music and dance."

LET'S MOVE 

1. Set up drummers and dancers in **group formation** and combine the Yankadi and Macrou dance choreographies into one performance piece. Yankadi is danced first, followed by Macrou. The Yankadi ending arrangement is used as a transition from Yankadi to Macrou. The Macrou choreography begins at the end of Part 3, after the break, as shown in the following example and on the DVD. The dance continues through the Macrou ending break.

Yankadi to Macrou Transition: Part 1a (bars 1–2)

	1	2	3	4	5	6	7	8
Arms	CLAP			HIGH/ LOW				HIGH/ LOW
				L / R				R / L
Feet	JUMP			STEP STEP	STEP			STEP STEP
	B			L R	L			R L

Yankadi to Macrou Transition: Part 1b (bars 3–4)

	1	2	3	4	5	6	7	8
Arms				HIGH/ LOW				DOWN
				L / R				
Feet	STEP			STEP STEP	STEP			UP
	R			L R	L			(R)

Yankadi to Macrou Transition: Part 2 (bars 5–6)

		1	2	3	4	5	6	7	8
Arms		UP	DOWN	UP	DOWN	UP	DOWN	UP	DOWN
Feet		STEP	UP	STEP	UP	STEP	UP	STEP	UP
		R	(L)	L	(R)	R	(L)	L	(R)

Yankadi to Macrou Transition: Part 3 (bars 7–8)

					BREAK			
	1	2	3	4	1 (5)	2 (6)	3 (7)	4 (8)
Arms	Circle BWD				CLAP			SIDE
	(R)	(L)	(R)	(L)				
Feet	BWD	BWD	BWD	BWD	JUMP			BWD
	R	L	R	B	B			R

Macrou Ending Dance Sequence

						BREAK				
	8	1	2	3	4	1 (5)	2 (6)	3 (7)	4 (8)	1
Arms	DOWN	UP	DOWN	UP	DOWN	FWD	FWD	FWD	KNEES	FWD
		(R)				(R)	(L)	(R)	B	**
Feet	LIFT	STEP	LIFT	STEP	LIFT	FWD	FWD	FWD	JUMP	
	(R)	R	(L)	L	(R)	R	L	R	B	

**Heads up and hands forward. Smile!

2. Use the performance track on the CD so all students get the opportunity to dance through the entire choreography. Concentrate on dancing in time with the music and making fluid transitions between each step. Students should dance with full extensions and with lots of energy as if this were a real performance.

LET'S DRUM ♪2 ♪5

1. Arrange drummers for performance according to the performance staging diagram in Lesson 18. Students who are not at an instrument can stand behind those playing and sing the vocables and/or play the body percussion patterns until it's their turn.
2. Begin from the Yankadi break, having all instruments enter at the same time.
3. Have the lead drummer play the Yankadi échauffment/break-combination pattern after several bars to signal the group to transition into Macrou via the Yankadi to Macrou Transition arrangement.
4. Play through the entire Macrou rhythm and end with the échauffment/break combination into the Macrou Ending Dance Sequence.
5. Rotate students through the instruments and repeat from step 2.

Note: When using this arrangement as a transition between the Yankadi and Macrou rhythms, all instruments except the lead jembe should rest on bar 8 (not playing the downbeat as they did in the Yankadi ending arrangement). The lead jembe should play the break instead, transitioning the group immediately into the Macrou rhythm with the pickups in the sangban and krinyi patterns.

The krinyi matches the seke-seke patterns for the Yankadi ending/transition and Macrou ending arrangement.

Yankadi to Macrou Transition Arrangement

Briefly review the Yankadi and Macrou songs using their respective xylophone patterns as an accompaniment. Concentrate on proper pronunciation of words and projecting voices over the instruments, as if performing for an audience.

Arrange the group for performance. Rehearse the entire Yankadi-Macrou performance as many times as possible. Invite students to treat this as they would a real performance. It's a great opportunity for them to demonstrate their knowledge of musical, movement, and performance skills learned over the Yankadi-Macrou course.

Let's Play Key

D=Dundunba S=Sangban K=Kenkeni J=Jembe X=Xylophone SS=Seke-seke KR=Krinyi
DS=Dance Step M=March SG=Song EM=Échauffmant

LEADER	BREAK	BREAK	EM	BREAK	BREAK	BREAK	BREAK	BREAK
DRUMMERS	All Yankadi	Volume Down	Volume & Tempo Up					
DANCERS	DS1	DS1 + SG	Stop SG	DS2	DS3	DS4	DS5	DS6

LEADER	EM/ BREAK	BREAK	BREAK	EM	BREAK	BREAK	BREAK	BREAK
DRUMMERS	Yankadi-Macrou Transition	All Macrou	Volume Down	Volume & Tempo Up				
DANCERS	Yankadi-Macrou Transition	DS1	DS1 + SG	Stop SG	DS2	DS3	DS4	DS5

LEADER	BREAK	BREAK	BREAK	BREAK	EM/ BREAK
DRUMMERS					Ending Arrangement
DANCERS	DS6	DS7	DS8	DS9	Ending Arrangement

Wrap-Up

- Invite students to store the instruments and straighten up the room for the next session.
- Ask students to get their Student Enrichment Books and gather for discussion.
- Review and clarify the assignment in the Student Enrichment Book for this lesson.

Evaluation

Were students able to

- combine both rhythms and perform Yankadi-Macrou all the way through? If not, have students identify what aspects of the program need practice or clarification. Focus on those elements outside of class and during the next class session.
- demonstrate knowledge of performance techniques and stage presence? If not, show the Yankadi-Macrou performance from Guinea (on the DVD), and have students identify which performance aspects could be used in their own performances.
- demonstrate the ability to work together within the ensemble? For example, are the parts being played at the same relative volume? Are students able to stay focused on their pattern or movement with everything else going on?

Discussion

- How does the energy level change from Yankadi to Macrou?
- Ask for student input based on previous lesson discussions. You may wish to ask for student volunteers to facilitate the discussion.
- Evaluate the session using P.R.I.D.E. (the WRAP core values and best practices) as discussion points.

LESSON 20: THE YANKADI-MACROU PERFORMANCE CELEBRATION

Performance and Events Instruction and Tips

Number

Susu/ Phonetics	English
mokhonyén *(MOI-kho-yen)*	"Twenty"

Dialog

Susu	English
Guiné anun khamé wo nusanén fa fera mukhukha Yankadi-Macrou. Khulunyi, fare anun sigui na kui khakhili n ara (koé, yanyi, gésségé) kelifera Guinée, West Africa. La Guinée na kui na makhasé anun fare abara findi baloe ra n'de bé. Na makhase munsema, di nu bari, khili safe, futi khiri, wali anun fe gbétée. Yankadi-Macrou makhase anun fare a ma senkhiné won n'tan nyama néné na na ralan anun won kha bore compininya nyi takhun. Mu kha kolon wo ma nyakha mané mukha makhase anun fare ra.	"Ladies and gentleman, welcome to our Yankadi-Macrou celeration. The music, dance and song that you will experience (tonight, day, morning) comes from Guinea, West Africa. In Guinea, there are special rhythms and dances for almost every event in life. There are rhythms for birth, naming, weddings, working and more. Yankadi-Macrou is a special rhythm and dance for meeting new people and sharing with friends. We hope you enjoy our music and dance."

Creating Your Event

With the skills learned during this course, WRAP students are now able to perform both traditional (village style) and modern (ballet style) events. In this section, you will learn how to customize your WRAP curriculum to meet the needs of your school, community, and education partners.

Yankadi-Macrou Performance

Event Type	Audience-based performance.
Occasions	School assemblies, concerts, festivals, any event where a cultural performance is needed.
Suitable Venues	Auditorium, gym, cafeteria, commons area, classroom.
Time	10 - 20 minutes.
Description	This is the full culmination of the performance aspect of the Yankadi-Macrou program. It is staged for an audience and is typical of the type of choreographed performance pieces played by performing groups such as ballets from Guinea.
Setup Suggestions	Arrange the stage with African props. Make and wear ballet or traditional Guinean costuming. (See "Your African Village" in appendix L.)
Other Ideas	Have students and parents make traditional African food and drink to share with the students and guests. (See "Recipes" in appendix I.) Play African music in the background before and as guests are eating, and/or show the "Inside of the Culture" feature on the DVD.

PREPARATION

1. Arrange musicians on stage according to their normal performance setup. (See diagram below.)
2. Dancers can begin the program off-stage, for a more dramatic entrance. Arrange dancers on one side of the stage and have them enter together as a group performing Yankadi Dance Step 1. Alternatively, dancers can enter from opposite sides of the stage and cross each other to take their marks (see below). This technique is visually impressive for the audience.
3. Have students introduce the performance using the Susu dialog learned in lessons 11 through 19.

Yankadi Dance Entrance

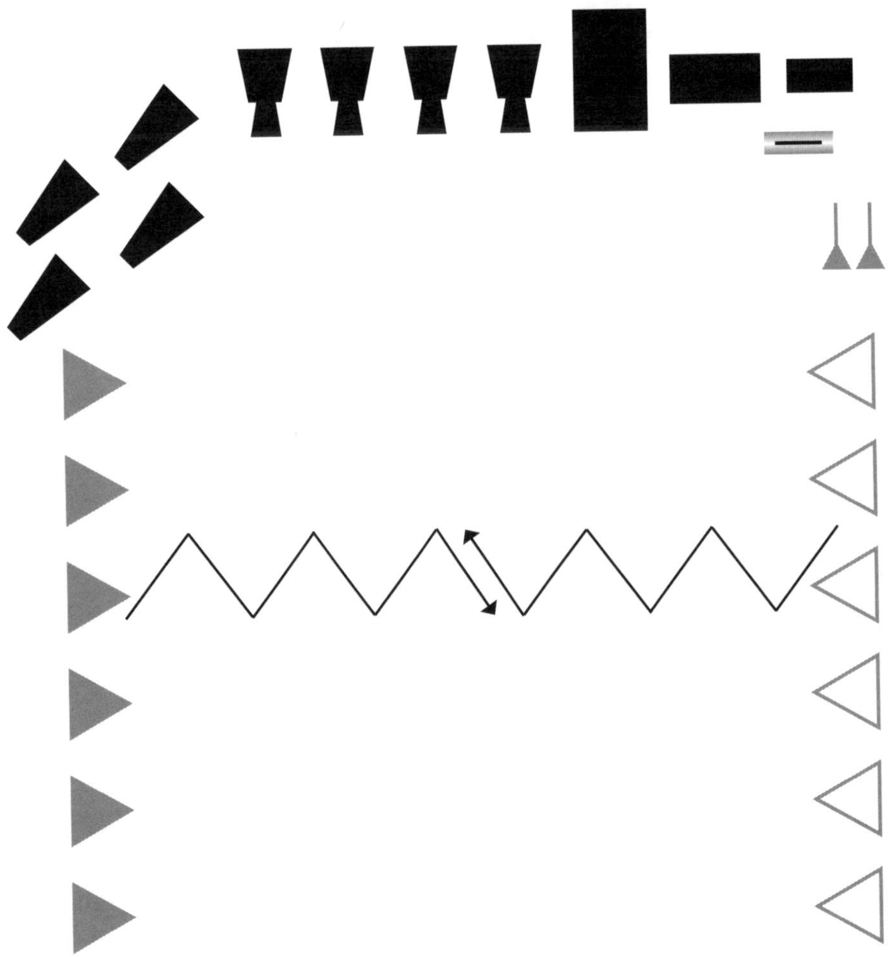

Dancers enter both sides from off stage, crossing in the middle.

PERFORMANCE

1. Begin playing Yankadi from the break with just the musicians on the stage.

Tip: Alternatively, have the musicians play a few measures of Macrou at a fast tempo, to get the audience's attention, before beginning Yankadi.

2. Have dancers enter the stage on a jembe break cue and begin singing the Yankadi song.
3. Continue through the Yankadi-Macrou performance as rehearsed in lesson 19. After the final Macrou ending arrangement break (and huge applause!), musicians can begin playing Macrou again as the dancers bow and exit the stage. If you are performing at an auditorium with a curtain, it can be lowered during this time. If not, play through the Macrou ending arrangement again.

Tip: During the dancer bows, play the music at a slightly faster tempo to add excitement and energy.

Theatrical Performance

The following are examples of how adding a variety of entertaining theatrical aspects can make your WRAP curriculum into a longer production play, highlighting the music, dance, and culture of Guinea.

- Create a village environment on stage. Bring the village alive by playing musical patterns used in the World Rhythms program on traditional village tools. For example, three students could be pounding millet in a mortar (a filled-in jembe shell) to the Macrou dundunba pattern. Several students could pose as "numu" (blacksmiths) and pretend to carve an instrument by hitting a large log in the rhythm of the sangban pattern for macrou.
- Create a scene on stage where a group of students are chopping wood in the forest. (Can you use some of the rhythm patterns?) Have another group of students walk by and invite them to a Yankadi-Macrou celebration in their village.
- Use the Susu greeting dialog learned in lessons 1–10 to have an authentic conversation. (See appendix H.)

The Traditional Village Celebration (With or Without Performance)

Event Type	Participatory cultural celebration.
Occasions	Back-to-school night, open house, parent-teacher night, African history month celebration, lunch-time activity, meet and greet, community event.
Suitable Venues	Classroom, cafeteria, football field, park, community center, commons area.
Time	30-90 minutes.
Description	This event most closely resembles the traditional West African Yankadi-Macrou ceremony. There is no audience! All guests become participants in the reenactment of this traditional cultural celebration and experience the music, dance and culture of Guinea in a fun and informal community setting.
Setup Suggestions	Arrange your room or space like an African village. See the suggestions in appendix L. Have students make and wear traditional African costumes and decorate the room with art and facts about West Africa that they learned in the student workbooks.
Other Ideas	Have students and parents make traditional African food and drink to share with the students and guests. (See "Recipes" in appendix I.) Play African music in the background before and as guests are eating, and/or show the "Inside the Culture" feature of the DVD.

PROGRAM OVERVIEW

- Have students introduce the Yankadi-Macrou celebration, instruments, and cultural facts about Guinea.
- Use some of the Susu language dialog learned throughout the lessons.

Tip: To get the event off to a bang, you can have your students perform the full Yankadi-Macrou Ballet program while guests finish eating. Although a performance wouldn't typically be part of a traditional event, this can really set a great tone for the celebration and gives your students a chance to show off their stuff.

PREPARATION

1. Set up instruments along the far end of the room according to the Performance Staging Diagram.
2. Have dancers and guests form a large circle in the middle of the room. (Intersperse WRAP students throughout the circle, and spread out adults and students so the circle is balanced.) Create concentric circles if space is limited or if the single circle is larger than 20 feet across.

PERFORMANCE

PART 1

1. The lead jembe signals the start of the Macrou rhythm.
2. WRAP students lead the group in the circle march configurations and Macrou Dance Step 1. Invite guests to join in. Assign a WRAP dancer to play the one-and two-bar break cues on the whistle.
3. Begin the Macrou song and encourage guests to sing along in the response section.
4. After the song, increase tempo if desired.
5. End the Macrou rhythm with the échauffment and break.

PART 2

1. The lead jembe signals the start of Yankadi.
2. Students and guests form lines at far ends of the room, facing each other.
3. On the jembe break, students begin Yankadi Dance Step 1. Guests match the movements.
4. On the jembe break, begin the Yankadi song. Invite guests to sing along in the response sections (or at least "A wayire").
5. The lead drummer plays the échauffment and Yankadi jembe break. On the break, students and guests perform Yankadi Dance Step 2, traveling in a zig-zag pattern to the opposite side of the room.
6. Lines turn to face each other and transition back to Yankadi Dance Step 1.
7. On subsequent jembe breaks, invite guests to match students in Yankadi Dance Steps 3 and 4 while still facing each other in lines.
8. To transition back to Macrou, the lead drummer plays the Yankadi échauffment and break to signal the Yankadi ending arrangement.

PART 3

1. Upon returning to Macrou, all dancers move from lines into a half circle facing the drummers and begin Macrou Dance Step 1.
2. One of the WRAP students approaches the drummers and performs a few solo movements from the Macrou choreography, using a piece of fabric as a prop (a handkerchief or scarf is perfect). Dancers face the lead drummer during their solo, interacting with him/her in a fun and playful way.
3. The lead drummer responds to the dancers by marking the steps and/or playing the breaks to change movements.
4. Once the solo dancer is finished, the scarf is passed to someone else in the circle who then takes over as the dance soloist.

Note: This is a fun improvisational section where you can do anything, although students should try to do at least a couple of the Macrou movements.

5. Pass the scarf until everyone has had a chance to do a solo, then invite everyone into the circle and perform Macrou Dance Step 9 (lesson 6), waiving goodbye to the drummers.
6. The lead drummer plays the échauffment and ends the music with the Macrou Ending Break. WOW! What a fun event!

Tip: During the solo section, WRAP students can switch between dancing and drumming so all have a chance to demonstrate their skill at both.

These are the two most popular ways to share the World Rhythms Arts Program. Remember that the WRAP curriculum is designed to be very flexible. The individual rhythms can be played on their own for events requiring shorter performances. When instruments are not available, just the dance routine can be performed with CD accompaniment. Conversely, your group could present a drumming performance utilizing all the breaks and arrangements. For more tips on using the World Rhythms Arts Program, visit the World Rhythms website (www.drum2dance.com).

Appendix A: Lead Jembe Patterns

Below are some lead jembe phrases that you can use for soloing and to accompany dance steps. Each of these can be heard on the CD in the performance tracks for each rhythm.

Yankadi Lead Phrases

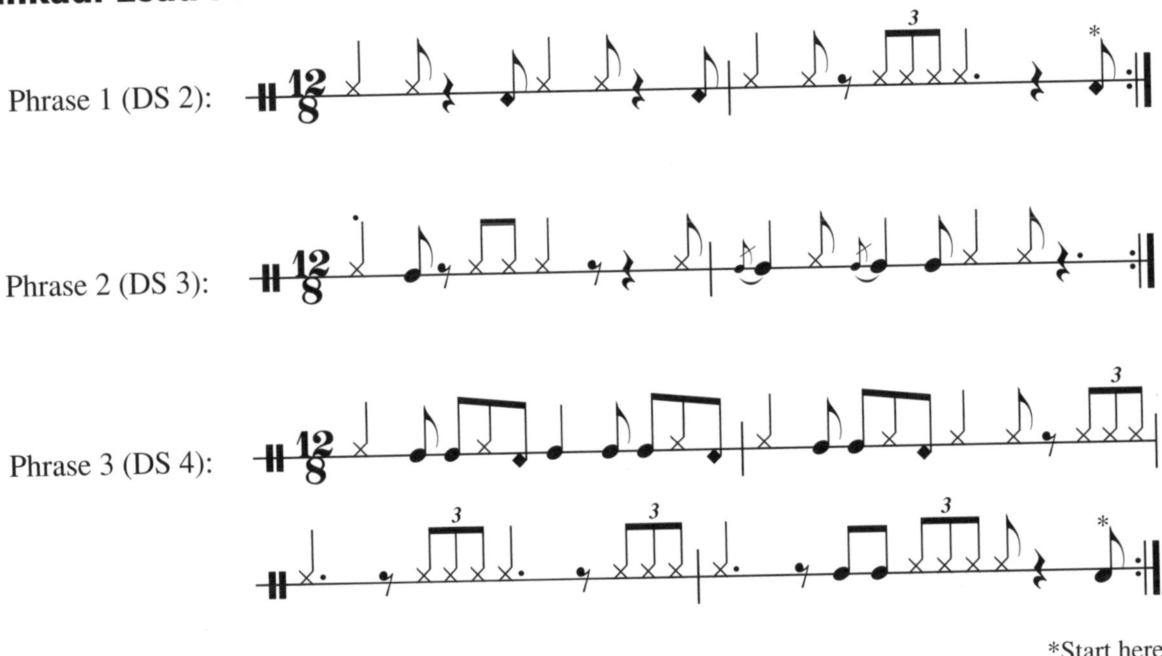

Macrou Lead Phrases

Appendix B: Instrument Cross-Reference Chart

Traditional Instrument	Substitute 1	Substitute 2
Jembe	Ashiko	Conga
Dundun	Drumset Toms*	Surdo or other large drum
Kenken	Cowbell or similar bell	A metal plate or tube
Krinyi	Temple blocks or woodblocks	PVC tubing
Seke-Seke	Caxixi	Rattle
Bala	Orff xylophone	Marimba**

* Mute with tape or fabric to reduce sustain.
** If xylophones or marimbas are unavailable, a synthesizer may be used.

Tip: We recommend using Orff instruments for the xylophone parts because they may be modified to facilitate learning and playing the patterns. (Orff instruments are specially designed for children and beginning students and feature removable bars and lightweight construction.) However, students may also use and share a standard xylophone and/or marimba.

Appendix C: Tuning Your Drums

Mali-Weave Tuning

Although the pattern of rope that runs up and down a traditional Mali-weave drum can look a little confusing at first, tuning up the jembe is simple once you know how to do it. As long as the drum hasn't been tuned up to the end of the rope, you should have a couple extra feet of horizontal rope running around the drum. (You don't want to start this process if you are at the end of your rope!) If you don't have any rope to work with, you have three options:

1. You can add some rope by lacing it into the current pattern.
2. Remove all the weaving until you're left with only verticals, then tighten the verticals by hand or use a rope-puller. This should free up more rope for use in tightening the head. Once the verticals are as tight as you can make them, you can create the Mali-weave pattern to raise the pitch of the head.
3. Send your drum to someone who specializes in jembe tuning and repair. (See drum2dance.com for links.)

To Tighten the Head

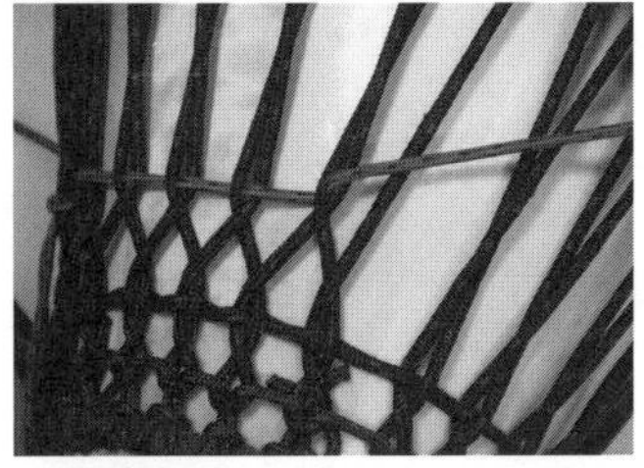

1. Start with the rope so it's coming out from the last diamond knot. Take the end of the rope and place it underneath the next two vertical ropes.

2. Feed the rope under the verticals and pull it down and tight. Feed the end of the same rope through the middle of the two ropes you just went under—so it's moving in the opposite direction.

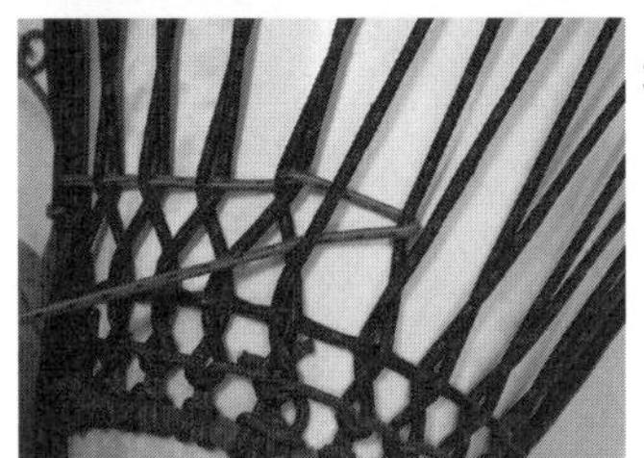

3. Place the horizontal rope so it's coming out below the section you just fed under the two verticals, and pull out any slack. This helps keep the diamonds compact as you work your way around the drum.

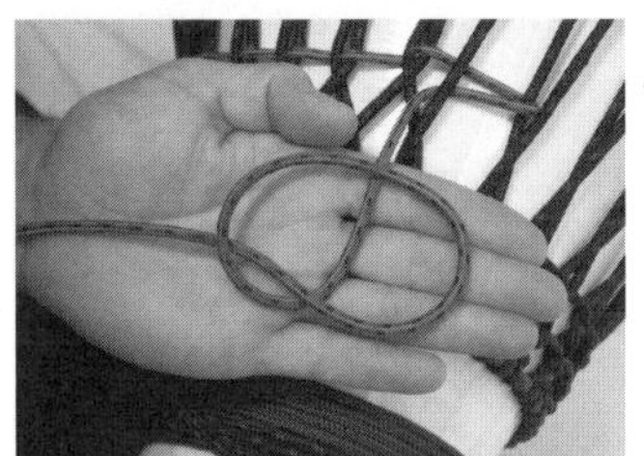

4. Now you're ready to pull this diamond. A good way of doing it is to create a loop and then fold that loop over the rope.

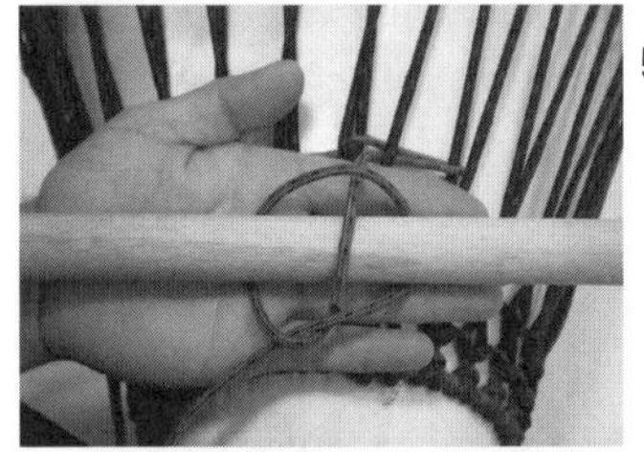

5. Feed a stick in one side and out the other. This will make a very good handle that can be used to pull the diamond.

6. Brace the bowl by sitting over your drum. Place one hand at the top of the shell to hold it down and pull with your other hand. If you need to pull with both arms, you can try placing your knees on the sides of the bowl to brace it. Pull the rope away from the shell with a firm movement until the two vertical ropes flip over.

Note: You can also wrap the rope around a stick or your hand. If using your hand, be careful not to pull too much as this will create blisters!

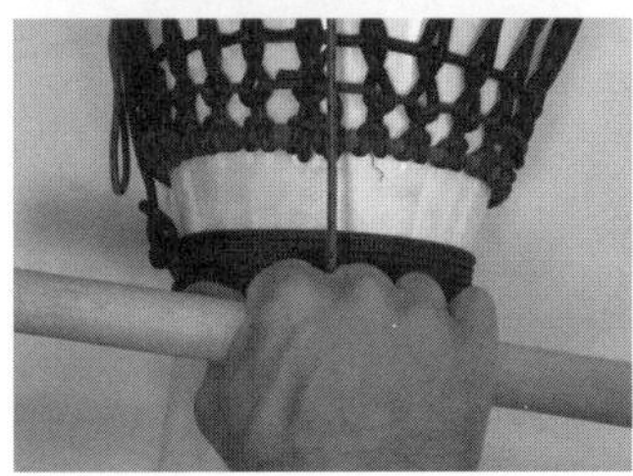

7. Remove the stick; the knot will fall out freely.

8. Continue Steps 1 - 7 until you reach the desired pitch.

9. When you've finished tuning up the head, feed the rope through the next vertical to secure it. Wrap the excess rope around the foot or body of the drum and tie it off.

Note: As the head gets tighter, the tension on the ropes may cause a new diamond knot to come undone. One way to prevent this is to hold the new knot in place until you can feed the rope under the next two verticals to hold it. An alternative solution would be to feed the rope through the next two verticals before you pull the knot. You may also want to try another similar tuning pattern where the rope is fed over–through–under. This method locks the knot in place as it is pulled.

To Loosen the Head

To release tension, simply work backwards, removing diamond knots until you've reached the desired pitch.

Many players like to tune their drums up quite high to eliminate any excessive ringing. One of the disadvantages of tuning the drum too high is that you run the risk of the head breaking from excessive pressure. How high is too high? Unfortunately, the only way you'll know is by going too far. The best way to get a feel for how experienced players tune their drums is by listening to recordings and live performances. Once you've listened to a lot of jembe playing, you'll be able to determine what the preferred sound is, and when your own particular drum sounds and feels right. There are many recordings of jembes, from solo drums to full ensembles.

Conga-Style Tuning

Non-traditional jembes that have conga-style lug tuning can be tuned using a 1⁄2-inch (13mm) open-ended crescent wrench. Tune the drum up by tightening each lug one-half turn at a time. Work your way around the circumference of the drum until you come back to where you started. There's no need to tune the drumhead using a star-like pattern (as with a snare drum). Be careful to keep the rim parallel with the top edge of the shell and check the pitch so you don't over-tighten it. Never use pliers on the drum as it can damage the lug nuts. If the lugs become too hard to turn or they start squeaking, loosen the nuts and place some heavy oil or grease on the threads of the tension rods.

Note: Always use a wrench that fits your lug nut. A wrench that is too big can slip over the nuts, rounding off the corners and making them less effective over time.

Appendix D: Myths and Misconceptions ♪8 ♪9

The following are some myths and misconceptions we have noticed in books, websites, and through word of mouth. We hope you join us in our mission to correct these and provide accurate information whenever possible.

JEMBE RHYTHMS ARE USED TO SEND MESSAGES FROM ONE VILLAGE TO ANOTHER.

Certain types of large log drums, played with sticks, are known to have been used in West Africa to send messages short distances. There is no evidence, however, that jembes or jembe rhythms were ever used for this purpose. Some jembe teachers have called the drum "a form of communication," but they are most likely referring to the universal language of music and not specific coded messages. When specific rhythms are used, it is usually within a village population and not between villages.

THE JEMBE IS A SACRED INSTRUMENT THAT IS CARVED FROM WOOD THAT IS HARVESTED AFTER SPECIAL RITUALS.

Our West African teachers retell histories of special ceremonies done for a tree before it is cut and again before a skin is attached to the carved-out shell. These ceremonies would involve cola nuts, singing, dancing and other rituals. These rituals are (or were) done for personal jembes and not for all of the commercially available instruments bought in music stores or other retailers.

JEMBE PLAYERS ARE ALSO TRAINED IN THE HEALING USES OF HERBS.

Some sources indicate that Mandé blacksmiths were trained in the use of herbs. Blacksmiths did create the first jembes; however, the jembe is an instrument that is free from hereditary restriction, and therefore not all jembe players are from the blacksmith caste. Some jembe players are probably trained in the use of herbs, but not all are.

EVERYONE IN A VILLAGE KNOWS HOW TO PLAY DRUMS.

Being a drummer was not always looked highly upon in villages. While everyone in the village participates in the ceremony of drumming-related events, only a very select few undergo the training and apprenticeship to become a drummer. Traditionally, drummers have another job like farming or fishing, and only perform music when called upon to do so.

THE JEMBE IS RELATED TO THE EGYPTIAN TABLA OR DOUMBEK.

While the "goblet shape" of the jembe is similar to that of the doumbek, there is no evidence to support any connection between the two. The jembe was derived from large mortars, while the doumbek, made of clay, most likely has its roots in pottery vessels used to carry water or store goods. In addition, the playing style and traditional rhythms are very different.

THE JEMBE IS FROM AFRICA.

Yes, the jembe is from Africa! Africa, however is a very large continent with many varied and diverse ethnic groups. The jembe comes from a very small area of Africa and is native to only a few ethnic groups. The jembe originates among Mandé-speaking peoples that occupy portions of present-day Guinea and Mali and very small areas of Cote l'voire, Burkina Faso, and Senegal. (See the instrument guide.)

JEMBES ARE TRADITIONALLY PLAYED WITH MUSICIANS SITTING IN A CIRCLE.

The events or ceremonies that the jembe and dundun drums accompany are usually done in a circle, however the drummers are located in a small area on one arc of the circle. See the WRAP DVD or the performance diagram for examples.

THE DIFFERENT SOUNDS OF THE JEMBE ARE CALLED "GUN, DUN, GO, DO, PA, TA."

The "Gun, Go, Pa" terminology was originated by Nigerian artist Babatunde Olatunji. It is a phonetic system using Yoruba (a Nigerian language) consonant sounds to vocalize drum patterns. While many students and teachers of hand drumming find it useful, it has no traditional relationship to the jembe or ethnic groups that play jembe. Jembes are not native to Nigeria or to the Yoruba people. While the technique of vocalizing drum patterns is an important part of learning jembe in West Africa, there is no set system of vocalizations in the jembe tradition. Jembe teachers in different regions use their own phonetic system for vocalizing the sounds on the jembe, and students in the WRAP curriculum are encouraged to make up their own as well.

The Olatunji System

TONE	BASS		OPEN		SLAP	
HAND	Dominant	Secondary	Dominant	Secondary	Dominant	Secondary
VOCAL	GUN	DUN	GO	DO	PA	TA

Appendix E: Rhythm Games

The following drum circle games provide you and your students with a means to explore and familiarize yourselves with the instruments, while creating a sense of group cohesion and camaraderie.

You can use these activities as icebreakers, energizers, and impromptu activities before or after your lessons, or for any gathering you wish to infuse with a sense of musical play and creative improvisation. Remember—a drum circle is not a **drum class** that is set up in a circle. It's a place of exploration, free from judgment, right and wrong, and practicing. It's more about encouraging self-expression, communication, and creativity than teaching specific techniques or rhythms. You do that by taking off your teacher hat and joining the circle as a facilitator of creativity and PLAY.

Rhythm Wheel

Focus: Cooperation, creativity, validating original ideas

1. Ask for a volunteer to begin playing a steady rhythm on their instrument. Let them play anything they want, as long as it's clear and steady.
2. Invite the person to one side of them to add their own rhythm.
3. Continue around the circle until everyone is playing.
4. After a few minutes of playing, end with a countdown, segue to another activity, or continue changing your patterns around the circle.

Tip: Let students know that it's OK to match someone else's pattern, but they can add any pattern they want such as clapping, vocalizing, moving—even passing altogether and just listening.

Orbit Echo

Focus: Active listening, creativity, support

1. During a rhythm or from a stop, play a 4-beat phrase and invite everyone to echo you. (Hold a hand to your ear as if to say "I'm listening to you.")
2. Continue playing and echoing a few more times, then choose someone to take over the lead.
3. Pass the lead to the next person by pointing to their instrument during one of the group echoes. Have them play one phrase. While the group is echoing, point to the next person's instrument to indicate that they will be next.
4. Continue echoing each new person as the lead travels (orbits) around the circle.
5. During one of your turns, transition to a groove or end.

Rhythm Teams

Focus: Diversity, mutual support, appreciation

1. During a groove, group several members of a particular trait (such as jembes) by pointing to their instruments and making the "continue cue" (rolling the hands forward around each other).
2. Stop the rest of the group and motion for the sub-group to continue playing.
3. Invite the rest of the group to clap their hands to a steady beat and listen to the sub-group.
4. When ready, cue everyone to start playing and join in. Or, choose a new sub-group (such as dunduns) and have them take over the groove. Rotate through all instrument groups so everyone gets to play and be heard.

Tip: There are two main ways to "group" the circle: by location (whole-, half-, quarter-circle, etc.), and by traits (instrument type, timbre, gender, playing style, etc.). Experiment with other groups and have students choose different groups to be featured. Discuss the differences in sound quality, volume, and dynamics of each group to expand students' awareness of the various sounds in the ensemble.

Solo Toss

Focus: Sharing, improvising

1. With everyone playing or clapping a steady beat, play a 4- or 8-beat "solo" phrase on your instrument.
2. Just before the end of your phrase, "toss" the solo role to another person in the circle by making eye contact with them to indicate that it's now their turn.
3. Continue tossing the solo role randomly around the circle until everyone has had a turn.

Tip: Challenge the group to play this game without repeating a member until everyone has had a turn.

4. Segue into a group rhythm, speed up to a new tempo, or count down to end.

Option: Challenge the group to rearrange themselves around the circle in the order of the solos.
Repeat this game, or change to another.

Tip: For more games like these, or to learn how to facilitate drum circles, read *Together in Rhythm: A Facilitator's Guide to Drum Circle Music* and *The Amazing Jamnasium: A Playful Companion to Together in Rhythm* (both from Alfred Publishing).

Appendix F: Healthy Music Making

People Health

- Allow ample room for movement. Be aware of anything in the room that could interfere with a swinging arm or leg, such as desks, tables, chairs, instruments, and other people.
- Prepare the body before drumming and dancing. Begin with gentle stretching, followed by light movement to warm the body. Develop a warm-up routine and ask students to volunteer to lead the group.
- Protect the hands and fingers by removing rings and bracelets and/or using hand drumming gloves when playing jembes.
- Don't push through pain. If you or someone in the group feels pain, have them take a break to assess their condition. Pain is often an indicator of improper technique. Reduce swelling with ice and/or aspirin.
- Discourage the consumption of sugar-heavy foods before drumming and dancing. Sugar provides a quick boost of energy followed by a longer period of sluggishness. Eating during class is also distracting. Encourage and allow students to drink lots of pure water instead.
- Breathe! Dancing and drumming is physical exercise. In order to do both well and sing at the same time, the body needs an ample supply of oxygen. Practice and develop deep-breathing techniques. You may wish to include breathing techniques as part of your warm-up routine.

Instrument Health

- Use care when moving instruments. Jembe heads are thin and can be punctured by sharp objects. Keep dundun heads from being scraped on the ground by moving them on a cart or having two people carry the larger drums.
- Changes in temperature and humidity can affect the tightness of jembe heads, causing them to break in some cases. To protect the heads, detune them a little if moving from cool to warm, or from humid to dry, conditions.
- Never play a jembe with anything other than your hands. Sticks and beaters can break a head, even with light pressure.
- Avoid leaving jembes in direct sunlight or in places that can get very warm, such as a parked car.

WRAP for Health and Fitness

It should come as no surprise that the costs of obesity greatly outweigh the costs of presenting enriching, health-promoting activities such as the World Rhythms Arts Program. With health-care prices rising in the same tide as obesity-related diseases, the more we can do to help our children develop active lifestyles, the greater chance they will have to be free from the added costs and restrictions of poor diet and inactivity later in life. Obesity is a community problem that needs a holistic solution. It's not enough to only consider what foods to eat. We must also consider what to avoid eating (sugar, salt, caffeine, etc.) and what action to take. The World Rhythms Arts Program is about taking action, making good choices, and working together. Before you begin your program, consult your peers in physical education, dance, and counseling. Work together to provide your students with a comprehensive program that is based on healthy habits, good choices and exercise!

Appendix G: Glossary of Terms

PERCUSSION

alto xylophone: The mid-sized xylophone, often abbreviated AX.

bala *(BAH-lah)***:** A melodic West African idiophone (xylophone) featuring graduated bars and gourd resonators.

bass: The lowest-pitched sound, produced by striking the jembe near the center of the head with the hand.

bass xylophone: The largest and lowest-pitched xylophone, often abbreviated BX.

chest: A common body percussion technique of patting the upper chest.

clap: A common body percussion technique of striking the hands together.

dundun *(DOON-doon)***:** A barrel-shaped drum with two heads, played with wooden sticks.

dundunba *(doon-DOON-bah)***:** The largest member of the dundun family.

flam: A rhythmic figure of two notes, where one note occurs slightly before the other.

jembe *(JEM-bay)***:** A mortar-shaped drum made of wood that features a goat-skin head.

kenken *(KEN-ken)***:** A rectangular bell, often mounted on the dundun.

kenkeni *(ken-ken-nee)***:** The smallest drum of the dundun family.

krinyi *(kree-nyee)*: A small log drum played with sticks. Also called **krin** *(KREEN)*.

mallet: A special stick used for playing barred instruments. It features a ball at one end, often made of rubber and wrapped with yarn.

muted stroke: Played by dampening the head after the strike by leaving the stick or hand on it.

open stroke: Played by bouncing off the head to allow it to vibrate freely.

Orff xylophone: A specially made xylophone featuring removable bars, well-suited for children.

pat: A common body percussion technique of patting the thighs.

sangban *(sahng-bahn)***:** The mid-sized drum of the dundun family.

seke-seke *(seh-keh seh-keh)***:** A basket-shaped shaker from Guinea.

slap: The highest-pitched sound of the jembe, produced with the fingers in a slight curve.

soprano xylophone: The smallest and highest-pitched xylophone, often abbreviated SX.

stamp: A common body percussion technique of stepping to produce an audible sound. (Also **stomp.**)

tone: The middle-pitched sound of the jembe, produced by striking the head with the fingers.

vocables: A system of vocalizations designed to emulate and teach drumming sounds and rhythms.

DANCE

Feet

BACK: A step that passes behind the other foot.

BACKWARD (BWD): A step away from the audience (up stage).

BALL-CHANGE: A rapid weight transfer from the ball of one foot to the other.

CLOSE: Moving the foot towards the other to bring the feet together.

CROSS: A step that passes in front of the other foot.

FORWARD (FWD): A step towards the audience (down stage).

HOP: Landing on one foot.

JUMP: Landing on both feet.

SIDE: Horizontal movement with weight transfer.

STEP: A touch with weight transfer to the foot.

TOUCH: A touch of the heel or toe without weight.

TURN STEP: A rapid rotation of 180° to face the opposite direction.

Arms

BACKWARD (BWD): Rotating the arms from the shoulder in a "backstroke" motion.

CROSS: Crossing the arms in front of the torso.

FORWARD (FWD): Rotating the arms from the shoulder in a throwing motion.

OPEN: Extending the arms to either side of the body.

SWING: Moving the arms as if walking.

Appendix H: Susu Pronunciation Guide

The WRAP curriculum introduces students to the Susu language through common greetings (lessons 1–10) and a short program introduction (lessons 11–20). Proper greetings are important Susu social customs. Greetings can last for several minutes, and it is considered very impolite not to properly greet people any time you meet or see them. Several basic greetings are learned and can be used in conversation. The following chart shows some of the most difficult to pronounce sounds in the Susu language and their phonetic English equivalent.

Spelling	Pronunciation	Explanation
mu	*moo*	The u is pronounced like the oo in "food."
kh and x	*kh*	The kh sound is sometimes written as x in Susu. Both are pronounced like saying the h in "hot" in the very back of your throat.
aa	*ah*	The use of aa denotes a short sound in English, like the ough in "ought."
ui	*we*	The ui is pronounced like the e in "we."
é	*eh*	The é is pronounced like the ey in "hey."
n'	*nn*	Meaning "I" in Susu, the n' sound is held briefly with the tongue against the top of the mouth before a word.
i	*ee*	Any word ending in "i" is pronounced like the e in "we."
gb	*gbé*	One of the more difficult sounds to make in Susu, the g is produced in the back of the throat before the bé. (See the é pronunciation above.)
nd	*ndé*	Combines the n' sounds and the é sounds. The n is held briefly before the dé, like saying the ay in "day."

Just as learning to play the three notes on a jembe would be difficult from just reading about it and never hearing it, pronouncing Susu words would be almost impossible. All of the Susu text found in the WRAP curriculum is clearly spoken on the CD by native speakers. Look for the CD icon and track number in each lesson's "Dialog" section.

Susu Dialog Review

The Susu Dialog Review is designed to be used along with the Susu language tracks on the CD. All of the Susu language taught in the 20 individual lessons is summarized here, along with the corresponding track numbers, for easy reference. We recommend the following "language-learning techniques" process when using the Susu review.

1. First listen to each CD track while reading along with the Susu text.
2. Listen to each track and say the Susu word or phrase along with the speaker.
3. Listen to each track and try to say each Susu word or phrase before the speaker says it. (You can use the pause button on the CD player if necessary.)
4. Practice the dialog without use of the CD.

NUMBERS

Track 50 allows you to hear the correct pronunciation of each of the 20 numbers learned in the WRAP curriculum. Each number is spoken first in English, followed by its Susu equivalent.

English	Susu	Phonetic
one	**keren**	*KER-ing*
two	**firin**	*FIR-ing*
three	**sakhan**	*SAH-xan*
four	**naani**	*NAN-nee*
five	**suli**	*SU-ly*
six	**senni**	*SEN-nee*
seven	**solo feren**	*SO-lo FIR-ring*
eight	**solo masakhan**	*SO-lo MAS-sah-khan*
nine	**solo manani**	*SO-lo MAN-na-nee*
ten	**fuu**	*FOO*
eleven	**fuu anun keren**	*FOO ah-NOON KER-ring*
twelve	**fuu anun firin**	*FOO ah-NOON FIR-ring*
thirteen	**fuu anun sakhan**	*FOO ah-NOON SAH-khan*
fourteen	**fuu anun naani**	*FOO ah-NOON NA-nee*
fifteen	**fuu anun suli**	*FOO ah-NOON SU-ly*
sixteen	**fuu anun senni**	*FOO ah-NOON SEN-ee*
seventeen	**fuu anun solo feren**	*FOO ah-NOON SO-lo FI-ring*
eighteen	**fuu anun solo masakhan**	*FOO ah-NOON SO-lo MAS-sah-xan*
nineteen	**fuu anun solo manani**	*FOO ah-NOON SO-lo MAN-na-nee*
twenty	**mokhonyén**	*MOI-kho-yen*

GREETINGS

Track 51 contains the Susu dialog learned in lessons 1–10. Each word or phrase is spoken first in English, followed by the Susu greeting.

English	Susu	Phonetic
How are you? Also, Thank you.	**I nu wali?**	*IN-nu-wa-ly*
What's happening?	**Arabakhadi?**	*ah-rah-BAH-kha-di*
Nothing bad is happening.	**Amurabakhi kioke.**	*ah-mur-ah-BAH-kha Key-oh-key*
There are no misfortunes?	**Tana mu na?**	*TAH-na MOO nah*
No misfortunes.	**Tana yo mu na.**	*TAH-na YO MOO nah*
How is it going?	**Anyéreéfe?**	*an-yer-re-FEE*
Little by little (okay).	**Dondorunti, dondorunti.**	*DON-dor-un-tee*
And you?	**I tan go?**	*EE TAAN GO*
What is your name?	**I khili di?**	*EE KHI-lee-dee*
My name is ______.	**N'khili ______.**	*N KHI-lee*
Where do you come from?	**I kelikhi minden?**	*EE KE-la khee MIN-de*
I come from ________.	**N'kelakhi ________.**	*Nn – KE-la KHEE*
See you later.	**Won na temui.**	*WON NA TEM-we*
Okay, see you later.	**Awa, won na temui.**	*AH-wa WON NA TEM-we*

GREETINGS DIALOG

Track 52 allows you to hear all of your new Susu greetings used in an actual conversation.
Follow left to right from person 1 to person 2.

Person 1	Person 2
I nu wali?	**I nu wali?**
Arabakhadi?	**Amurabakhi kioke. I tan go, arabakhadi?**
Amurabakhi kioke. Tana mu na?	**Tana yo mu na. I tan go?**
Tana yo mu na.	**Anyéréfe?**
Dondorunti, dondorunti. I tan go?	**Dondorunti, dondorunti.**
I khili di?	**N'khili Kadiza*. I tan go? I khili di?**
N'khili Baba*.	**I kela khee minden?**
N'kela khee Americ. I tan go? I kela khee minden?**	**N'kela khee la Guinea**.**
Won na temui.	**Awa, won na temui.**

* The names of the speakers. "Baba" means father and also "adopted family." It is the name that Ryan M. Camara and his adopted Father M. Lamine Dibo Camara call each other. Kadiza is a common nickname in Guinea for Kadiatou. Kadiatou "Kadiza" Camara Grace performed the Susu Dialog for the WRAP project.

** The names of the countries of origin of the two speakers. "Americ" is how Susu speakers say America and "la Guinea" is how they pronounce their own country.

PERFORMANCE INTRODUCTION WITH TRANSLATION

Track 54 allows you to practice each sentence of the performance introduction individually with translation. Each sentence is spoken first in English, then in Susu.

English	Susu
Ladies and Gentlemen, welcome to our Yankadi-Macrou Celebration.	**Guinè anun khamè wo nusanèn fa fera mukhukha Yankadi-Macrou.**
The music, dance and song that you will experience (tonight, day, morning) comes from Guinea, West Africa.	**Khulunyi, fare anun sigui na kui khakhili na ara (koè, yanyi, gèssègè) kelifera Guinée, West Africa.**
In Guinea there are special rhythms and dances for almost every event in life.	**La Guinée na kui na makhasé anun fare abara findi baloe ra n'de bè.**
There are rhythms for birth, naming, weddings, working and more.	**Na makhase munsema, di nu bari, khili safe, futi khiri, wali anun fe gbètèe.**
Yankadi-Macrou is a special rhythm and dance for meeting new people and sharing with friends.	**Yankadi-Macrou makhase anun fare a ma senkhinè won n'tan nyama nènè na na ralan nun won kha bore compininya nyi takhun.**
We hope you enjoy our music and dance.	**Mu kha kolon wo ma nyakha manè mukha makhase anun fare ra.**

PERFORMANCE INTRODUCTION MONOLOGUE

Track 53 is designed for you to hear the entire performance introduction spoken as it would be used to introduce the Yankadi-Macrou performance. This is ideal for memorization, if one student will be introducing the performance in Susu.

Susu Performance Introduction

Guinè anun khamè wo nusanèn fa fera mukhukha Yankadi-Macrou. Khulunyi, fare anun sigui na kui khakhili na ara (koè, yanyi, gèssègè) kelifera Guinée, West Africa. La Guinée na kui na makhasé anun fare abara findi baloe ra n'de bè. Na makhase munsema, di nu bari, khili safe, futi khiri, wali anun fe gbètèe. Yankadi-Macrou makhase anun fare a ma senkhinè won n'tan nyama nènè na na ralan anun won kha bore compininya nyi takhun. Mu kha kolon wo ma nyakha manè mukha makhase anun fare ra.

Like all Guinea languages, Susu was never written until the French began colonizing Guinea in the 1800s. While the French promoted and taught the French language in schools, they adapted traditional Susu words to certain French language conventions and invented new language rules for sounds that didn't have a French-language equivalent. One example of this is the spelling of the jembe drum. It is very common to see jembe spelled "djembe." Because French doesn't use a hard j sound, as in the word "jump," a French speaker would pronounce the word "jembe" with a soft j sound, as in the name "Jacques." In order to correct this, French linguists introduced the hard j sound in the written form "dj." In the United States and other non-French speaking countries, this has led to the gross mispronunciations. It is still common for people to see the word "djembe" and pronounce it "DUH-jem-bay" instead of "JEM-bay."

Appendix I: Traditional West African Recipes

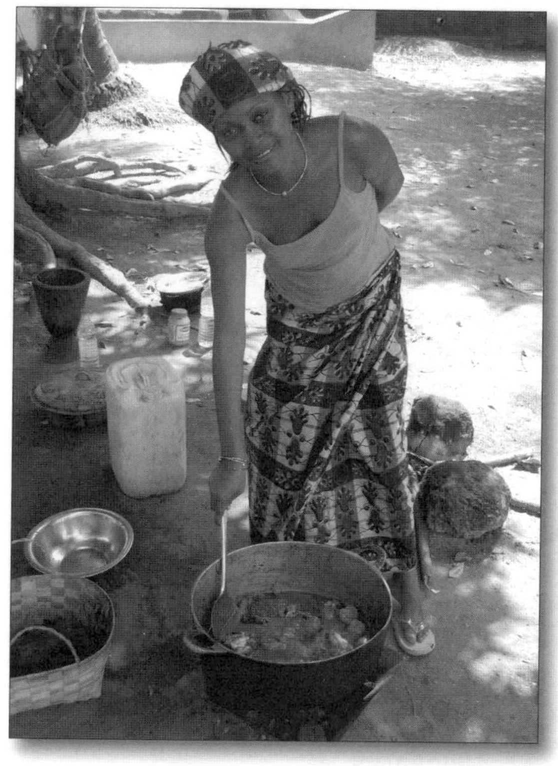

Canci Ye (khan-see-YEH)

Canci ye (literally translated as meaning "peanut water") is the Susu version of a famous West African staple, peanut sauce. Canci ye is very popular throughout the Susu region and is usually cooked with fresh fish, chicken or goat and a variety of fresh vegetables. The following recipe is adapted slightly to reflect the difference in availability of particular items between Guinea and the U.S. This delicious recipe will feed 12 to 15 people.

Heat in a large saucepan:
¾ cup vegetable oil (palm oil is traditional)

Sauté:
3–4 cloves minced garlic
1 large chopped onion (brown or white)

Stir in:
⅔ cup (6 ounces) tomato paste
1 ½ cups (12 ounces) stewed tomatoes
4 cups chicken or vegetable broth
1 chicken bullion cube (or substitute)

Add (in reverse order of cooking time):
Assorted cut vegetables (3–4 kinds is adequate)
Potatoes (4–5 medium)
Yam (1)
Yucca (1)
Eggplant (1 medium)
Carrots (5–6)
Squash (2–3)
Cabbage (1 head)

Simmer on medium heat, stirring often, until fully cooked (45–60 minutes).

Reduce heat and add:
4–5 whole habañero peppers*
1 cup of natural smooth peanut butter
Salt to taste

Cook separately:
3 cups of white jasmine rice

Meat-dish options:
Brown and add with peanut butter
1 pound chicken (brown first) *or*
1 pound fish (cook first)

When habeñero peppers shrivel, remove from sauce and place in a separate bowl. Turn heat off. Your canci ye sauce is ready! Serve sauce over rice. For spicier food, break open a cooked habeñero pepper on your plate and add very small amounts at a time. Enjoy!

Fire Warning!
Habenero peppers add a wonderful flavor, similar to that of the bengbe peppers of Guinea, which are an integral component to canci ye; however, habeñeros are extremely hot! You may wish to skip them if cooking for those with sensitive palets, such as the elderly or young children. If you do add habeñeros, handle them with care and try not to break them open in the sauce.

Eat smart and healthy:
Always use fresh, locally and/or organically grown ingredients whenever possible!

Guinea Sorrel (Bisap)

Guinea sorrel, more commonly known as bisap, is a popular drink throughout Guinea and all of West Africa. Made from dried hibiscus flowers, it is the perfect traditional beverage for your canci ye.

Ingredients:

2–3 cups of dried hibiscus flowers
2 quarts of drinking water
1–2 cups of sugar or equivalent sweetener (honey or stevia)

Optional:
Sprig of mint
½ teaspoon vanilla extract

Gently rinse hibiscus flowers (sorrel or roselle) and set aside.

Bring water to boil in a large saucepan.

Add hibiscus leaves. Remove from heat and allow flowers to steep for approximately 10 minutes.

Strain water into a pitcher and add sweetener to taste.

Serve chilled or over ice.

While the mint/vanilla combination is the most popular, other flavorings are added in some parts of West Africa. These combinations include the following:
1 teaspoon orange-flower water, or
½ cup lemon juice, or
1 cup pineapple juice or orange juice.

Tip: This drink is similar to the popular Mexican drink *jamaica* (HAH-my-kah). Herbal tea may be substituted for hibiscus flowers. To match the color, use tea that has a reddish hue.

Appendix J: Other Popular Traditional Instruments in Guinea, West Africa

There are many other instruments found in Guinea and the surrounding region. The following is a brief description of some of the most popular.

KORA

A harp-lute with 21 strings arranged on both sides of a notched bridge, the kora's body consists of half a large calabash partially covered in calf-skin and a large, rounded wooden neck to which the strings are attached. The kora is played with both the thumb and index finger of each hand and originates from the Griot or Jeli caste.

BOLON

The bolon is a type of harp comprised of a large calabash and curved wooden pole to which three or four strings are attached. The bolon can be played standing, or by holding one hand on the neck and plucking or pinching the strings with the thumb of the other hand. It can also be played the more popular way, seated with the thumbs of both hands plucking the strings. The bolon was said to have been used traditionally in hunting ceremonies, but is now heard in all types of popular Guinean music.

SICO (SIKO)

Originating from the Temné ethnic group is Sierra Leone and quickly adopted by the Susu ethnic group of Guinea, the sico is a flat square-shaped drum with goat skin attached to one side. Sico's are usually played in a set of 5 or 6. The largest sico, called baba, are played upright with one hand. The smaller doumblock and solo are played with two hands, with drums held between the legs, and the mid-sized rollin is played on the ground with two sticks.

BOTÉ

The bote is a small, bowl-shaped drum from the Susu ethnic group in Western Guinea with cow skin stretched over one side and played with a flat mallet in one hand. The other hand plays a bell hanging from one finger, and is played with metal rings attached to the others. The boté is often used to accompany the bala for wedding and other celebrations.

GONGOMA

The gongoma is a popular instrument from the western coast of Guinea, consisting of a large half calabash with a thinner piece of wood affixed over the open part. Three to four sawblades are then attached and plucked with the fingers of one hand while the other hand taps on the calabash or wood top. The gongoma is played to accompany singing.

FULÉ (MALINKÉ, SUSU) TAMBIN (FULA)

This type of transverse flute is made from the conical vine and is popular among the Fula (Peul) ethnic group of the Fouta Djalon region of Guinea. It has three finger holes and can produce one complete diatonic scale. Typical keys include F, F♯, G, A♭, and A.

WASSAKHOUMBA

This hand-held clapper/rattle is made from curved or angled sticks onto which several calabash discs are attached. Popular among the Peul (Fula) and Susu of Guinea, they are traditionally played for circumcision ceremonies.

Appendix K: Instrument Kits for Your WRAP Ensemble

Mini (minimum to make music)

- → 1 whistle
- → 2 jembes
- → 1 dundunba with sticks
- → 1 pair caxixi (seke-seke)
- → 1 woodblock with sticks (krin)
- → 1 xylophone with mallets (alto or soprano)

Standard (minimum to play all parts)

- → 1 whistle
- → 4 jembes
- → 3 dundun with sticks (dundunba, sangban, kenkeni)
- → 2 bells with beaters (kenken) for sangban and kenkeni
- → 1 pair caxixi (seke-seke)
- → 2 woodblocks with sticks (low & high)
- → 3 xylophones with mallets (bass, alto, soprano)

Deluxe (allows greater participation)

- → 1 whistle
- → 7 jembes
- → 3 dundun with sticks (dundunba, sangban, kenkeni)
- → 2 bells with beaters (kenken) for sangban and kenkeni
- → 1 pair caxixi (seke-seke)
- → 2 woodblocks with sticks (low & high)
- → 8 xylophones with mallets (2 bass, 3 alto, 3 soprano)

Traditional instruments (dundun, jembes, bala, krin, & seke seke).

Other Options

Kalani Hand-Drumming Gloves

Benefits:

- ◎ Allows new or periodic players greater stamina and comfort while playing.
- ◎ Helps keep both the hands and drumhead safe.
- ◎ Produces authentic tones.

Kalani Dundun Sticks

Benefits:

- ◎ Consistent size, finish and professional quality.
- ◎ Exclusive bevelled shaft makes them easy to hold and play.
- ◎ Works with all sizes and types of drums.

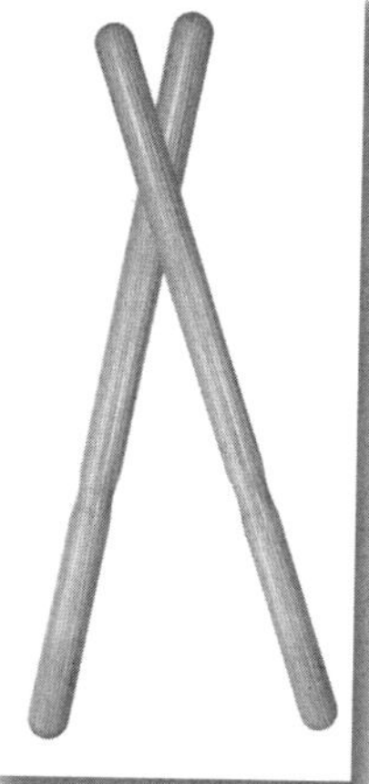

Appendix L: Your African Village 7 9

Tips for Bringing More Culture to Your Classroom

Discovery Center

You may wish to dedicate part of your music room to creating a "World Rhythms Discovery Center" by decorating it with props, fabric, maps, and other items you feel will be enriching for students and visitors to your music room.

Some things you could include:

- Wall treatment (reed fence treatment or African-themed wall paper)
- Cloth/fabric (mud cloth or African print)
- Mask/art project (wood or paper mache)
- Map of Africa or West Africa with ethnic groups, cities, and countries
- Guinea flag
- Drums and percussion instruments

Authentic Village Dress

Bring your performances to life with traditional West African costumes. Authentic girls' *dugis* and boys' *goubahs* can be easily made or purchased for your students. For more information and resources, check the WRAP website at www.drum2dance.com.

Girl's dugi (DOO-gee): shirt, skirt "lapa," and head wrap.

Boy's goubah (GOO-bah): pants, shirt, and head wrap

Appendix M: Working with Stakeholders

As you develop your World Rhythms Arts Program, you will want to share the benefits of music making, dance, and singing with members of your community who have a vested interest in your students' education, your school, and community. Just as the country of Guinea uses its National Ballet as ambassadors to surrounding countries and the rest of the world, you will use your WRAP ensemble to reach out to the people in your community and beyond.

Stakeholders are

- ☐ parents, relatives, and the extended family of your students
- ☐ school staff, administrators, board members, and district representatives
- ☐ fellow teachers, their students, and families
- ☐ other local schools
- ☐ organizations (clubs, groups, non-profit organizations, events)
- ☐ business owners and their customers

Like you, stakeholders have a vested interest in the education of your students. They want to know what is being taught in school and to see the results.

Needs of Stakeholders

- ☐ Families want to know what their children are learning and how they can share the positive experiences with their children.
- ☐ Other teachers want to know about alternative and enriching learning strategies that are being used in their school.
- ☐ Administrators want to be able to showcase enriching programs to their community—especially those that foster cultural competency and appreciation of diversity.
- ☐ Support staff and counselors want to see programs that promote teamwork, cooperation and life skills development that result in a drop in discipline problems.
- ☐ School staff like to see programs that teach a broad range of social skills such as listening, cooperation, discipline, teamwork, and respect.
- ☐ Other schools want to know about programs that promote school spirit, a sense of pride in the school community, and cross-cultural awareness.
- ☐ Local organizations are often looking for ways to infuse their events with energy, focus, and fun. They will want to know how they can work with your WRAP ensemble to promote both their cause and music in our schools.
- ☐ Businesses love to support positive programs that bring out the best in our youth and bring attention to the good things that are happening in the community. They will work with you to spread the word and help grow your program.

One of the best ways you can support arts education in your school and district is to have a robust arts program. There's no better tool for advocacy than energized, involved, and successful students. Need more ideas for music advocacy? Visit *supportmusic.com*, *amc-music.com*, or *menc.org*.

Start Spreading the News

When your World Rhythms Arts Program has developed to the point that it is meeting the needs of stakeholders, you will want to share the news with as many people as possible. You can use the WRAP Core Values (page 9) along with your group's unique success story as a guide for a press release.

SHARE THE GOOD NEWS ABOUT YOUR WORLD RHYTHMS ARTS PROGRAM THROUGH

- school assemblies
- fairs and festivals
- PTA meetings
- choral events
- churches
- dance events
- school board meetings
- professional development workshops
- conferences
- community events
- concerts
- radio/TV stations
- message boards
- list-serves/chat groups
- newsletters

Developing Program Support

Once you have an established World Rhythms Arts Program, you can offer special sessions to involve, educate and gain further support from specific groups within your community. The following session outlines are designed to help you develop key relationships with three member groups: administrators, teachers, and parents.

Tip: You may also incorporate one or more of the drum circle games during any of these sessions as an icebreaker, energizer, or community-building activity.

ADMINISTRATOR SESSION

1. Use the CD for accompaniment, and invite everyone to join you in Macrou Dance Step 1 (2–3 minutes).
2. Add the Macrou song (first part only from lesson 1), and initiate a call-and-response with the group (2–3 minutes).
3. Discuss the movement experience. Ask questions about how they might feel different after the group dance as opposed to when they arrived. How did they feel while dancing? Where did they look, listen, and focus?
4. Discuss connections to other areas of the curriculum: focus, teamwork, listening, etc.
5. Describe your World Rhythms Arts Program and some of the benefits that you've experienced. Remember to talk about your experience. Have positive statements from your students on a handout or presentation slide.
6. Use a transparency or PowerPoint (Keynote for Mac) presentation to outline several key objectives of the World Rhythms Arts Program, and note how you have met them.
7. Discuss cross-curricular connections and how they support the students' complete education and social development.
8. In what ways can administrators support the WRAP ensemble and promote the benefits to other teachers, schools and the community?
9. How can they work with you to present a developmental (team-building) session for teachers, staff, and parents later in the school year?
10. If appropriate, close the session with more dance and song. Add the dundunba part (played on any drums you have available), and invite others to join you.

TEACHER SESSION

1. Play the CD for accompaniment, and invite everyone to join you in Macrou Dance Step 1.
2. Add the Macrou song (part 1 only from lesson 1), and invite call and response.
3. As you are singing (with everyone still dancing), stop the CD and play the dundunba rhythm.
4. Invite teachers to move to the other drums and make up any parts they like. (Remember to remove rings, watches, and bracelets.)
5. Stop and discuss the experience. What was fun or challenging? How do they feel different now than before?
6. Describe your World Rhythms Arts Program and some of the benefits you have experienced. Remember to talk about your experience and not simply describe what it could do.
7. Take a few minutes to brainstorm with a focus on other benefits.
8. Ask teachers if they are interested in getting together periodically to drum together. (This helps staff development and teambuilding, but just tell them it's for fun!)
9. Designate someone to organize the group drumming schedule.

PARENT SESSION

1. Have students provide Macrou rhythm accompaniment, and invite everyone to join you in Macrou Dance Step 1 (2–3 minutes). Have students teach the steps to the parents.
2. Add the Macrou song (part 1 only from lesson 1), and invite call and response (2–3 minutes).
3. As you are singing (with everyone still dancing), invite everyone to clap the dundunba pattern with you (2–3 minutes).
4. Pause to process the activity with the group.
5. Provide a brief overview of the WRAP ensemble (objectives) and the benefits you have noticed, and allow student testimonials.
6. Ask parents if they can identify other ways the World Rhythms Arts Program could benefit their child's development.

As you work with different community-member groups, you will fine-tune your presentation to best address their concerns, but there are universal messages that work with all groups.

Five Key Messages for Gaining Support

→ According to a Gallop Poll, 95 percent of Americans believe that music is part of a well-rounded education, and 93 percent think music education should be part of our public schools' core curriculum.

→ A cross-cultural music and movement program develops the whole student by incorporating multiple intelligences and learning styles.

→ Students who study music score higher on their SATs, and do better in math, science, and language.

→ Students learn more than music. They learn important life skills such as teamwork, discipline, creative thinking, and improvisation.

→ Playing music and dancing helps students gain confidence and self respect, and provides them with a creative outlet they can use for the rest of their lives.

Appendix N: Educational Resources

World Rhythms! Arts Program

http://www.drum2dance.com

WRAP offers materials and workshops that support the WRAP curriculum. Educators are encouraged to join the WRAP user group to receive special membership benefits, additional resources and information.

Company Forè-Foté

http://www.fore-fote.com

An educational and performance organization dedicated to preserving and promoting the traditional music, dance, and culture of Guinea, West Africa. Founded by Master Drummer M. Lamine Dibo Camara, Company Forè-Foté offers professional drum and dance performances, workshops, school and university demonstrations, residencies, CDs, videos, and more. Forè-Foté also hosts drum and dance workshops on the island of Roume in Guinea, West Africa, suitable for teachers, performers and recreational drummers and dancers.

Denbaya, Inc.

http://www.denbaya.org

A 501c(3) non-profit cultural arts organization based in Ashland, Oregon, offering school and university programs, community celebrations, courses and workshops for the northwest United States. Denbaya (which means "family we care for" in many West African Mandé dialects) is committed to building intercultural understanding through the medium of performing arts and education.

Djembelesson.org

http://www.djembelesson.org

Ryan M. Camara's educational website offering complete jembe and dundun drumming lessons online. Using advanced audio, video and multimedia, djembelesson.org offers students and teachers from around the world the type of quality instruction previously only available through ongoing master classes or special workshops.

Drum Camp

http://www.drumcamp.com

Drum Camp is a week-long retreat for beginning to advanced drummers and dancers. Classes feature techniques, history and applications, improvisation, skills development, and more. Healthy meals and comfortable housing in a beautiful forest setting are included.

Drum Circle Music

http://www.drumcirclemusic.com

Kalani Music offers training and certification, based on Kalani's award-winning book and DVD *Together in Rhythm*. Drum Circle Music™ (DCM) is an innovative and effective approach to group music making and expressive movement that fosters important life skills and musical intelligence. DCM is used by drum circle facilitators, educators, therapists, activity directors, healthcare workers, and community music instructors.

Rhythm Gym

http://www.rhythmgym.org

A 501c(3) non-profit, Rhythm Gym provides children and communities with healthy music-based programs that promote core timing, physical fitness, and social skills development. Founded by Kalani, Rhythm Gym features unique "Fitness Drumming" activities that combine movement, playing drums and percussion instruments, and exercise. Programs, training opportunities, and resources are available on the Rhythm Gym website.

Additional Websites:

alfred.com (music books and media)

vicfirth.com (sticks, mallets, drumming gloves)

kalanimusic.com (educational, professional, therapeutic, and recreational drumming programs and media)

Appendix O: Track List

WEST AFRICAN DRUM AND DANCE: A YANKADI MACROU CELEBRATION CD

Performance and Practice

1. Yankadi Macrou Performance 08:35
2. Macrou Practice Track 05:16
3. Yankadi Practice Track 05:07

Macrou

4. Macrou Break Slow Tempo 00:12
5. Macrou Break Fast Tempo 00:12
6. Macrou Dundunba Slow Tempo 00:45
7. Macrou Dundunba Fast Tempo 00:28
8. Macrou Sangban Slow Tempo 00:45
9. Macrou Sangban Fast Tempo 00:28
10. Macrou Kenkeni Slow Tempo 00:45
11. Macrou Kenkeni Fast Tempo 00:28
12. Macrou Jembe 1 Slow Tempo 00:45
13. Macrou Jembe 1 Fast Tempo 00:28
14. Macrou Jembe 2 Slow Tempo 00:45
15. Macrou Jembe 2 Fast Tempo 00:28
16. Macrou Jembe 3 Slow Tempo 00:45
17. Macrou Jembe 3 Fast Tempo 00:30
18. Macrou Krinyi Slow Tempo 00:45
19. Macrou Krinyi Fast Tempo 00:30
20. Macrou Drums Layered 02:35
21. Macrou Xylo 1 Slow Tempo 00:46
22. Macrou Xylo 1 Fast Tempo 00:29
23. Macrou Xylo 2 Slow Tempo 00:46
24. Macrou Xylo 2 Fast Tempo 00:29
25. Macrou Xylo 3 Slow Tempo 00:46
26. Macrou Xylo 3 Fast Tempo 00:29
27. Macrou Xylophones Layered 01:16

Yankadi

28. Yankadi Break Slow Tempo 00:15
29. Yankadi Break Fast Tempo 00:12
30. Yankadi Dundunba Slow Tempo 00:42
31. Yankadi Dundunba Fast Tempo 00:30
32. Yankadi Sangban Slow Tempo 00:42
33. Yankadi Sangban Fast Tempo 00:30
34. Yankadi Kenkeni Slow Tempo 00:42
35. Yankadi Kenkeni Fast Tempo 00:30
36. Yankadi Jembe 1 Slow Tempo 00:42
37. Yankadi Jembe 1 Fast Tempo 00:30
38. Yankadi Jembe 2 Slow Tempo 00:42
39. Yankadi Jembe 2 Fast Tempo 00:30
40. Yankadi Jembe 3 Slow Tempo 00:42
41. Yankadi Jembe 3 Fast Tempo 00:30
42. Yankadi Drums Layered 02:29
43. Yankadi Xylo 1 Slow Tempo 00:42
44. Yankadi Xylo 1 Fast Tempo 00:30
45. Yankadi Xylo 2 Slow Tempo 00:42
46. Yankadi Xylo 2 Fast Tempo 00:30
47. Yankadi Xylo 3 Slow Tempo 00:42
48. Yankadi Xylo 3 Fast Tempo 00:30
49. Yankadi Xylophones Layered 01:21

Susu Language

50. Susu Numbers 01:08
51. Susu Greetings 01:05
52. Susu Greetings Dialog 00:48
53. Performance Intro Monologue 00:53
54. Performance Intro w/ English 01:27

Macrou Instrumental Score

Yankadi Instrumental Score
Jembes
1:
2:
3:
Dunduns
K:
S:
D:
Xylophones
3 (SX):
2 (AX):
1 (BX):
Seke-Seke:
Jembe Break:
*Start here.

ACKNOWLEDGEMENTS

The authors extend their gratitude to the following people, companies, and organizations for their contributions to this project.

FROM KALANI

Thank you to the following people, companies and organizations for their contributions to this project and our mission of promoting drumming and dance.

Drum teachers: M. Lamine "Dibo" Camara, Abdoul Doumbia, Mohamad "Joh" Camara, Jimo Kouyate, Mohamed DaCosta, Ladji Camara, Mamdy Keita, and my brother, Ryan Camara; Djibril "Jibi" Camara for his energetic dancing and spirit. Companies and the people that make them special: Sylvia and Andrew Perry and everyone at Peripole-Bergerault Educational Instruments; Dave Black, Andrew Surmani, and everyone at Alfred Publishing; Victor Filonovich, Steve Nigohosian, Ken Fredenberg, Kim Graham, Derek Zimmerman, West Wheeler and everyone at Toca Percussion and Kaman Music; Neil Larrivee, Marco Soccoli, Tracey and Vic Firth at Vic Firth, Inc.; the International House of Blues Foundation; the California Music Educator's Association; the Florida Music Educator's Association; the Oregon Music Educator's Association; the National Association of Music Education; the American Orff-Schulwerk Association; the American Music Therapy Association; Katy Winter and the students at Frost Middle School, Granada Hills, CA; Margaret Jerz and the students at Evergreen Elementary School, Wasau, WI; the students at Markham Middle School, Watts, CA; Pam Herzog and the students at Cold Spring Elementary School, Santa Barbara, CA; Betty Ann Bruno, Craig Scheiner, Yvette Ortega, Rocky Camara, Greg and Eva LaBonty at Camp Latgawa, Eagle Point, OR; Janet James at Camp de Bennevile Pines, Angeles Oaks, CA; Our Drum Camp family.

FROM RYAN

I would like to first and foremost thank my teacher, mentor, and "Baba," Master Drummer M. Lamine Dibo Camara, for his acceptance, love, patience and constant support, for entrusting me with the knowledge of his traditions, and encouraging me to find my own voice in sharing them. This project would not be possible without him. Inuwali kefanyi, Baba. Alah kha wo mali. (Thank you and may God help us.) To my teacher and friend, Kalani—thanks for the opportunities, the loyalty, and most of all your love and support. To all the people of the Republic of Guinea and especially the wonderful families on the island of Roume who have so graciously opened their homes and hearts, who shared everything with me even when there was hardly anything to share—Wonuwali. Allah kha wo mali. (Thank you all. May god bless you all.) A very special thanks to my amazing drum and dance teachers: Mamady Keita, Boka Camara, Ousmane Sylla, Sekouba Camara and Ballet Matam, Lansana Camara, Fanta Camara, Mabinty Soumah (Konkacere), Nene Soumah, and Yamoussa Soumah. To Sharon Holland, Dane and Sierra Stinson—thanks for your constant support, encouragement, friendship, understanding, and most of all, your love. My thanks and love to Nancy Mehlmauer, Ann "Bubba" Mehlmauer, Mary Blackburn, Seth and Tisha Blackburn, Rocky Camara, Aboubacar Camara, Abdourahamane Camara (Ro), all the Forè-Foté family in Europe, Africa and the U.S., Elizabeth and Scott Whitman, Sean Grace and Kadiatou Grace, Paul Riley, Adam Frisch, Culture Den, and all the Denbaya family in Ashland, all the Almamya family in Conakry, Afia Walkingtree, and all of the artists who participated in the making of this project on Roume and in the U.S. To Lezlie Green—thanks for the photos, video, and most of all your unwavering support and friendship. Dedicated to N'namuso (my wife) Ai'cha Kaba and son Aly. M'bi Fe, I dumanye. Alla i kendeya. Alla i here ye fulen. Alla si jan di i ma. I love you!

Performers from Roume, Guinea (DVD)

Musicians
Mohamed Lamine "Dibo" Camara (organizer)
Lamine Bangoura
Alassane Soumah
Mohamed Camara
Amara Soumah Bassir Toure "Ilo"
Issa Kouyate (Jack)
Daouda Camara
Moussa Camara (M'Mayele)
Ibrahima Sakho (Ibro)

Female Dancers
Mafoule Camara
N'Konie Bangoura
Zehab Camara
Aminata Sylla (Amizo)
Aminata Bangoura

Male Dancers
Mangue Smoumah
Mohamed Sylla (Gongona)
Sekou Conte
Alseny Sylla
Mangue Bangoura

School Teachers
Mr. Facinet Camara (directeur)
Mr. Alexandre Bazil Morgan (instructor)

Village Chief
Mr. Moussa Camara (Tomy)

Dance Model
Kadiatou Camara Grace "Kadiza"

Photos
Ryan Camara, Kalani, Afia Walkingtree, Lezlie Green, Elizabeth Whitman, Paul Riley, and Adam Frisch

Music Consultant
Sharon Holland

Additional Video Credits:

Background and title audio courtesy of:
Company Foré-Foté from the CD, "Wonbere."

"Inside the Culture" artists:

A special thanks to the following performance groups:
Ballet Matam, Boka Jr., Kaly Multicultural, Ballet Bassikolo

and the following performers:
M. Lamine "Dibo" Camara
Lansana Camara "Sagatella"
Ousmane Sylla
Fanta Domini Camara
Mabinty Soumah

Dedicated in memory of:
Bangaly Bangoura and Kemoko Sano